Agile exists as both a collection of practices and the principles that underlie those practices. Teams need both. But practices change over time—today's state of the art is passé tomorrow. And while Agile practices may change, the principles never do. That's what makes this book so valuable. Lynda and Simon provide plenty of time-proven practical advice—specific things you can begin doing immediately. But practices are always presented with a helpful dose of principles. You'll finish this book knowing what to do today and how to adapt those practices in the future.

Mike Cohn, *Mountain Goat Software, Co-Founder of the Agile Alliance and the Scrum Alliance*

First principles are regularly overlooked when people start with Agile, and also seemingly forgotten by many who profess to be experienced with Agile. This book delivers both a fantastic introduction and very insightful reminders as to why these first principles are essential to 'being Agile', all supported with real experience and insightful research. Essential reading.

Julian Holmes, *Principal Transformation Consultant, Thoughtworks*

Agile from First Principles is an essential compendium for delivery professionals, intuitively weaving together concepts from Agile, Lean and product development disciplines. It provides accessible expertise for teams starting their journey, insights into the daily challenges of working in rapidly changing environments, the spectrum of practices available to experienced Scrum Masters, and a library of nuanced learnings, grounded in the fundamentals of modern product delivery that will resonate with leaders. A highly recommended addition to an Agile coach's toolkit.

Tom Hoyland *(Expert Coach), Principal Agile and DevOps Consultant, That Agile*

This book is essential reading for anyone practising in an Agile context. The authors share their vast experience and knowledge in a compelling and accessible way starting at first principles. Along the way they summarise key concepts, techniques and 'antipatterns' (warning signs). The book is written in a refreshingly hands-on, practical way which cuts through the buzzwords and gets straight to the point. Highly recommended!

Adrian Reed, *Business Analyst at Blackmetric Business Solutions, Author of* Business Analyst *(BCS)*

This is a convincing commentary on successful Agile methods. *Agile from First Principles* gets to the heart of what being Agile really means: a focus on people and practical solutions. It explains why the Agile Manifesto and the principles behind it matter so much. An excellent orientation for beginners which will help avoid common pitfalls. For experienced hands, a fundamental study of wide application, Agile leadership and culture.

Toby Jones, *founder of the Accelerated Capability Environment (the government's innovation engine)*

This is an excellent book for people both starting their Agile journey and those experienced practitioners who are looking to either deepen their knowledge or in need of a little reminder of the core principles that make Agile such a powerful and effective delivery approach. The book has a great blend of background context and practical examples, demonstrating why Agile is so effective in today's information and technology-based world.

James Burton, *Director Consulting Expert and UK Career Champion for Agile at CGI*

Agile from First Principles is the guide for advancing your Agile journey. The book, as its name implies, goes from principles to specific techniques in a framework-agnostic manner making it a valuable resource irrespective of whether you use Scrum, Kanban, XP or any of the scaling models. This book is highly recommended for both Agile beginners and experts.

David Bulkin, *Managing Director, Grow-Lean LLC*

Some books can't be written until most other books on the subject already have been written. *Agile from First Principles* is such a book. In an easy-to-understand way, the book presents the journey Agile has taken from its first stumbling steps to where it is today, having penetrated much of industry and academia. 'Now this is not the end', as Churchill might have said, but we are at a point in time where an elegant summary of the mess in which Agile is will help us to successfully move forward to a better future. And the book points to this future with discussions on leadership, the challenges of scaling and a subject closer to my own heart, Essence.

Dr Ivar Jacobson, *Chairman and CEO, Ivar Jacobson International*

Agile from First Principles is the perfect guide to understanding Agile and what is truly different about Agile approaches. The in-depth explanation of values and principles is far from theoretical. Lynda and Simon use loads of examples, as well as common traps and anti-patterns, to help you understand what it really means in practice, going far beyond the usual applications and methods (they do an excellent job covering them too, by the way). This book has already changed how I teach Agile!

Joakim Sundén, *Agile Transformation Coach/Specialist,*
Co-creator of the 'Spotify Model', Co-author of Kanban In Action

As the title promises, Lynda and Simon introduce the underlying principles and values of Agile, emphasising the benefits of adopting an Agile mindset and attitude, alongside a straightforward guide to popular Agile methods and tools used within software development. Anti-patterns identified throughout the book help challenge common attitudes and behaviours that can limit and sabotage our ability to be Agile. The book invites the reader to reflect on what we need to do more of, but also what we need to do less of, and stop doing to improve our agility! An easy-to-read guide for anyone interested in understanding the fundamentals of Agile and identifying ways to improve their own agility personally, within their team, and as a leader.

Belinda Waldock, *Being Agile, Author of* Being Agile in Business

An expertly crafted go-to manual for both seasoned professionals and those just starting out in the world of Agile. An easy read, full of practical hints and tips that will empower you to overcome the issues that hinder so many Agile teams. Well written and full of rich examples, it is sure to become your primary Agile reference book.

Martin Maya, *Founder, Amatis Training Ltd*

Finally, everything is in one place. *Agile from First Principles* has quickly become my go-to Agile resource book. I have long been a fan of Lynda and Simon's work and their endless comprehensive knowledge of Agile models, frameworks, values, principles, examples and thought leaders. As expected, this book does not disappoint. This book is well structured and pitched perfectly for anyone entering an Agile environment or those who are experienced and looking to refresh and expand their knowledge.

Kylie Yearsley, *Director, Agile Games Ltd*

As the Agile movement enters its third decade, it has grown and moved into dimensions and directions never thought of by the writers of the Agile Manifesto. The success of Agile as a business has often corrupted the original ideas behind Agile, imposing it in domains where its application is not the optimal solution to the problems at hand. The questions of where Agile practices and techniques make sense, where they are out of place, and where and how they might be altered and extended are valid questions that require reflection on the original ideas and intent of the Agile founders. This book, written by two knowledgeable and experienced Agilists, provides the foundation for self-reflection on the basic principles and the what and why of Agile, to help ensure that future advancements maintain both the word and the spirit of the Agile Manifesto.

Joseph Pelrine, *Agile Psychologist*

This timely book exposes many stubborn myths around Agile and highlights the potential dysfunctions when seeking to achieve greater agility. In jargon-free language, it outlines a path for leaders and practitioners alike to thrive in an ever more turbulent climate. I would highly recommend this book to anyone seeking to move beyond tools, and to understand the true spirit of the Agile movement.

Karim Harbott, *Co-Founder, Agile Centre,*
Author of The 6 Enablers of Business Agility

AGILE FROM FIRST PRINCIPLES

BCS, THE CHARTERED INSTITUTE FOR IT

BCS, The Chartered Institute for IT, is committed to making IT good for society. We use the power of our network to bring about positive, tangible change. We champion the global IT profession and the interests of individuals, engaged in that profession, for the benefit of all.

Exchanging IT expertise and knowledge
The Institute fosters links between experts from industry, academia and business to promote new thinking, education and knowledge sharing.

Supporting practitioners
Through continuing professional development and a series of respected IT qualifications, the Institute seeks to promote professional practice tuned to the demands of business. It provides practical support and information services to its members and volunteer communities around the world.

Setting standards and frameworks
The Institute collaborates with government, industry and relevant bodies to establish good working practices, codes of conduct, skills frameworks and common standards. It also offers a range of consultancy services to employers to help them adopt best practice.

Become a member
Over 70,000 people including students, teachers, professionals and practitioners enjoy the benefits of BCS membership. These include access to an international community, invitations to a roster of local and national events, career development tools and a quarterly thought-leadership magazine. Visit www.bcs.org/membership to find out more.

Further information
BCS, The Chartered Institute for IT,
3 Newbridge Square,
Swindon, SN1 1BY, United Kingdom.
T +44 (0) 1793 417 417
(Monday to Friday, 09:00 to 17:00 UK time)
www.bcs.org/contact
http://shop.bcs.org/

AGILE FROM FIRST PRINCIPLES

Lynda Girvan and Simon Girvan

Published by BCS Learning and Development Ltd, a wholly owned subsidiary of BCS, The Chartered Institute for IT, 3 Newbridge Square, Swindon, SN1 1BY, UK.
www.bcs.org

Paperback ISBN: 978-1-78017-5799
PDF ISBN: 978-1-78017-5805
ePUB ISBN: 978-1-78017-5812

British Cataloguing in Publication Data.
A CIP catalogue record for this book is available at the British Library.

Disclaimer:
The views expressed in this book are of the authors and do not necessarily reflect the views of the Institute or BCS Learning and Development Ltd except where explicitly stated as such. Although every care has been taken by the authors and BCS Learning and Development Ltd in the preparation of the publication, no warranty is given by the authors or BCS Learning and Development Ltd as publisher as to the accuracy or complete- ness of the information contained within it and neither the authors nor BCS Learning and Development Ltd shall be responsible or liable for any loss or damage whatsoever arising by virtue of such information or any instructions or advice contained within this publication or by any of the aforementioned.

All URLs were correct at the time of publication.

Publisher's acknowledgements
Reviewers: Andy Smith, Alistair Corrie, Margaret Morgan
Publisher: Ian Borthwick
Commissioning editor: Rebecca Youé
Production manager: Florence Leroy
Project manager: Sunrise Setting Ltd
Copy-editor: The Business Blend Ltd
Proofreader: Barbara Eastman
Indexer: Matthew Gale
Cover design: Alex Wright
Cover image: iStock/iagodina
Typeset by Lapiz Digital Services, Chennai, India

CONTENTS

LIST OF FIGURES AND TABLES

ABOUT THE AUTHORS

Lynda Girvan is the head of Agile and Business Analysis for CMC Partnership Consultancy Ltd, which specialises in Agile and business transformation services. She is a Chartered Fellow of BCS, BCS subject matter expert in Agile and business analysis, holds the coaching certification Certified Scrum Professional with the Scrum Alliance and is working towards Certified Enterprise Coach. Lynda has extensive experience of adding value to organisations, from coaching Agile development teams to advising and coaching on board-level change programmes. Lynda's particular strength is applying her knowledge of change, business analysis and Agile to help organisations overcome challenging business problems, such as Agile transformation and organisational agility. Lynda co-authored the BCS book *Agile and Business Analysis*[i] and is an experienced and keynote speaker on these subjects at international conferences.

Simon Girvan is a principal consultant and Agile coach with Ivar Jacobson International, where he helps organisations to improve teams and products agnostic of the framework they are using. He holds the coaching certification Certified Scrum Professional with the Scrum Alliance and is working towards Certified Enterprise Coach in addition to being certified in various other methods, including Scrum, Kanban, Scrum@Scale, LeSS and SAFe. He is a Chartered Fellow of BCS and the Institution of Engineering and Technology (IET), and is a BCS subject matter expert in Agile. Simon has significant experience working with teams, leaders and organisations to help them adopt an Agile mindset. Having spent many years in the public sector leading Agile teams and coaching leaders, he is now applying his knowledge and experience in the private sector. Although he has an engineering background, Simon enjoys working with non-technical teams and with organisational agility initiatives. He is a regular speaker and author on Agile topics.

---

i   https://shop.bcs.org/store/221/detail/workgroup/?id=3-221-9781780173221

FOREWORD

ABOUT THE AUTHOR

Over the last decade and more, my passion has been in supporting other Agile practitioners in their growth and development. I have spent much of that time helping those who work in service to their teams, organisations and, most importantly, colleagues in creating better workplaces – those more suitable for the challenges of the 21st century and more respectful of our humanity.

In that time, as a coach, consultant and trainer, I have collected many certifications, not for the recognition but for the platform they have given me to broaden my reach. My work as the managing partner of Agile Centre in both leading an organisation built on Agile principles and supporting other organisations in adopting those same principles comes with challenges many of you will have faced. It comes with great benefits too.

One of those benefits was meeting Simon and Lyn. What started as coaching and mentoring relationships quickly evolved into a relationship of peers. A meeting of minds and a differing of opinions. A place where I could challenge, and be challenged, across the broadest of horizons in the Agile discipline.

Over the last four years, I have had the privilege of witnessing both Lyn and Simon's knowledge, and understanding of the Agile mindset and philosophy crystallise. Already experts in other fields, it has been with great pleasure that I spent time working with them to synthesise their understanding and apply it to the context in which they have worked. This combination of clarity of thinking and deep experience and practice has come together in this book. The first on Agile, I suspect, of many to come.

I have enjoyed many conversations covering the esoteric to the mundane in the Agile world throughout the years. The ones that stay with me are not those where we spent time exploring some dark corner of thought related to team dynamics or social complexity. The ones that stick are invariably related to the core of Agile: the values and principles. The few words of the Agile Manifesto cut to the core of product development and knowledge working, and I find them still ringing true two decades later.

It will be no surprise then that the sections that stand out for me are the values and principles. Extraordinarily few books deal with the values and principles of the Agile Manifesto in a way that is both insightful and practical. Yet, they are the foundations on which we build our practice.

When introducing the Agile Manifesto, many texts give at best a second thought to the values, simply saying 'we prefer the ones on the left' or something equally as helpful. Instead, Simon and Lyn have tackled these powerful statements in a new and insightful way. They examine each value, look deeper into the meaning, uncover why many organisations and teams find it hard to live up to them and call out the anti-patterns and problems they have observed in working with teams aspiring to the values.

Suppose you have found this book during your first steps on the Agile journey, congratulations. Adopting a new way of working, especially one as alien to the typical organisation as Agile is, is a daunting task. Take heart that practitioners such as Lyn and Simon have gone before you and drawn a map to help you on your journey. Your journey won't be the same, but there will be similarities. Please read the text carefully, make notes, take your time to understand the concepts and how they relate to your team and organisation. Which practices and ideas resonate with you? Which will be harder to bring to life?

If this book found you further on your Agile journey, you may look at the title and dismiss the content as irrelevant. I implore you to reconsider. As practitioners, we fall foul of hubris as easily as anyone else. If nothing else, revisit the values and principles and create time to reflect on what Simon and Lyn have to say and how your views have changed over the years of practice. What has changed for you? Why?

In the time I have known Lyn and Simon, we have debated every aspect of Agile conceivable, from the humble user story to the implications of true business agility on organisations and society via change management and business analysis. And I've enjoyed every minute.

In your hands is an invitation to join that discussion.

John McFadyen
Managing Partner, Agile Centre

ABBREVIATIONS

2FA	two factor authentication
3Cs	card, conversation, confirmation
API	application programming interface
BDD	behaviour driven development
CD	continuous deployment
CI	continuous integration
CTO	chief technical officer
DDaT	Digital, Data and Technology Framework (UK Government)
DoD	definition of done
DoR	definition of ready
DSDM	Dynamic System Development Method
GDPR	General Data Protection Regulation
HiPPO	highest paid person's opinion
HR	human resources
INVEST	independent, negotiable, valuable, estimable, small, testable
LeSS	Large-Scale Scrum
MI	management information
MMP	minimum marketable product
MoSCoW	Must have, Should have, Could have, Want to have but Won't have this time
MUST	Minimum Usable SubseT
MVB	minimum viable bureaucracy
MVP	minimum viable product
NFR	non-functional requirement
OKRs	objectives and key results
OMG®	Object Management Group®
PDCA	plan-do-check-act
PDSA	plan-do-study-act
PI	planning increment
RAD	rapid application development
RUP	Rational Unified Process

SAFe®	Scaled Agile Framework®
SCARF	status, certainty, autonomy, relatedness, fairness
TDD	test driven development
UI	user interface
UML	Unified Modelling Language
UX	user experience
VUCA	volatile, uncertain, complex and ambiguous
WiP	work in process (Lean), or work in progress (Kanban)
WSJF	weighted shortest job first
XP	extreme programming

GLOSSARY

Acceptance criteria: The criteria that specify whether a feature or work item will be accepted by the customer.

Agile board: A physical or electronic board that displays the current work of the team. A public way to share the work of a team.

Agile Manifesto: The result of the meeting that defined Agile and described it as a set of values and principles.

Agile practice: A concrete, specific thing that Agile teams do that helps them with an Agile mindset, includes techniques, approaches, processes, patterns, models or maps.

Anti-pattern: A pattern that describes a way something is done, organised or happens that is detrimental to the intended outcome.

Application programming interface: A set of functions or services that allow separate software systems to connect and interact with one another.

Backlog: A list of work items or ideas that could help achieve value for the customer.

Backlog refinement: Periodic review of the backlog to keep it up to date.

Behaviour driven development: A way to provide a shared understanding between the different perspectives of developer, end user and tester.

Big Bang delivery: Waiting until the entire product is complete before the customer can use it.

Big room planning: An event used in scaled approaches to bring together multiple teams for collaborative planning purposes.

Component team: A team that works on a single component as part of a wider solution, in contrast to a Feature team.

Context diagram: A diagram used to show the interactions between a product, or structure, and the things outside that product/structure.

Continuous deployment: Deploying new capability as soon as it is available, often combined with continuously integrating small pieces of work frequently.

Continuous integration: Integrating work into the main workflow as soon as it is complete. Often done with very small pieces of work, perhaps many times a day.

Customer journey map: Technique that maps the path a customer takes to achieve a goal or objective.

Daily stand-up: Daily team event to discuss and share what they have been doing, what they will do next and any blockers. Often conducted while standing to help ensure it remains short.

Definition of done: Criteria to verify that quality-driven activities are in place and completed for a work item.

Definition of ready: Criteria that describe what must be in place before work can commence.

Development team: The people in the team that are committed to creating any aspect of a usable increment in each iteration.

DevOps: A contraction of Development and Operations. The combination of cultural philosophies, practices and tools that bring together development and operations in the same team in order to deliver software at a faster pace.

Empathy map: Technique to help teams obtain a shared understanding and empathy for others and improve customer experience.

Empiricism: The theory that all knowledge is based on experience derived from the senses.

Essence: An open standard for defining methods and practices.

Feature: Functionality within a product that offers significant value to the customer.

Feature team: A team that delivers working features for the customer, in contrast to a component team.

Functional requirement: A way to express what the product needs to do.

Gantt chart: A popular way to describe a project plan where each activity is shown as a bar against a schedule. Tasks to be performed are on the vertical axis and time duration on the horizontal.

Increment: A step towards a usable product.

Iteration: A time-bound cycle, usually within a broader delivery life cycle, delivering a version of the product or service.

Kaizen: Japanese word for continuous improvement or 'change for the better'.

Kanban board: Physical or digital board used by teams to visualise the flow of work by the team to provide value to the customer.

Kanban Method: A method to optimise flow of work by a team.

Lean wastes: The seven wastes, identified by Taiichi Ohno, that should be identified and minimised in order to speed work by a team.

Linear approach: A software delivery approach that completes each step sequentially before starting the next (e.g. Waterfall approach).

Minimum marketable product: The minimum set of functionality for a product that could permit the product to be sold or used operationally by a customer.

Minimum viable product: The minimum set of functionality for a product such that the product can be used to run experiments and generate feedback.

Non-functional requirement: A way to express how well the product/programme will achieve functionality.

Persona: An archetype used to understand the motivation and drivers from a customer perspective.

Planning Poker®: An Agile estimation approach based on Wideband Delphi trademarked by Mountain Goat Software LLC and widely used by Agile teams.

Product: The solution that Agile teams are producing.

Product Owner: The role in Scrum that is accountable for maximising the value of the product resulting from the work of the team. Also widely used in non-Scrum teams.

Programme increment: An 8–12 week planning horizon used within SAFe.

Refactoring: The practice of restructuring existing solutions (e.g. computer code).

Requirement: Feature or need that has been requested by a stakeholder.

Retrospective: Regular event enabling the team to reflect, over a specified time period, on their ways of working and identify opportunities for improvement as part of their continuous improvement.

Roadmap: A way to describe the vision and/or goal for the work and a rough order.

Scrum: The most commonly used Agile framework for development teams.

Scrum Master: The role in Scrum that is accountable for establishing Scrum as defined in the Scrum Guide.

***Shu Ha Ri*:** A Japanese concept that describes three stages on the path to mastery of a skill.

Spike: A short, time-bound task within an iteration that is not critical to the iteration goal. Often used to restrict time spent on open-ended tasks like research.

Stakeholder: Anyone who has a vested interest in, or is affected by, the product.

Story Points: A unit of measurement used by a team to size user stories in a Product Backlog to aid planning and forecasting.

The three pillars: The 'Empirical Scrum Pillars' from the Scrum Guide: transparency, inspection, adaptation.

Time boxing: The act of restricting a task, activity or event by a time limit.

T-shaped professional: People who are competent in a range of skills and have one or two areas where they have deep expertise.

Two factor authentication: A security feature that requires a user to have an additional form of identification to log into a system beyond just a username and password. For example, a token, mobile device, authentication app, and so on.

Use case: A lightweight, iterative way to describe a specific situation in which a product or solution could potentially be used.

Use case diagram: Model to visualise and express the scope of the endeavour showing use cases and their actors.

User role: Defines a single user group that interact with a product or solution.

User story: Short description of user value used in Agile approaches.

User story mapping: Technique to visualise user stories across the whole product or solution.

UX design: Design of the user experience elements of a product such as the graphical interface or web pages.

Velocity: The average number of Story Points (or other metric) per iteration that a team has completed.

Waterfall: A linear software development approach.

Wideband Delphi: A collaborative approach to estimate work.

Working solution: A working product that achieves value for the customer, but is not necessarily the final solution.

PREFACE

A quick search will reveal that there are already many books on Agile, covering a wide range of topics. Many focus on Agile methods and approaches; others on specific topics or techniques. Some books expect little prior knowledge; others expect at least an appreciation or understanding of the basic concepts.

In this book we have attempted to live up to the title *Agile From First Principles* and cater both for those new to Agile and more experienced practitioners who would benefit from a refresher. We incorporate both theoretical and practical application of Agile, combining our experience and stories with external references and guidance.

In this preface we provide a brief overview of Agile, provide indications about who this book is for, introduce you to our case study and provide a short synopsis of what to expect of the rest of the book.

WHAT IS AGILE?

Before we start, it is worth considering what 'Agile' actually is. At its simplest, it is an approach to developing products, often but not always software products. It applies an iterative and incremental approach, favouring the release of versions of the product throughout the development process, seeking feedback on them and incorporating that feedback into the development process.

This means that the development cannot be planned far in advance, as we can't second guess the feedback. Therefore, Agile teams must be able to plan for short horizons and be able to respond to change. Agile teams typically work in short cycles, a few days to a few weeks, before pausing to reflect on how they are doing and replan for the next cycle.

Agile teams use certain frameworks and practices to help them plan and deliver the product. They form teams and assign roles in a particular way, adopt high levels of collaboration and tend to operate relatively autonomously.

Already, we can see this is different from how many products are developed. We are used to projects deciding the product specification at the start and releasing the product, when it is complete, at the end.

Agile emerged in the early 2000s and initially had quite a niche following. However, over the intervening years it has grown in popularity and influence. As we write in 2022 it is extremely popular, well known and widespread – not only for software products, but for solutions and projects of all shapes, sizes and types.

IF IT'S SO POPULAR, WHY DO WE NEED THIS BOOK?

You may be wondering why, if Agile is so widespread, this book is necessary? As you will discover, despite Agile being simple to understand, in practice it is very hard to do well.

Over the years, we have witnessed many teams struggle to apply Agile concepts consistently and successfully even with experienced teams. One of the reasons for this is that many people focus on the mechanics of Agile methods and don't give enough consideration to the underlying principles and values. The problem is that it's easy to apply the mechanical elements in ways that don't embody those values, and can even undermine them.

That's why we have called this book *Agile From First Principles* – we believe successful Agile adoption starts with a solid understanding of the fundamentals, and only once these are mastered can you expect to apply any Agile method or framework successfully.

WHO IS THIS BOOK FOR?

The short answer is that this book is for anybody who wants to understand Agile better. That includes those who are brand new to the subject. It also includes coaches like us who value a single book that reminds us of what is important and is a handy reference to a broad range of Agile concepts. This is the sort of book we would buy and use ourselves.

More specifically, there are certain groups of people to whom we particularly recommend this book.

Those new to Agile

This book provides a comprehensive introduction to Agile with a base of knowledge that makes learning and applying any Agile approach easier and more likely to succeed. The important elements are highlighted and reinforced together with examples and stories that help bring it to life.

Leaders and managers

Even if you are not involved in the day-to-day work of Agile teams, leaders and managers have an important role to play. Bringing out the best of Agile teams requires different sorts of leadership from what you may be used to. This type of leadership will feel uncomfortable and perhaps counter-intuitive. This book will help you to understand why it is important to lead differently and help you work out how. Of course, it will also help you to understand what's going on in Agile teams, demystify some of their language and behaviour, and help you to lead and manage them better.

Business stakeholders

Agile teams exist to provide value to customers. In order to provide the maximum value, those customers and other stakeholders need to understand how Agile teams work. Whether you are representing a direct user, or are a conduit to external customers and users, this book will help you to understand why Agile teams can be more effective and what you need to do to help them. This will usually involve some changes in behaviour and perspective. This book will help you with ideas and tools that can help you to achieve that.

Project managers

Being thrust into Agile can be confusing and bewildering for project managers, particularly those who are experienced and skilled. The Agile ceremonies, language and assumptions can be very alien when compared to best practice in project and programme management.

This book will help you to understand how Agile teams work and why they do some of the things they do. It will help you to understand how project managers can help Agile teams succeed, and why some things that project managers can expect may not be helpful for Agile teams. If you are taking on an Agile role, this book will help you to understand what is expected of you and give you the knowledge and understanding to perform it well.

Students and trainers of the BCS Foundation Certificate in Agile

The BCS Foundation Certificate in Agile is an excellent certification that gives a broad grounding in Agile concepts and practices without focusing on a particular method or practice. This book covers the whole syllabus, although it isn't written in quite the same order.

The 2020 version of the syllabus was written by one of this book's authors and one of its reviewers, so the perspective of the book represents what the syllabus intends to convey.

Agile practitioners and coaches

It may sound odd that a book that addresses first principles, and is suitable for novices, should also be valuable to experienced practitioners. However, there are two good reasons why this is the case and why this is exactly the sort of book we would buy for ourselves.

First, this book covers a lot of ground to explain the principles and practices of Agile. There are dozens of techniques, ideas, methods and practices described; many in brief detail with references to more detailed descriptions. As such, this one volume contains just enough information to be useful but references a huge body of knowledge that is invaluable to any Agile practitioner.

Secondly, even experts in Agile practices are not immune to falling into the traps and anti-patterns that we discuss. Having a reminder of the core principles of Agile to hand helps to keep us grounded. The discussions on the values and principles will be particularly useful to help Agile teams improve.

WHAT TO EXPECT?

This book is a mix of fact, opinion, guidance and stories. Agile emerged as a short website in 2001 with just 68 words describing its values and a further 186 covering the principles.

We help you to understand those values and principles from our experience as Agile practitioners and coaches with many years of experience. We have tested our opinions with reviewers, colleagues, peers and others. We think that understanding what's behind Agile and what it means in practice is important. That's why we have devoted so much space and effort to explaining what we think they mean. We have illustrated this with examples of anti-patterns and problems we have experienced and use them to show not only why it's so easy to get Agile wrong, but ways that you can avoid making those same mistakes yourself.

We wanted reading this book to feel like a conversation with an experienced Agile coach. One who can explain new things to you, share their experiences, point you towards some good books or references, suggest new ideas and, most importantly, challenge you and make you think. You may not agree with all of our opinions, and you may speak to other Agile coaches who have different ideas. That's fine. Just treat this as new information to add to your existing knowledge and opinions and perhaps you will formulate a slightly new and evolved opinion. As you will read, we call this inspection and adaptation, and iterative development. It can apply just as much to ideas and beliefs as it can to products or processes.

It is worth mentioning that this book is unashamedly about Agile – the word is used over 900 times. This book is definitely about Agile delivery, Agile teams and for people interested in Agile. However, we are not trying to tell you that Agile must be the approach to everything, or that it will be the best choice for every endeavour. Agile is an excellent choice for many types of project and deliveries. It is the best choice for some; one of several good choices for others; and a poor choice for some. There are many situations where a well-executed alternative approach will be better than a poorly executed Agile approach. There are many scenarios where either a traditional or Agile approach can work well, provided they are executed well. Poor application of any approach will lead to poor results, even if that choice of method is ideal for the situation.

This book isn't about encouraging you to use Agile when it isn't appropriate. But any time you **do** choose Agile, this book will help you to execute it well and maximise the value you will achieve. By understanding the principles of Agile, you will also be able to judge when Agile will be appropriate to use and when it is not.

HOW TO READ THIS BOOK

We have written the book to flow logically: it starts with the background and history of the Agile movement, describes the main concepts, then goes into more detail on some specific, important areas in the later chapters. Thus, you can start at the beginning and the book will make sense.

However, you can also jump into a chapter that interests you and it should still make sense without having read the previous chapters. For example, much of the leadership chapter stands alone, as does the chapter on managing the product. This does mean there is a little repetition, particularly in the chapter on Agile practices. This is because we feel it is useful to have a summary or introduction to a practice even when we later expand on it in more detail.

Later in this preface, we provide a summary of each chapter to help you work out where to start. The table of contents and index will also help. However, we would urge you to spend some time on the values and principles chapters. Even if you think you know the Agile Manifesto – and, perhaps, **especially** if you think you know the Agile Manifesto – these chapters contain a wealth of experience and discussion on how the values and principles can be applied well and, importantly, how they are commonly misapplied. We are confident even experienced Agile practitioners will find something of value.

AN INTRODUCTION TO AG STORES

Having an example always makes things easier to understand. In this book, we have tied most of the examples to a fictional product that we hope you will be able to relate to.

AG Stores is a chain of large superstores that sell a variety of products, including food, hardware and home decoration products. Having relied for years on a loyal customer base, AG Stores are experiencing increased competition from other shops and also from online competitors. They believe that introducing a loyalty programme will allow them to reward their existing customers, dissuade the customers from shopping elsewhere and provide a rich set of data that they can use to improve marketing, store layout and stock control.

To cater for some customers, they will need physical cards and telephone-based account management, but they also want an electronic solution that can be more tightly integrated to their other IT programmes, allowing real time data analytics and personalised content such as offers or adverts. The proposed solution will include:

- a mobile app for customers to manage their account, view offers and discounts and present at the till;
- a website for managing accounts and viewing discounts and offers;
- integration between the loyalty programme and the till structure so that points can be accrued and spent;
- data analysis components that can generate insights into customer spending habits, steer marketing campaigns, assist with financial analysis and help with product placement;
- offline support for customers who don't want to use the app, including physical membership cards.

This scenario allows us to explore many aspects of product delivery, including how non-IT elements (such as marketing) can be included. There are many ways to deliver such a solution, and many ways to split up the work. We don't pretend our examples are the perfect answer (if such a thing even exists) and there are many alternative ways we could have chosen. We hope that the examples will help bring some of the concepts to life.

A BRIEF WALKTHROUGH

In this section we provide a brief walkthrough of the chapters in this book to help you decide where to start.

Chapter 1 – The importance of Agile today

This chapter explains why Agile approaches are still important today – despite emerging over 20 years ago, the conditions that led to Agile are not only still present but have intensified. Agile has matured beyond its origins in software to many other fields, and modern leadership theories are converging with the types of leadership advocated by Agile approaches. Coupled with Agile's growing dominance in the technology sector, it is clear that Agile is still relevant and the ability to apply Agile well has never been more important.

Chapter 2 – The origins of Agile

Here we discuss the theories and practices that have influenced Agile, some of which date back centuries. We discuss how non-Agile teams plan and manage their work and tell the story of how the Agile Manifesto came to be created in a ski lodge in Utah in 2001.

Chapter 3 – Projects and products in Agile

One of the ways that Agile bucks the trends set by traditional development approaches is that it has a product focus rather than a project focus. In fact, not only is the term 'project' not even mentioned in many Agile approaches, we suggest its use can actually be harmful – encouraging an unhelpful focus on tasks and milestones and minimising the importance of responding to change. We explain how Agile delivery is incremental and iterative and this is how we can deliver more value. The 'Product Backlog' is introduced as an important artefact.

Chapter 4 – Understanding the Manifesto for Agile

This chapter, along with Chapter 5, is one of the two cornerstone chapters in the book. The Agile Manifesto defines what we mean by 'Agile' so, to apply Agile well, it is critical that we understand what is meant by the Agile values to understand how we can apply and reinforce them.

A recurring theme throughout the book is that Agile is difficult to do well and we have seen many teams struggle. Even though the values look like common sense, they are not always commonly applied. Therefore, we look at common challenges and anti-patterns we have seen through the lens of each value, showing how they can be reinforced or undermined. There are plenty of references and further reading offered here too.

Chapter 5 – Understanding the Agile principles

Similar to Chapter 4, here we explain and examine each of the Agile principles in turn. We share our perspectives on what they mean and why each is important. We focus on particular words and phrases and drill down to consider them more deeply. This allows a far greater insight into what Agile means and how we can apply it ourselves and with our teams.

Additionally, we unpick the intent behind each of the 12 Agile principles and explore anti-patterns that may prevent you from applying Agile as it was intended.

Chapter 6 – Fundamental concepts in Agile

There are several common themes and concepts that run through the values, principles, core behaviours and mindset that underpin any Agile approach. This chapter introduces and discusses them. They are: empiricism; the three pillars of transparency, inspection and adaptation; lean approaches and wastes; incremental and iterative delivery; customer centricity; and self-organising, empowered teams. The chapter explains with some examples how these reinforce the values and principles.

Chapter 7 – Agile delivery

Agile teams need some defined approach to help them apply the values, principles and fundamental concepts to deliver value to their customers. There are several common patterns and techniques that are present in most Agile methods and frameworks. This chapter shows the delivery approach in a generic way, agnostic of any specific approach.

We discuss the overall life cycle; how to get started; how Agile delivery differs from a traditional approach; how to measure progress; getting to the first delivery of value; how to include continuous improvement; how iteration works; and how the team behaves and is organised. We introduce some of the other roles commonly found, including some that are specific to a particular method or framework.

Chapter 8 – Agile practices

Here we discuss and briefly describe a range of practices, techniques, methods, approaches and other ways of working that Agile teams commonly use. They are grouped into categories covering the following areas: leadership; ways of working; requirements, estimation; prioritisation; software development; and measuring success. We briefly describe two of the most common Agile approaches used by teams: Scrum and the Kanban Method.

Chapter 9 – Agile leadership

The easiest way to make an Agile team fail is to surround them with poor leadership and management that don't understand Agile. This chapter will help to address that by helping leaders and teams develop the kind of leadership that will help Agile teams to deliver the best results.

We describe the evolution of leadership and how many management techniques that evolved in early 20th-century manufacturing are still prevalent today, despite the conditions that Agile teams operate in today being vastly different from those factories or mines. Agile leadership needs to be different; ironically, we look to a German field marshall from the 1800s for a description of what it should be.

For many leaders, effectively leading Agile teams requires a shift in mindset, and we identify and discuss our six key leadership outcomes that leaders should strive for: servant leadership; psychological safety; intrinsic motivation; trusted, empowered people; self-organising teams; and creating strategic alignment. Many of these are not unique to Agile leadership, and we share stories and references that show how these leadership outcomes bring value to many different types of teams. We talk about the importance of creating the right culture and why Agile coaching is a powerful path to success.

Chapter 10 – Managing the product

One of the biggest differences between traditional and Agile delivery is how the product requirements are understood and managed, in particular how the customer is involved and how teams cope with changes to the customer needs. This chapter looks in detail at how Agile teams understand their customers and manage their product and their stakeholders using techniques such as roadmaps, backlogs and story mapping. Some of these techniques have entire books to describe them, so there are lots of examples and references to help bring the ideas to life and point you towards further information.

Chapter 11 – Beyond the basics

Finally, in this chapter we introduce scaling. We have consciously left it until last because we think it is important to properly understand the basics before trying to scale.

It is also important to only introduce scaling when you need it, so we devote the bulk of the scaling discussion to ways that you can avoid the need to scale, even when you have large products or lots of teams. We show ways you can reduce the drivers for scaling by reducing complexity, decoupling everything, managing the product differently, splitting goals, refactoring, using feature teams and shortening the cycle time. If you really, really want to scale, we also cover that briefly.

A second practice that you should only embark upon when you understand the basics is tailoring a process. An aspect of tailoring is the use of specialist roles or teams that can sometimes be sensible to use.

We finish by describing in brief some of the more commonly used Agile methods and frameworks, including references to their source to allow you to find the current versions.

LET'S GET STARTED

We set out to write this book with the expectation that it would mostly involve writing down what we had learned and experienced through our years working with organisations, teams and individuals. In fact, it's been much more than that. Thinking through the Manifesto values and principles in detail, and spending time reflecting on ways that we have seen them reinforced and undermined, has improved our own understanding of them immensely. Similarly, researching more in-depth leadership and managing the product chapters has improved our understanding and knowledge of those important areas. As a result, this book is far more than an expression of our experience – it is a book that we will refer to, recommend and use in our day-to-day work with Agile teams and others.

We hope you will find it as useful and as illuminating as we have.

1 THE IMPORTANCE OF AGILE TODAY

It has never been more important for teams and leaders to understand Agile and how to apply it well

This chapter explains why Agile approaches are not only still important today but are more important than ever. We will explore why:

- Despite emerging over 20 years ago, the conditions that brought about the movement towards Agile development are still present and have intensified.
- Agile approaches are being applied in a growing range of areas and becoming commonplace, although they are also hard to do well and often applied poorly.
- Agile approaches, which began with software projects, are being applied to a wider range of business problems and are well matched to them.
- The secret to applying Agile well is to focus on acquiring a deep understanding of the underpinning fundamentals of Agile rather than just learning a framework.

WHY ARE WE HERE?

Before we start to consider the importance of Agile today, let's look back at why Agile emerged.

In the late 1990s, development of new IT systems was characterised by large, expensive projects that seemingly took a long time to deliver. Teams would often attempt to understand the totality of the solution before any of the ideas had been tested. The result of this was lots of time spent ensuring a full set of requirements were documented up front before a line of code was written.

This approach is reasonable when there is little change and when you can be confident that your requirements are right. This may have been true for some of the systems and projects in the late 1990s, such as tax systems or banking systems that had a lifetime measured in years, but even then it was still a bit of a gamble. It is much less true now. Today, even a tax system requires regular changes to keep pace with the changing world that it supports.

In the mid-1990s huge organisations such as Lockheed, Chrysler, Xerox, Honda and Borland were trying things differently and getting better results. As we will explore in Chapter 2, those pioneers and innovators joined forces with others, also doing things differently, to create the paradigm shift of Agile development.

At the heart of this paradigm shift was the belief that reducing lead times, embracing changing requirements and improving customer buy-in was possible and would provide the ability for technology to create solutions faster than had been possible in the past. These core factors are not only still true today but have become orders of magnitude more significant.

We live in an increasingly VUCA world

The term VUCA emerged from the US War College in the wake of the collapse of the USSR and the end of the cold war. It was inspired by the leadership theories in the 1985 book *Leaders: Strategies for Taking Charge* by Warren G. Bennis and Burt Nanus.[1] They recognised that what had been a relatively stable and predictable state was suddenly anything but that; things had become volatile, uncertain, complex and ambiguous. This predicated an entirely different military approach.

What is meant by a VUCA world? It's one that has the characteristics set out in Table 1.1.

Table 1.1 VUCA

Volatility	The world is constantly changing. Change, both large and small, is more unpredictable and happening more frequently. This instability results in unforeseen, dramatic changes with cause and effect difficult or impossible to analyse at present.
Uncertainty	It is more difficult than ever to anticipate events. Attempts to use historical data to predict what will happen next fail as the past is no longer a good predictor of the future. This makes it extremely difficult to plan with any certainty.
Complexity	The world is more complex than ever. Problems are layered, nuanced, have more dimensions and are harder or impossible to truly comprehend. Information to support decisions is incomplete, contradictory and untrustworthy. There isn't always a single right decision and, if there is, the answer is difficult to reach through analysis.
Ambiguity	There is rarely a single right answer or unique best practice; everything is shades of grey. Decisions, plans and advice exist in an environment of contradictory, missing and extraneous data. Operating like this requires courage when taking decisions, and a willingness to accept you may turn out to be wrong.

The COVID-19 pandemic that began in 2020 is the perfect example of a VUCA situation. The situation was complex and constantly changing; large amounts of data were available, but they were contradictory and incomplete. The political challenge of balancing economic impact, protecting society, preserving medical capacity and managing infection rates was an impossible task. Any solution that helped in one dimension caused harm in another. As more data emerged, previous decisions needed to be revised.

---

1 Bennis, W. G. and Nanus, B. (1985) *Leaders: The Strategies for Taking Charge.* Harper & Row, New York.

It is easy to find other examples of a VUCA world, particularly with knowledge work (i.e. work that is non-routine and requires divergent and convergent thinking to solve problems). We have learned to construct complicated physical solutions such as bridges and electronics dependably, yet even the most experienced and skilled teams struggle to deliver IT or business change projects without exception reports, changes to requirements and rework. This isn't a failure of their management approach or poor quality implementations – this is because the problems being solved exhibit VUCA.

We find it hard to predict the future at the best of times. That's why IT projects are so difficult. They generally depend on user requirements being an accurate prediction of what users will need – yet, people are very bad at accurately predicting this. The problem is exacerbated when the data that are informing the prediction keep changing. This is true of non-IT projects, such as business change or service delivery projects, too.

When a problem is a VUCA problem, you cannot follow the current plan or analyse your way to a solution using traditional methods. When problems happen – the requirements change or the solutions don't work – it isn't generally a failure in planning or implementation; instead, it is often an acknowledgement that the problem wasn't capable of being analysed in advance. More or better analysis probably wouldn't have resulted in a successful delivery – it would likely have resulted in different things going wrong.

When we are confronted with VUCA problems, we need to solve them in different ways, and that's where Agile comes in.

Converging leadership approaches

The problems of a VUCA world are not restricted to areas where Agile is traditionally used, so it should be no surprise that the direction of travel of Agile leadership and more general management theories are converging. Leadership experts and gurus who have never even heard of the Agile Manifesto are coming to conclusions about how best to lead teams that are very similar to those of Agile thought leaders.

Joost Minnaar and Pim De Morree quit their corporate jobs and embarked on a mission to meet the people behind the world's most inspiring organisations and understand what makes them think differently. They documented their findings on their website[2] and in their inspiring book, *Corporate Rebels*.[3]

The organisations that inspire them include clothing companies, bus manufacturers, public sector organisations and banks. Few would describe themselves as an 'Agile organisation', yet the practices, behaviours and cultures they have created resonate strongly with those described in the Agile Manifesto.

---

2   https://corporate-rebels.com.

3   Minnaar, J. and de Morree, P. (2020) *Corporate Rebels: Make Work More Fun*. Corporate Rebels, The Netherlands. https://corporate-rebels.com.

David Marquet's book, *Turn The Ship Around*,[4] describes how he transformed his leadership from one of command and control into what he calls 'Intent Based Leadership'. Team members at all levels are empowered to take decisions; rather than waiting to be told what to do, they know what the overall vision is, decide what they need to do to move towards it and share what they intend to do with their colleagues and leaders. What's even more remarkable is that Marquet did this in the most surprising of situations – as commander of a nuclear-powered submarine in the US Navy. Although not labelled as an 'Agile' transformation, many of the changes Marquet made are the same ones we would recommend to organisations trying to be more Agile.

Agile leadership isn't just for small teams either. Jeff Sutherland, one of the creators of the most widely used Agile approach, Scrum, was part of the team that applied Agile approaches to the development of a military jet fighter – the JAS 39E Saab Gripen.[5] As on David Marquet's submarine, decisions were given to the team to make wherever possible. They operated to short three-week iterations with higher level coordination happening quarterly – orders of magnitude more frequent than most military procurements. They had a strong focus on continuous improvement and ensured frequent customer engagement by having pilots available on the same site to provide feedback.

In his book *Implementing Beyond Budgeting* and his work with the Beyond Budgeting Institute,[6] Bjarte Bogsnes describes how it is possible to run huge traditional businesses in radically different ways. He explains that organisations don't need to focus on short-term financial targets or plan around fixed dates (such as financial year boundaries). They don't need to set targets and cascade them to teams or control their people with detailed rules and performance evaluation. Instead, they can have teams with high degrees of autonomy over their work that organise around business-centric rhythms and events. They draw down resources when they are needed and are aligned and driven by high-level strategic objectives. Organisations operating successfully like this include large banks, petrochemical companies and manufacturers.

When author Dan Pink researched 50 years of behavioural science and psychology to understand what motivates us, he discovered that it's not what many people think. His book[7] explains why trying to motivate teams with money or promotions not only doesn't work, it can actually make us perform more poorly, especially for knowledge work. Instead, he found the key drivers of intrinsic motivation are autonomy, mastery and purpose.

4   Marquet, L. D. (2013) *Turn the Ship Around*. Penguin, London and New York.

5   Furuhlelm, J., Segertoft, J., Justice, J. and Sutherland, J. (2015) Owning the sky with Agile: Building a jet fighter faster, cheaper, better with Scrum. scruminc.com. https://www.scruminc.com/wp-content/uploads/2015/09/Release-version_Owning-the-Sky-with-Agile.pdf.

6   Bogsnes, B. (2016) *Implementing Beyond Budgeting*. John Wiley & Sons Inc, Hoboken, NJ. https://bbrt.org/.

7   Pink, D. H. (2011) *Drive: The Surprising Truth About What Motivates Us*. Canongate Books Ltd, Edinburgh.

These are just a few examples of advances in leadership and management theory that share many attributes with an Agile mindset. We will explore them in more detail in Chapter 9. Just as these approaches can support and enable Agile teams, so too can Agile approaches be valuable to leaders in any sector. As these examples show, you don't have to be applying an Agile methodology to benefit from Agile leadership approaches.

Technology – friend or foe?

Technology is advancing at an incredible pace. In particular, the development of cloud technologies, and their ability to rapidly provide processing capacity, have revolutionised our ability to deploy IT solutions. This advancement in technology has tremendous benefits, but it also brings threats. User expectations are shaped by their experiences with other products. We interact with high quality, easy to use products in our social lives and we expect the same at work.

The barrier to entry for competitors is set by their rivals; and the ability of new entrants into a market to change, evolve and respond to new opportunities can give them a competitive advantage over existing incumbents. We have seen examples of this behaviour in banking, with the arrival of digital-only challenger banks; in media, with streaming services and digital journalism; and in the public sector, with the digitisation of formerly paper-only forms. Starling Bank went from hiring its first technical team to launching current accounts in less than a year.[8] That's a pace that traditional banks could only have dreamed about.

This advance in the pace of technology makes it hard to keep up – particularly if you are working on systems that take months or years to get to market; any technology choice you make will almost certainly be out of date before it gets used. Agile's focus on releasing value quickly and iterating frequently is well suited to this trend in technology.

Another attribute of Agile development is the expectation that designs and architectures evolve and are refactored. Iterative development means that a given component or function is frequently revisited to add new capability. Each time this happens is an opportunity to refactor the component to take advantage of advances in technology.

Agile products constantly evolve.

THE DOMINANCE OF AGILE

In recent years, Agile approaches have become dominant for IT. In 2007, software vendor VersionOne began an annual 'State of Agile' survey. The first version had 722 respondents, of whom 84 per cent were in organisations that had adopted Agile in their software development. Their average length of experience with Agile was less than two years. In the 15th survey, published in 2021, 95 per cent of organisations were practising Agile, with around a third doing so for more than 5 years.[9] A quarter of those surveyed

---

8   https://www.starlingbank.com/about/road-to-starling/.

9   Digital:ai (2021) 15th annual state of Agile report. https://stateofagile.com/.

were in organisations with over 20,000 staff, showing that the move towards Agile over traditional approaches is not just for small startups.

But it is not just the development of software products where Agile is growing. A quick search for books published on Agile will show that Agile approaches are being applied to business analysis, systems engineering, human resources, IT service management, business change, sales, marketing, organisational culture and, of course, project management. Applying Agile to project management means that pretty much anything that could be a project can now be 'Agile'.

One area of growth is in applying Agile approaches at an organisational or business level, operating whole teams, divisions or companies along Agile principles. This is usually because organisations realise that they are operating in a VUCA world and it isn't just their products and services that need to respond to change and complexity, but the organisation itself.

Agile organisations don't just optimise their current state, they adapt, pivot and revolutionise their whole mission. Well publicised examples include Netflix, FujiFilm and Amazon, but the global COVID-19 pandemic provided an opportunity for Agile organisations to change and flourish in ways that just aren't possible when you are driven by three- to five-year strategic plans and fixed approaches.

Some businesses that rely on face-to-face interaction with customers decided to sit out the pandemic and wait for the world to get back to normal. Others didn't. British farmhouse cheese specialists The Courtyard Dairy[10] saw demand for cheese tastings plummet. They reacted by changing to an online model where they post the cheese and wine out to participants who join their experts for an online tutored cheese tasting.

Many training organisations pivoted to online training. Some just moved their existing courses online; others, including Agile Centre,[11] completely revised them to adapt to the differences in learning online, which had both advantages and disadvantages. For instance, they found that learning is more effective with two half-day sessions rather than one full day.

This ability to pivot demonstrates an underlying belief in the principles set out by the Agile Manifesto and provides the flexibility within the organisation to make such changes; changes that other organisations, big and small, have found difficult to make.

SIMPLE TO UNDERSTAND, DIFFICULT TO MASTER

If Agile is being applied to everything, does that mean that it is successful everywhere? Sadly, it doesn't. Agile projects also struggle and fail, just like any other type of project. However, that does not necessarily mean that Agile is not suited to those situations. More often we see examples where Agile is a good choice, but poor or naive implementation

---

10 https://www.thecourtyarddairy.co.uk.

11 https://www.agilecentre.com.

has caused problems. This is most common with inexperienced teams, but we frequently see badly executed Agile approaches by experienced and well-trained people.

In particular, it is common to see Agile teams revert back to traditional linear project approaches even though they are following an Agile approach such as Scrum. Such projects may default to capturing all the requirements at the start, then spend months of development effort without producing anything that a customer can trial or use. These projects inevitably end up with delays as the requirements and understanding evolves, resulting in changes and additional work at the end to get approval for a formal 'go live'. All too often the customer buy-in so readily available at the beginning has been lost, and trust between the customer and the development community is broken. This demonstrates that blindly following an Agile approach is not the answer. Rather, the fundamental principles and behaviours need to be embraced by people in the project and in the work that is carried out.

This paradox – Agile is simple to understand yet difficult to apply – runs through many of the challenges teams and organisations face when trying to adopt Agile frameworks or methods and is a theme we will revisit.

Why is it so hard?

There are many reasons why Agile is so difficult to adopt. It suffers from the same factors that any large change suffers from: organisational resistance, Conway's Law[12] and other systemic issues. Yet, with Agile's people and team-centric focus, you may be surprised that, even within a team, Agile adoption is still difficult. We have identified three main factors within teams that contribute to Agile failures.

One – Comfort in the familiar
The Agile Manifesto is only 68 words and seems like common sense. This can lull us into a false sense of security. If it's common sense to us, then surely we will be adhering to its values by default? An Agile mindset, however, is quite a large paradigm shift from where most people's default behaviours lie. We are comforted by following plans and processes; we are used to there being a single correct answer that we can find if we try hard enough; we have been consistently rewarded for individual performance over team performance throughout our academic and work careers; we value big projects and big change more than small increments and partial solutions.

These are just some of the things that make us naturally resistant to the values and principles of Agile and why it is so easy for us to veer away from good Agile practice without realising it.

Two – Too quick to customise
Teams can often rush to change and customise an approach too quickly. This is partly the fault of some Agile trainers and coaches who (rightly) say that there may be some 'tailoring' required to match the approach to the situation. While this is true, most Agile

---

12 Melvin Conway observed in 1968 that 'Any organization that designs a system (defined broadly) will produce a design whose structure is a copy of the organization's communication structure.' Conway, M. E. (1968) How do committees invent? *Datamation*, 14 (5), 28–31.

practices are quite widely applicable and seldom need much 'tailoring' when they are applied correctly. The problem is that they are often not applied well. Therefore, before tailoring and changing (or omitting) an element of an Agile approach, we would always advise making absolutely certain you are applying it properly in the first place.

Three – It would be easier without the people

The third factor that makes Agile hard in practice is that it is a highly people-centric approach, and people are complex, unpredictable and wilful. Agile doesn't have formulae and detailed analysis that will tell you the right answer; it gets people together to share knowledge and understanding before selecting a way forward that might be right or might not. It doesn't put individuals in absolute charge – it expects teams to collaborate to reach decisions – and it doesn't assume things are going to go well – it expects problems to arise and for teams to identify constant improvements to the way they work. All these things are unusual for many people, and counter to much of our experience and training to date. That makes it hard to apply well.

These three reasons are why getting a firm grip on the fundamental principles of Agile is so important. When we deeply understand Agile and why it works so well when applied properly, we are in a far stronger position to identify when things start to go wrong and adapt. When we understand why Agile approaches work, it is easier for us to hold faith when it feels uncomfortable and to make adaptations that reinforce the Agile values rather than undermine them or revert to the familiar.

SUMMARY

The Agile Manifesto is coming of age. It is no longer only relevant to software products or small organisations. A much wider range of organisations, leaders, teams and projects can benefit from a more Agile approach.

Through its focus on dealing with complexity and change, there are more and more business problems that suit an Agile approach. Through its focus on people, interactions and collaboration it is converging with evolutions in leadership theory, making Agile relevant to business change and enabling change to organisational culture and behaviours. But it won't be easy. Adopting an Agile mindset will challenge decades of cultural norms and business behaviours. There is a strong tendency to 'snap-back' to traditional approaches, which are comforting and familiar. Even when we know they don't work well, it is easy to presume that this time might be different. They appeal to our logical brains. It makes sense that we should be able to conduct the right analysis, define the right plan and execute it to succeed; however, now, more than ever, we are realising that it's just not possible to do that. Even for relatively simple problems, there are too many variables, too little we can trust to remain the same and too many people involved. This environment is where Agile approaches thrive. For example:

- having a clear vision but achieving it with small iterations of value;
- continually testing whether you are doing the right thing through real-life problems;
- expecting to be wrong and having the ability to adapt and change;
- assuming you can get better and looking for ways to improve;

- trusting people to do the right thing and empowering them to make decisions;
- sharing what you are doing;
- being transparent and asking for feedback so you can get better;
- stopping when you aren't making things better, or where your time is better spent on a different problem.

There isn't anything software-specific about the above statements. They can apply in a wide range of situations and be applied at any level of an organisation. This book will delve into this in more detail and help you to understand Agile principles so that you can apply them to your situation, whatever it is.

2 THE ORIGINS OF AGILE

Agile emerged as a response to a myriad of processes, influences and ideas dating back decades

Agile didn't begin as a single idea or as the product of a single person's experience – it evolved over decades, and we can trace elements of Agile to numerous other ideas, approaches, concepts and theories dating back as far as the 1600s. However, it was at a single event in 2001 when the word 'Agile' came to be applied to these things.

The mid-20th century saw the early days of software development, and the methods being used tended to mirror those of earlier manufacturing and hardware approaches. They were linear, with each aspect of development being completed before the next would begin. This made sense with hardware, but some of those applying this approach to software began to see problems with it. They started experimenting with different methods to order and manage the work, and they began to talk about their findings with each other. The ideas emerging from this small minority of developers gradually spread through papers, articles, conferences and word of mouth.

As their ideas matured, many of them began developing those ideas into brands and methods they could market to others. Yet, despite their differences, these people and their approaches shared much in common. One trait they shared was their desire to be collaborative and the notion that working together can reach a better outcome than working individually. This was partly what drew them together in February 2001 at a ski lodge in Utah, where the common ground they shared emerged as the Agile Manifesto.

This chapter explores that journey and helps you to understand how the richness of Agile's heritage can explain why it is so successful. We describe the traditional, linear, 'heavyweight' approaches that were (and to some extent still are) dominant, and explain some of the alternative approaches that influence Agile. Finally, we describe how the 17 authors of the Agile Manifesto managed to reach such profound and influential common ground despite seemingly being in competition with one another.

Even 20 years ago, the only thing new about 'Agile' was its name. This chapter helps you to understand why and provides you with a solid basis to the rest of the book where we help you to understand Agile in more depth.

THE ESTABLISHED APPROACH TO DEVELOPMENT

Before we start to think about Agile, it is worth first considering the alternatives to developing systems and solutions prior to the Agile Manifesto. These are still relevant and have their place in systems development today.

The linear approach

There are many approaches to delivering solutions, but they mainly break down into two types: an Agile approach or a linear approach. Prior to the emergence of Agile, most development took a linear approach in which the main building blocks of the solution were carried out sequentially, with one being completed – and usually signed off – before the next was started. By putting enough effort and talent into each stage, and by applying rigorous processes and scrutiny, the team expectation is that each element (requirements elicitation, analysis, design, test, etc.) will be correct and therefore flow into the next step. Change is managed as an exception activity within the steps and is minimised so as to not cause delay. If there are multiple versions or releases, each version would follow its own linear approach.

In 1970, Dr Winston Royce wrote a paper in which he reflected on the previous nine years he had spent at Lockheed building software packages for spacecraft mission planning, commanding and post-flight analysis.[13] In the paper he drew several diagrams to illustrate his points. One has proved particularly influential and been coined the Waterfall model (see Figure 2.1).

Figure 2.1 Royce's Waterfall diagram (Adapted from Royce, 1970)

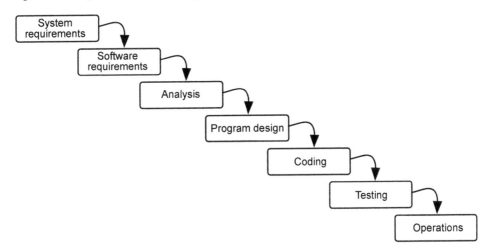

This model describes the seven steps that are required to successfully deliver a software system. Although Royce did not intend this to be a recommendation of how software should be built, that is how it was interpreted and how many organisations apply it. In fact, Royce describes this approach as 'risky and invites failure' and that it has 'never worked on large software development efforts'. The rest of his paper proposed alternative approaches that bear more similarities to Agile approaches than most people think.

---

13 Royce, W. W. (1970) Managing the development of large software systems. *Proc. IEEE Wescon*, 26, 328–388. https://www-scf.usc.edu/~csci201/lectures/Lecture11/royce1970.pdf.

There are other approaches, such as the V-Model for systems engineering, which also set out steps that are executed in a linear fashion with delivery to the customer at the end. The V-Model is so called as it is presented as a V with the left side describing the decomposing of business need to system and component requirements, the right side building up testing of components, integration, system testing and business case validation and verification, and component implementation at the base. It can be thought of as an extension of the Waterfall process with added layers of testing, since each layer of testing on the right side maps across to a requirement description on the left.[14]

Despite his reservations at the time, Royce's Waterfall model is still a popular way to develop software and deliver solutions. Even when teams try to be Agile, they often end up with an approach that resembles the Waterfall, with most of the analysis at the start and delivery delayed until the end.

When considering linear approaches, there are two main facets that are distinctly different from Agile approaches. They are:

- how the work is decided;
- how teams are managed and led.

How the work is decided

In linear approaches, such as Waterfall, the work is decided in advance based on up-front requirement and analysis steps. This aims to achieve a level of certainty and accuracy through rigorous analysis. In some ways this makes sense: do each stage once and do it well. It will be cheaper to fix mistakes in analysis than in design and cheaper to fix mistakes in design than after release.

So, it makes sense to put a lot of focus on getting analysis and design correct before moving onto implementation, test and release. However, as we will discuss throughout this book, this depends on it being possible for up-front analysis to be (and remain) true. This is increasingly rare in today's real world projects and distinctly different from the pace of change encountered through the mainframe systems of the 1960s and 1970s. Deciding a complete project's worth of work in advance seems implausible in the volatile, uncertain, complex and ambiguous world we live in today and hence why Agile adoption has become far more appealing.

How teams are managed and led

Management in linear approaches is typically top-down command and control, with managers instructing team members what to do. Work is planned in advance, assigned to teams and monitored by managers. More experienced engineers are promoted to lead or manager roles, and it is generally assumed that the more senior you are, the more skilled and experienced you are. Decisions tend to be escalated up to managers

---

14 Jesko, G., Lamm, S. R. and Walker, M. (2016) *Model-Based System Architecture*. John Wiley & Sons, Hoboken, NJ.

to make and cascaded down to the workers to implement. Chapter 9 discusses this type of leadership (Theory X) in more detail.

Work is typically managed as a project, with each step detailed in a plan, usually in advance. The project manager creates a product breakdown structure and a work breakdown structure. Each work item is then estimated and a project duration established. To reduce risk, each stage includes completion sign-off, after which the artefacts created are generally not changed without invoking a change process. Since change gets more expensive the further down the waterfall you go, change is heavily resisted and getting confidence in each step before starting the next is really important.

INFLUENCES ON AGILE

There is a rich mix of influences on Agile, dating back to 1620 when Francis Bacon first described the scientific method of empiricism that is at its heart (see Chapter 6). Many of the influences are from the software world, but by no means all of them. Rigid production lines with each machine carrying out a fixed task may seem like the antithesis of Agile, but the early 20th-century pioneers of manufacturing such as Henry Ford laid some of the foundations for it. Their focus on efficiency, standardisation and automation made sense for relatively simple problem spaces; so too with Agile, where continuous improvement and delivering value as quickly as possible means automating processes where possible.

The Toyota Production System

The Toyota Production System evolved from Toyota's origins making weaving looms and creating automated production lines for textile mills.[15] Based on the philosophy of eliminating all waste, it has a strong culture of continuous improvement and empowering workers on the production line.

One example of empowerment is the Andon Cord – a rope or button that will stop the production line. Any worker who spots a problem is expected to pull the Andon Cord so that the abnormality can be addressed. Any use of the cord results in a 'thank you', not a reprimand, thus encouraging workers to pull the cord not just when they are sure something is wrong, but as soon as they suspect something is not right. This focus on quality over speed is what sets Toyota apart from its competitors.

However, Toyota also focuses on speed. The philosophy of *jidoka* (automation with a human touch) means that the ingenuity of humans design the system, but once shown to have value, processes are automated. Then a *kaizen* (continuous improvement) approach is applied to steadily simplify, improve and make the element more efficient. Many of these improvement ideas come from the workers, who are empowered to suggest and test possible improvements.

The Lean movement was largely born out of the innovations of Toyota and has itself been hugely influential, not just on Agile but throughout manufacturing and beyond.

---

15 https://global.toyota/en/company/vision-and-philosophy/production-system/.

The New New Product Development Game

In 1986 the *Harvard Business Review* published an article by Hirotaka Takeuchi and Ikujiro Nonaka called The New New Product Development Game.[16] They had observed that the rules of the game of product development were changing. It wasn't good enough to take years to bring a new product to market anymore; the most successful companies were bringing products to market much more quickly, and they were cheaper and better.

When they looked at some of these products, they found that none of them were applying a linear approach to development – that is, one where research and development pass ideas onto engineering, who pass designs onto production, who pass products into marketing, which they characterised as being like a relay race, where the baton is passed from one team to another. Instead, products were being developed by an integrated team; one that behaved more like a rugby team, all moving forward together, passing the ball between them.

The paper didn't just introduce the rugby metaphor that would inspire Scrum, it also described several core behaviours that can be found in the Agile Manifesto and in the Agile methods that would follow:

- self-organising teams;
- iterative development;
- subtle leadership;
- empowered teams;
- engineers encouraged to go out and talk to customers;
- striving for constant iteration in a world of constant change.

What's interesting about the New New Product Development Game is that none of the products investigated were software products – they were paper copiers (Fuji-Xerox), cameras (Canon), a car (Honda) and a PC (NEC) – yet their conclusions were remarkably similar to those from the software community who created Agile.

Iterative development

The integrated 'rugby' method recommended an iterative approach to development with overlapping development phases and iterative experimentation. Sixty years earlier, at Bell Labs, the engineer and scientist Walter Shewhart was describing the scientific method as 'specification – production – inspection' and using a scientific, empirical approach to improve manufacturing quality. His success led to him publishing a book in 1931,[17] and later turning his control chart ideas into the Shewhart Cycle in 1939.[18]

---

16 Takeuchi, H. and Nonaka, I. (1986) The new new product development game. *Harvard Bus. Rev.*, January. https://hbr.org/1986/01/the-new-new-product-development-game.

17 Shewhart, W. A. (1931) *Economic Control of Quality of Manufactured Product*. Van Nostrand Co. Inc., New York. Reprinted in 2015 by Martino Fine Books, Eastford, CT.

18 Shewhart, W. A. (1939) *Statistical Method from the Viewpoint of Statistical Control*. Graduate School, Department of Agriculture, Washington, DC.

W. Edwards Deming would later popularise this in Japan in 1950, where it became known as the Deming Cycle, and as the plan-do-study-act (PDSA) cycle that defines continuous improvement[19] (see Figure 2.2).

Figure 2.2 Deming's plan-do-study-act cycle of continuous improvement (Adapted from Shewhart, 1939 and Deming, 1982)

This iterative approach was also advocated for large software projects. In 1986, Barry Boehm was working on US defence software projects when he published a paper on his 'Spiral Model' (see Figure 2.3).[20] The solution is developed across several iterations, each going through the same development stages with each iteration building on the lessons learned from the previous iterations.

Around the same time, Dr Ivar Jacobson was using his experience at Ericsson to come up with a new way to manage requirements he called 'Use Cases'.[21] A decade later he joined forces with James Rumbough and Grady Booch to create the Rational Unified Process – a tailorable framework for iterative software development with a focus on modelling and component architectural design.[22]

The lightweight software development methods

Over the 1990s, software development exploded in popularity and sophistication. What had been the preserve of large organisations with large mainframe computers and bespoke languages was democratised with the advent of the PC. Even within those large organisations, pioneers were finding alternative ways to develop software that didn't follow the traditional linear and Waterfall development approach.

Approaches such as rapid application development (RAD), extreme programming (XP), Crystal, feature driven development, adaptive software development and Scrum were emerging. They were termed 'lightweight' development methods as they were not as 'heavyweight' as the established approaches such as the Waterfall approach or the V-Model.

---

19 Deming, W. E. (1982) *Out of the Crisis*. MIT Press, Cambridge, MA. Earlier in Deming's career he used plan-do-check-act (PDCA) but changed 'check' to 'study' as he felt that 'check' emphasised inspection over analysis.

20 Boehm, B. (1986) A spiral model of software development and enhancement. *ACM SIGSOFT Software Eng. Not.*, 11 (4), 14–24.

21 Jacobson, I. (1992) *Object Oriented Software Engineering: A Use Case Driven Approach*. ACM Press, Addison-Wesley, Boston, MA.

22 Jacobson, I., Booch, G. and Rumbaugh, J. (1999) *The Unified Software Development Process*. Addison Wesley, Boston, MA.

Figure 2.3 Boehm's Spiral Model (Adapted from Boehm, 1986)

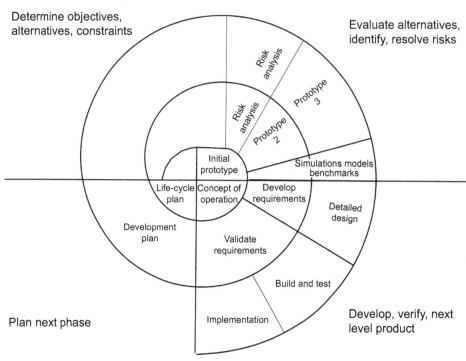

Although 'lightweight', many of these approaches emerged from large product development activities: XP from the C3 Project at Chrysler (a payroll system);[23] Scrum from the New New Product Development Game, meeting culture at Borland[24] and the complex process control theory at DuPont;[25] and DSDM (formally known as the Dynamic System Development Method) has its origins in RAD that emerged from blue chip organisations like British Airways, Oracle and ANZ Bank.[26]

THE MANIFESTO STORY

Many of the influences mentioned earlier had been around for a long time, but it was one event in February 2001 that catalysed them into what we now know as 'Agile' and resulted in the Agile Manifesto. On its 20th anniversary, Fadi Stephan published an article

23 https://martinfowler.com/bliki/C3.html.

24 Rigby, D., Sutherland, J. and Takeuchi, H. (2016) The secret history of Agile innovation. *Harvard Bus. Rev.*, April. https://hbr.org/2016/04/the-secret-history-of-agile-innovation.

25 http://leanmagazine.net/wordpress/wp-content/uploads/The-Scrum-Story.pdf; https://kenschwaber.wordpress.com/2010/06/10/waterfall-leankanban-and-scrum-2/; Highsmith, J. (2002) *Agile Software Development Ecosystems.* Addison-Wesley, Hoboken, NJ.

26 https://thedigitalprojectmanager.com/dsdm-consortium/; https://www.agilebusiness.org/page/history/.

describing the event from behind the scenes.[27] In that meeting, 17 people got together in a ski lodge in Utah where, over the course of three days, they managed to find common ground for their different perspectives and products and created the Agile Manifesto.

What is surprising is that they were able to find common ground at all, since they represented several different theories and approaches and were, in some respects, competitors of one another. Indeed, one of the participants, Alistair Cockburn, observed 'I personally didn't expect that this particular group of agilists to ever agree on anything substantive.'[28]

The various backgrounds

The original idea to get together to identify common ground came as a result of some discussions at an XP retreat about whether XP should extend beyond its focus on technical software practices. This led to Martin Fowler reaching out to Alistair Cockburn, who was developing the Crystal method and had arranged similar meetings in the past. They thought they should get themselves, and their respective contact lists, together to talk about this more.

The invite list grew, and included people such as Jeff Sutherland, Ken Schwaber and Mike Beedle (who were popularising Scrum), Joe Kern (feature driven development), Arie Van Benneken (DSDM), Jim Highsmith (adaptive software development) and many others, including some specifically to bring in different perspectives such as testing or more formal processes. 17 of the invitees were able to attend. They settled on Utah as the venue largely for logistical reasons (the airport was easier to get to and some of the main organisers lived there).

The lightweight methods conference

They arrived on Sunday 11 February and would spend the next three days in a fairly relaxed agenda that included time to ski and laze in the hot-tub but also several hours of discussion a day. The aim was to understand what everyone wanted to achieve, set up a website to share their thinking and to come up with a manifesto they could all commit to signing. In particular, they wanted to counter the notion that chief information officers needed large, heavyweight frameworks, lots of documentation and lots of people to ensure their projects would 'be safe' and deliver.

Having got to know one another better and learned about each other's different methods, they approached the first hurdle: what to call this thing. Nobody was keen on being described as 'lightweight', and some of the other candidates, such as 'lean' or 'adaptive', had already become associated with specific approaches – they settled on 'Agile'.

There was a lot of good discussion, but it took Dave Thomas and Martin Fowler to grab a pen and propose some values to catalyse the group into focusing on something tangible to agree on. The group discussed and iterated the values through several versions (including debating which order they should take) before settling on the four that we describe in Chapter 4.

---

27 Stephan, F. (2021) A behind the scenes look at the writing of the Agile Manifesto. Kaizenko. https://www.kaizenko.com/a-behind-the-scenes-look-at-the-writing-of-the-agile-manifesto/.

28 History: The Agile Manifesto. Agile Manifesto.org. https://agilemanifesto.org/history.html.

The idea of a set of principles was discussed, but they didn't have time to discuss them in more depth; that happened over email exchanges over the following weeks, with a draft published in April 2001. Ward Cunningham (inventor of the Wiki) then set up a website to promote the manifesto and allow visitors to show their support by signing up. They formed the Agile Alliance later that year as a non-profit organisation to further Agile methods.

SUMMARY

Although it formally emerged in 2001, the roots of Agile can be traced back as far as Francis Bacon's scientific method, first described in the 1600s, and to the manufacturing innovations that revolutionised textiles and motor manufacturing in the early 1900s.

However, it was the surge in new ways to develop software in the 1990s that were the strongest influences. As various innovators and pioneers of software rebelled against the established 'heavyweight' processes that dominated at the time, they came together and found that they could all agree on a simple expression of their values and beliefs that became the Agile Manifesto.

What is perhaps most remarkable is that 17 people with different approaches, many trying to sell or promote their approach in competition with one another, were able to agree on common ground in just three days. And that common ground has stood the test of time.

3 PROJECTS AND PRODUCTS IN AGILE

In Agile, the product is the key player; so what is an Agile project, and do we need one?

Many of us are familiar with using the term 'project' when delivering change or developing technical solutions. An Agile delivery is different and introduces some new language. This chapter explains why:

- 'Project' isn't always a helpful term to use for Agile work as it can lead to unhelpful assumptions.
- 'Product' is the dominant word used by Agile teams at it helps to maintain stronger customer focus.
- Agile applies both an iterative and an incremental approach to delivery, and this is key to how it delivers value.
- The Product Backlog is such a critical artefact.

WHAT IS A PROJECT?

The *Oxford English Dictionary* defines 'project' as:

> An individual or collaborative enterprise that is carefully planned to achieve a particular aim.[29]

The first challenge with this definition in terms of Agile delivery is the reference to 'carefully planned'. While Agile deliveries can be carefully led, the level of planning is usually very variable – tightly planned in the first couple of weeks; more loosely planned over the next couple of months; and barely planned at all over the next couple of quarters.

This doesn't mean they are poorly led – it is an artefact of Agile approaches being particularly well suited to problems where the detail of the problem isn't clear at the start, as we will see in Chapter 4. This means that we cannot 'carefully plan' to meet our 'particular aim' in advance. Instead, Agile teams must continually plan and adjust as we learn more about the problem we are solving and the solution we are developing.

As we described in Chapter 2, traditional linear projects begin with a requirement, analysis and design phases where the problem is thoroughly understood, requirements fully defined and a solution proposed and analysed. Once this is complete, the development of the solution starts.

---

29 https://www.lexico.com/definition/project.

In Agile deliveries, we begin developing a solution before we even know the detail and before we have thought through a detailed design. Furthermore, we expect the customers to start **using** the solution when we **know** it doesn't meet all their needs and that its design will likely change. Both these behaviours are profoundly different from classic, linear project management. Understanding that this is how Agile approaches work is critical to being able to understand or lead Agile work.

> You will note we have refrained from using the phrase 'Agile project'. This is for the reasons above. However, many teams and organisations still use the word 'project' and there are even some Agile methods that describe 'Agile projects'. We prefer not to. We feel it can be confusing and lead to a mismatch in expectations, particularly with stakeholders outside the Agile delivery team.

ITERATIVE AND INCREMENTAL

One of the fundamental properties of an Agile delivery is that it presents the solution to the customer in an **incremental** and **iterative** way. This means that:

- The solution is delivered in a series of iterations, usually time-bound, with each iteration delivering a version of the solution or product.
- The value of these versions to the customer incrementally increases with each iteration.

In other words, customers can start using the product very early in the project's life cycle, and each time a new increment is completed, it will add more value – usually through implementing more of the users' needs and improving existing features.

As customers use the solution, they understand more about what they need, and whether this version of the solution is meeting those needs. This feedback allows new ideas to be refined, and the next version of the solution to be better. This experience of the solution also improves the customer's understanding of what is important to them, and therefore what is important to deliver next, and enables prioritisation of the user needs to be achieved iteratively and incrementally.

This feedback loop is essential within Agile delivery as it enables the customer to evolve their ideas throughout. Collaboration between the team and the customer is encouraged so that the design and architecture of the solution also adapts and iterates throughout the development life cycle to support the evolved understanding.

This is particularly important for IT products, where priority of the user needs can be very volatile. The longer it takes to make a decision regarding implementation of a user need, the less likely it is that the user need will still be valid or a priority. In Agile delivery, it is advisable to use short iterations to incrementally deliver a small number of user needs that you are certain the customer has prioritised. Once this has occurred, the customer will be better placed to prioritise what they need next and provide feedback for any new ideas that have arisen from the first increment. This forms the basis for the next iteration and ensures that users' needs are being understood just enough and just in time.

Each iteration is like a short project

This iterative and incremental approach means that we should visit all aspects of the delivery life cycle in every iteration: understanding user needs, deciding our design options, implementing and testing a solution and deploying that solution for customers to use. That's why one of the most widely used Agile approaches, Scrum, states that each iteration 'may be considered [to be] a short project'.[30] This is a helpful way to think of Agile delivery and a good use of the word 'project'. It also helps us to understand the second fundamental difference between Agile and traditional projects – their duration.

Traditional projects are usually very time centric, with an emphasis on planning and achieving funding milestones. This depends on accurate estimation to ensure the time available will allow the scope to be delivered. Extending projects usually requires some form of change control providing additional layers of governance that make change harder rather than enabling flexibility. As projects are funded and planned for set periods of time, they are rarely stopped early unless there is some crisis. The fundamental flaw with this approach is that it doesn't work well in an environment where change is likely. We need to shift thinking away from fixed scope and big up-front planning to something that can adapt to change more readily.

Agile deliveries can achieve this as they don't have a fixed duration or long up-front planning and design sessions, as traditional projects do. Rather, every iteration provides an opportunity for the customer to decide whether they want to continue to invest in improving the solution. Since Agile teams always aim to deliver a solution that customers can use, this means that they can iterate until the customer needs have been met by the solution or until the customer decides to stop funding. Essentially, every iteration could be the last. Conversely, if an Agile team is considered to still be adding value to a solution beyond the originally anticipated duration, a customer can decide to continue investing in it.

This is why Agile deliveries can be better value than traditional projects. Because they focus only on delivering what the customer needs, they save time and money by not developing features that the customer identified at the start, but subsequently decides they don't need. In a traditional project, requirements are fully elaborated and documented at the start even if they turn out to be a low priority.

Even well-managed traditional projects can overrun. Customers often realise they need new or different requirements after the initial requirements have been agreed. This is usually due to not truly knowing what they needed at the start, or because things have changed since they initially provided their requirements. Agile teams try to avoid contracts around requirements and even try to avoid using requirements at all, instead referring to them as work items, ideas and customer needs. This avoids the contractual aspects often associated with requirements. With traditional projects they are agreed

---

30 Scrum Guides (2020) The 2020 Scrum guide. https://www.scrumguides.org/scrum-guide.html.

and signed off before the first line of code is written; in Agile this is simply managed through a prioritised backlog where less important work items are de-prioritised and the customer may decide they don't need them at all.

Managing work in this way enables time and effort only to be spent understanding and developing the items that are most important and provides the flexibility for when customers change their mind. This is discussed in more detail in Chapters 8 and 10.

Since the major cost in many Agile deliveries is people's time, this also means that Agile teams maintain flexibility with cost; it means that when we need to use cost as a constraint, we can be confident that we get the best value for our investment because we deliver the highest priority requirements first. Even in situations when they take longer than anticipated, we know that the requirements we don't have time for are certain to be less important than those we do.

Agile deliveries maintain a flexible approach to planning where the detail is understood only when a customer need has been prioritised. While this may look like short-term planning, there is still forethought and long-term planning in terms of roadmaps and a vision. It's just that the plans can change based on feedback and that the detail is developed just in time.

Of course, there are also many situations where the traditional, linear approach is the best choice to manage the delivery. Where we are certain the requirements will not and cannot change – perhaps a like-for-like legacy system replacement – then a traditional Waterfall approach is likely to be faster and cheaper. The frequent production of iterative versions of the solution and checking the priority of requirements will be wasteful and prevent the team delivering faster.

THE IMPORTANCE OF THE PRODUCT

Although the word 'project' still carries significance and weight in many organisations, in Agile teams the word 'product' is far more important. The seemingly insignificant difference signals an important shift in mindset:

- A **product** focus requires a focus on the customer, their needs and ensuring those needs are met by the product.
- A **project** focus implies a focus on the planned delivery approach and ensuring that we deliver what we are contracted to.

The term 'product' in Agile refers to whatever is providing value to the customer. Often it is a tangible product, such as some software, media or a physical item, but it can also be a service, business process, change initiative or organisational transformation. In short, it can be anything that the customer finds valuable.

This focus on the product is also reflected in Agile roles. In every Agile approach there is a significant role responsible for the ownership of the product, usually called the Product Owner. This is the person who is accountable for the product meeting the needs of the customer and for owning the Product Backlog – the list of things that the product could do.

The Product Backlog

The word 'backlog' is an unusual one, so it is worth explaining here. In simple terms, it is just the list of work items or ideas that will help to achieve value for the customer; but it is much more significant than it implies. The Product Backlog represents the **current** view on what the product needs to do to meet the needs of the customer. It is an ordered list, with the items at the top being those that represent the greatest value or are most urgent to address, and below that are things that are less important (see Figure 3.1). It is not a plan.

Figure 3.1 The Product Backlog

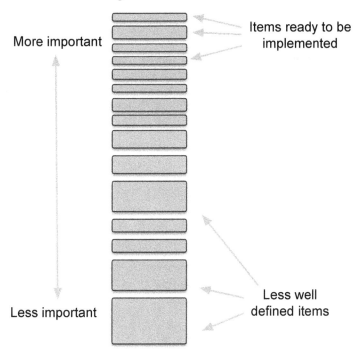

Product Backlog

Managing the backlog is an ongoing and crucially important task. Once the team is working on the current iteration, the Product Owner's role is to make sure that the backlog continues to represent the current view of what is important. That may mean things are shuffled around, added, changed, split, combined or even removed. In this way the backlog constantly represents the current priority and ensures the team is always working on the most valuable work.

The Product Owner must also ensure that the work at the top of the backlog – the things that are most likely to be delivered next – describes things that can be delivered and used by real users for real tasks. If it doesn't, the team won't be able to release versions of the solution (or product) that can be used, and the core premise of iterative **and** incremental delivery is lost.

This is surprisingly hard to do well, and it is easy to slip into bad habits such as treating backlog items as commitments rather than options, or describing technical components rather than user value. It is really important that each backlog item describes clear, genuine value for the users of the product. A good tip to test this is to ask someone outside the team (such as a director or user) what the backlog item means and whether they would benefit from it. If they can't answer, perhaps it isn't written in terms of customer value.

Since the items at the top of the backlog are those that need to be taken into the next iteration, they must be small enough to be completed in less than the length of the iteration; but, given that users' needs change, it would be wasteful to spend a lot of time elaborating things that won't be prioritised for delivery for a long time.

Good backlogs will have loosely defined, big items at the bottom and smaller elaborated items at the top. The bigger items represent larger pieces of work that are not yet fully understood, and perhaps contain complex user goals. As and when these items become important, they can be broken down into smaller goals and the detail and complexities will be uncovered at that point, and not before.

Crucially, the Product Backlog doesn't need to contain everything the product could ever do – it just needs to contain things that are potentially important enough to be delivered in the next few iterations. Things can always be added to it and longer-term planning can be carried out elsewhere. Approaches for this are covered in Chapter 10.

SUMMARY

Agile approaches introduce new language alongside new ways of thinking. Instead of thinking about a project, with clear aims and plans at the start, we think of a product, with a customer need that must be met.

Customer needs are described in a Product Backlog, which is a prioritised list of work items describing the value a customer can obtain. We often call these items 'stories', as they help to tell a story of what we intend the product to do. This is covered more in Chapter 10.

Because all Agile approaches expect change, we commit only to short timeframes – perhaps just a week or two – and leave everything else more fluid. That means we can introduce change late in the process as it arises, even late in the development. Conveying longer-term intentions may be hard, so other ways to achieve this are required, such as roadmaps. However, even roadmaps or release plans are just guesses – we still expect they may change, so we don't put in too much detail and we certainly don't expect them to be treated as commitments or promises, as traditional plans are. They are just well-intentioned, well-informed guesses that provide a snapshot of the future, which can change as we learn and evolve our understanding.

As work continues through the development of a product, it is essential that multiple versions of the product are delivered so that the customer can use it as early as possible, within the first few weeks if possible. Each version that the customer can use for their real business problems results in valuable knowledge and feedback. Without this feedback, an Agile approach is pointless.

The early deliverables enable the customer to work out whether the product is working for them and thus helps them to understand their needs better. Feedback on the product itself also helps the developers to improve its quality and evolve the architecture and design. As we get further into the development, our ideas of what still needs to be on the backlog improves and we get a better idea of when we may achieve the overall outcome.

This iterative and incremental approach provides the ability to be flexible with the cost, product features and schedule of the delivery. We can ensure each iteration delivers the customer needs on time or on budget because we focus on customer outcomes and ensure each iteration achieves the outcome even if it is a minimal viable solution.

This is why Agile teams can deliver more value in less time – delivering iteratively and incrementally enables tighter focus on delivering a working solution to the customer early, thereby giving insight into whether that solution is valuable much earlier in the project life cycle than traditional projects.

4 UNDERSTANDING THE MANIFESTO FOR AGILE

At the core of 'Agile' is the manifesto; it is crucial to understand it well

The term Agile began with the Manifesto for Agile Software Development: a powerful document that is the foundation of all Agile approaches and remains just as valid today as it was when it was signed in 2001. For many, the Manifesto is a footnote in an Agile training course or certification where the main focus is on applying a process or framework. Unfortunately, skipping over the Manifesto values, or giving then scant regard, risks misunderstanding or, worse, abusing them. This is a common problem. Many believe they are 'Agile' following completion of an Agile course, yet when we compare their behaviours against the Agile Manifesto values, we find that they are not really Agile at all.

Every Agile book will mention the Agile Manifesto, but most just list the values and principles with little regard for the changes in behaviours expected by the reader to achieve those values. We believe that the Agile Manifesto values are so critical that they deserve more explanation and consideration. This chapter takes you through the Manifesto and discusses each value statement in depth. As you will see, each value statement has two parts – one side, the left-hand side, is a statement that Agile teams value highly; the other side, the right-hand side, is a statement that Agile teams want to de-emphasise and value less.

For each value, we will help you understand it from three perspectives:

- What the value is all about and why it is useful.
- What people find challenging about the value.
- Some anti-patterns we have observed that cause people to value the left-hand side less or the right-hand side more.

By understanding the Manifesto in this way, you will gain a deeper understanding of what it means to **be Agile** and how the Manifesto values can help you achieve that.

THE MANIFESTO FOR AGILE SOFTWARE DEVELOPMENT

As we discussed in Chapter 2, the Agile Manifesto was the result of three days of discussions in 2001 between a group of thought leaders and development framework experts. Despite coming from different backgrounds and having different experiences, they agreed on a short form of words that summed up how they all felt software development ought to be done to have the greatest chance of success, as shown in Figure 4.1.

Figure 4.1 The Agile Manifesto

> We are uncovering better ways of developing software by doing it and helping others do it. Through this work we have come to value:
>
> Individuals and interactions over processes and tools
> Working software over comprehensive documentation
> Customer collaboration over contract negotiation
> Responding to change over following a plan
>
> That is, while there is value in the items on the right, we value the items on the left more.

In just 68 words they managed to convey a number of powerful concepts and proposed an approach to developing products, services and solutions that was radically different from how most projects were being run. Many teams and organisations still continue to value the attributes on the right-hand side of the Manifesto, even thought they would claim they are following an Agile approach. You will see us reiterate many times throughout this book the difficulty in adhering to the Agile Manifesto values and principles despite how straightforward it seems. In fact, they are very hard to stick to and we constantly see individuals and teams struggle with the concepts.

Each element of the Manifesto deserves some attention and thought, starting with the first sentence, which sets the tone:

> We are uncovering better ways of developing software by doing it and helping others do it.

It makes clear that we are practitioners that 'do' the development of software ourselves and not managers or consultants. We are directly involved in the work. Agile teams are teams where everyone is involved in creating the value. That doesn't mean everyone needs to be expert software coders, but it does mean there isn't room for people whose sole role is to set tasks for others or oversee the work.

THAT SOFTWARE WORD

Before we can discuss the Manifesto in depth, we must address the elephant in the room – that 'software' word. We have already said that Agile approaches work for many types of business problems, not just those that have a software product as their solution, so why does the Manifesto continue to include the word 'software'?

In practice, as we will explore later, the word 'software' is relatively meaningless; even software products often require additional, non-software elements to provide value, such as marketing, business change or user training. But it is also a reflection of the origins of the Manifesto and it is helpful to remember the context in which the Manifesto was written, particularly when we think of the Agile principles.

For many, replacing the word 'software' with another word, such as 'solution' is preferable so that those with non-software problems won't be put off, or consider that Agile can't help them. However, we prefer to stick with the original, and use it as a trigger to discuss what we mean by 'working software' and what 'emergent design' may mean for non-software teams.

THE VALUES

At the heart of the Agile Manifesto are four value statements. They are particularly powerful because of the way they are framed. Each sets out two contrasting viewpoints with one valued **more than** the other. Unlike most sets of values, this not only sets out what we should do, but also what we should try to avoid.

The final sentence of the Manifesto is often misunderstood:

That is, while there is value in the items on the right, we value the items on the left more.

While it is clear that the items on the right of the Manifesto have value, that doesn't mean that they need as much attention as those on the left. One reason for this is that many organisations and teams are already very comfortable with the items on the right; our working practices and management approaches overwhelmingly favour values such as planning, control, consistency and formal documentation. This means that, by default, many people will naturally favour the statements on the right of the Manifesto. The challenge isn't reminding teams that there is value in the items on the right – they already value those things. The challenge is in helping teams shift their default behaviours towards the items on the left.

We will now explore each of the values in turn, understanding what underpins them and why they are so significant. We will share practical advice and tips and look at common challenges of both the left- and the right-hand statements contained within the Manifesto.

Individuals and interactions over processes and tools

This statement is all about people – because it is people who make the biggest impact on the success of delivery (see Figure 4.2). It is people who create the solution, and it is people who will be using the solution. Getting from the problem to a good enough solution therefore requires lots of communication and interaction between lots of people. Some of this interaction can be automated or standardised, but it is possible to take this too far – to the extent that the process becomes more important than the people. You may have experienced this yourself if you have ever become lost in the multiple menus of automated call centre systems, struggling to find a combination of options to match the reason for your call.

To understand this value, let's consider the software domain that the Manifesto authors were familiar with. The creation of software products to meet a user need is a human endeavour. It requires people to make decisions, consider options and apply judgement. Every software product is the result of a unique combination of actions taken by people. This uniqueness means that what works well in manufacturing does not work well for software or other types of knowledge work; following the same standard process each time will not predictably meet the needs of the customer. Many people are engaged in knowledge work that, like software, overwhelmingly requires decisions to be taken, data to be analysed and judgement to be applied – work that is unique, just like the software domain the Manifesto originated from.

Figure 4.2 Individuals and interactions over processes and tools

This Manifesto value reaches far beyond the domain of software development. When we overlay the fact that our world is more VUCA – volatile, uncertain, complex and ambiguous – it is clear that trying to predict and codify everything into a standard process or tool will be futile. Tools and processes have their place, but can only help to a certain extent – delivering the best outcome for the customer will always rely more on people and human interaction.

Where we can get value from processes and tools is when we apply them to the right type of problem – those that are simple or repetitive, such as automating tests, tracking version control of artefacts, delivering simple training as e-learning or describing ways of working. They can also be valuable for more complicated situations that do not stretch into the complex – for example, tracking dependencies between system components, managing build pipelines, analysing performance data or controlling financial data.

Valuing individuals also means trusting them
An implication of valuing individuals is that we must also trust them. When things go wrong, it is rarely because people are not good enough, yet that's often our first thought. In his book, *The New Economics*,[31] Dr W. Edwards Deming attributes the blame for problems on the system, rather than other factors such as the people, 94 per cent of the time. We should assume noble intent in our people. The vast majority of us come to work intending to do a good job, are trustworthy and will make decisions we believe are the right ones. This is a powerful statement and important for Agile teams.

---

[31] Deming, W. E. (1994) *The New Economics*, Massachusetts Institute of Technology, Cambridge, MA.

Placing high degrees of trust in our people can be unnerving. We are used to systems that place protections aiming to prevent unwanted behaviour; however, such processes affect everyone, not just the few exhibiting such behaviour, and this can have a negative effect. Even seemingly benign processes exhibit this behaviour. For example, a human resources (HR) performance management process that rewards individual effort is intended to incentivise people to work to their maximum effort, but it can have a negative effect on overall team performance because people are not incentivised to work for the good of the team.

Instead, it is preferable to use processes that only trigger if the unwanted behaviour occurs. These then only affect the small minority of people who are not behaving with noble intent. Trusting people and balancing that trust with setting direction and leading is core to good Agile leadership, as we discuss in Chapter 9.

What makes this value hard to apply?
The key to this value is to treat people as people: value their opinion, remove barriers to communication and work collaboratively. However, this isn't always as easy as it sounds.

Existing processes constrain Agile behaviour   Many organisations have existing processes, some of which may be mandatory, that inhibit a focus on people. Some common examples include staff management processes, quality assurance checks, internal review stages, progress reporting, corporate tooling and standardised job roles.

Processes can become ingrained in organisational culture, which can lead to a focus more on adhering to the processes rather than adapting them or challenging them. Just because a process exists doesn't mean that it must be followed every time; not all processes are mandatory, and even those that are ought to be subject to review and continuous improvement. However, all too often that isn't the case, and it isn't always easy to propose changes.

Over-reliance on tools   Tools can also become dominant. When we are engaged in complex work, tools can help to manage the complexity and make things easier, but this is not always true. Sometimes tools can make work more complex, not less. One example is job tracking or work management tools. Because they can handle hundreds of tickets or thousands of work items, teams that use them can end up struggling to manage huge backlogs of work.

Teams that stick to simple processes – such as paper boards and sticky notes – can't track such volumes and so are forced to prioritise better and focus on finishing work to create space for new work to be captured. This makes them more efficient and more Agile, even when they are a similar size to the teams with hundreds of tickets in the job tracking tool.

Face-to-face collaboration isn't always feasible   Valuing individuals and interactions is easier when engaging with people face to face, where we can look each other in the eye and pick up non-verbal communication such as body language. Being physically in the same place enables humans to more quickly establish trust, which is essential to good team performance.

Remote collaboration and more distributed and homeworking has become more commonplace now. When teams are distributed, particularly over different time zones, it can be harder to work well together, and processes and common tooling can really help; however, be careful the tools don't dominate at the expense of human relationships.

It isn't just teams that can be more successful with high levels of interaction; products can be too. When a product is collaboratively developed by multiple people together, it tends to have higher quality, be easier to support and to perform better. This is because the constant communication within the team as they develop the solution brings quality reviews, redesigns and deeper customer understanding for free.

Anti-patterns

Table 4.1 shows some of the anti-patterns and problems we have observed when trying to value individuals and interactions or avoid over-valuing processes and tools.

Table 4.1 Anti-patterns for valuing individuals and interactions over processes and tools

The tool makes us Agile	Just because a process, framework or tool claims to be 'Agile', it doesn't mean that applying it will automatically mean you are Agile. In fact, quite the opposite. It is easy, and very common, to see a team take an Agile process, tool or technique and apply it in a very non-Agile way.
It's there so I must use it	This refers to using a tool or process that exists without questioning whether it is a good choice for the team or delivery. Good teams make a conscious decision on how they work and use tools and processes that support them, avoiding those that do not.
Over-utilisation of tools	Tools are valuable and can make teams much more effective, but they are often feature rich, with many additional capabilities and levels of detail beyond the basics. We frequently see teams seduced into making far more use of a tool (or process) than they need to just because the tool lets them.
	It's OK to use a complex tool for a simple task, but don't let a complex tool turn a simple task into a complex task.
Relentless automation	Just because we can automate something, doesn't mean we should. For instance, automating an infrequent process can be costly and divert the team from more valuable work.
	Replacing human interactions with machines can cause other negative impacts. For example, automation of customer service can affect customer experience and brand loyalty.
Bad execution vs bad process	When processes don't work, it can be easy to blame them. Often, however, the problem is bad execution. Ensure you are using a process or tool properly before ditching or changing it.

(Continued)

Table 4.1 (Continued)

Tool worship	Tools are valuable when they enable the team, but they do not have intrinsic value themselves. If there are better ways to enable the team, they should be considered. This is undermined when the tool becomes the centre of attention, as we see when there are guilds, communities of practice or other groups dedicated to a particular product or tool. This is a clear example of valuing the tool more than the people using it.
Hierarchies	Hierarchies of status, grade or title can inhibit communication paths and cause people to focus more on gaining promotion than delivering value to the customer. Even with a range of seniority or salaries in a team, you can still create flat hierarchies through good leadership and shared purpose.
Over-standardisation	Shared approaches and standardised ways of working can bring consistency and help new team members get up to speed quickly. Take it too far, and you can rob the team of the ability to be creative or to innovate. Even established standards should be reviewed and improved or removed.
Too busy to talk	If everyone in the team is working flat out, the team won't have any opportunity to get to know each other, talk about their work or find ways to help one another. Build time into the team rhythms and ways of working for the team to get to know each other better.
Focusing on individual performance	Collaboration doesn't just mean each person working on tasks towards the same product – it also means working together on the same task; but this doesn't happen when we value individuals more than teams, for example through performance management processes, bonus policy or task allocation that assumes one person for each task.
We are all experts	When everyone thinks they are an expert, there isn't any incentive to try to get better or to help others. Agile teams can always learn and improve.

Working software over comprehensive documentation

This statement is all about the specifics of what is delivered at the end of each iteration of work, and how valuable it is (see Figure 4.3). Unfortunately, the statement suffers from including the 'software' word, which can detract from its real impact, which is the other word – 'working'. 'Working' is the significant word. Software isn't working if users aren't able to use it to solve their problems, and that is true for all types of product or solution.

For users to get value from the solution, it must be available, they must be allowed to use it, and it must use real data to solve real problems. This can mean that in order to be 'working,' the solution requires a certain amount of documentation. For example, you may need to document data policies to be allowed to access another system, provide training material for users or create images for marketing.

Documentation is just another aspect of the solution and should be updated and evolve just like the other solution elements – with just enough documentation created just in time for the users who need it. Each iteration of the solution should include **just enough** documentation to support deployment, maintenance and customer needs.

Figure 4.3 Working software over comprehensive documentation

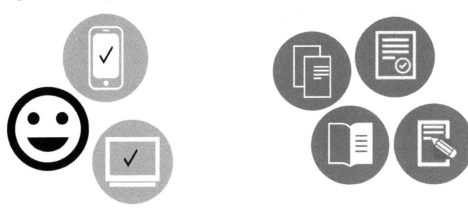

How much documentation is enough?

Achieving 'just enough' documentation is a delicate balance that requires constant iteration and evolution. There is often a tension between the team and their stakeholders over how much documentation is enough. If in doubt, identify who the documentation is for (e.g. users, system support) and ask them how much documentation is enough, and what format they want it in.

Too much documentation can be a poor investment of time, so how can we get the balance right? There are broadly two types of documentation most teams need to care about:

- governance documentation to provide information on the health, progress and viability of the work or delivery;
- product documentation to provide information to the users, supporters and future developers of the product.

Particularly in large organisations or the public sector, there can be higher-level governance structures that aren't as Agile as the delivery teams. These can have very fixed ideas of what progress reporting is necessary, and may not be willing or able to look at the team's dashboard. Persuading them otherwise can be difficult, so teams end up creating additional reports, updates or documents, often on a cadence that doesn't match the team's. This can lead to these artefacts becoming out of sync with the work of the team, and being a high overhead to maintain. If possible, align the rhythms of the team with the external processes and align as many of the reporting elements to existing team information as you can. Educating your stakeholders on your approach and helping them to understand the data the team uses can also assist.

Understand your audience

For both types of documentation, we should try to minimise the effort it takes to produce it. Often the development approaches chosen can be self-documenting, particularly for software products, removing the need for additional design documents; or, instead of creating a progress update report for a stakeholder, they could just be given access to the work tracking system used by the team, or come into their room and ask them.

Understanding your audience in this way is important for all documentation. For example:

- The needs of early adopters familiar with the problem space are different from customers forced to use a new tool they aren't used to.
- Technical users have different needs from non-technical.
- Documenting in an accessible way for disabilities requires additional thought.
- Expanding to new markets may require knowledge of different languages and cultures.

This variety of documentation should also be approached in an iterative and incremental way, with just enough documentation for the current product and its users. It can be tempting to do too much because you know it will be needed for later iterations – but that assumes later iterations will happen and they will be what you expect. Neither of these things are guaranteed, so it is better to wait until you are sure before creating that documentation.

One exception to this is accessibility. Even if you don't have any disabled users for early iterations, building in good accessibility at the start can make things much easier, and in some sectors (such as within UK Government[32]) can be a legal requirement. Meeting accessibility standards[33] tends to improve a product for all users, whether they need accessibility features themselves or not.

---

32 The 'Public Sector Bodies (Websites and Mobile Applications) (No. 2) Accessibility Regulations 2018' places a legal obligation on all public sector websites and mobile applications to be accessible and include an accessibility statement. https://www.legislation.gov.uk/uksi/2018/852/contents/made.

33 Such as the Web Content Accessibility Guidelines (known as WCAG 2.1). https://www.w3.org/TR/WCAG21/.

What makes this value hard to apply?

This should be one of the easier values to get right – after all, delivering a product to customers is clearly a beneficial thing to do – yet we frequently see teams spend months without their customers using the product. Additionally, development tools make it easy to produce lots of documentation that is tempting to publish and maintain.

We see documentation as more valuable than it is   One of the biggest challenges is that creating documentation and attaching importance to it has become commonplace in modern development practices. Traditional development approaches place high levels of value on documents, since they are deemed to be a primary way to reduce risk and ensure delivery, and are even used as a measure of progress. Documenting requirements, detailing a plan to deliver them and getting sign-off from the customer before the expensive work of development begins seems to make sense. It is only when you bring in the challenges of a VUCA world described in Chapter 1 that this approach seems wrong.

While documentation can often be an indicator of potential value, we can only confirm true business value when the solution is actually being used by a user or customer. No amount of documentation can achieve the same result.

Not delivering working solutions   The second major challenge we observe is teams who continue to deliver solutions at each iteration that cannot be used properly by their customer – in other words, they are not 'working'. A solution cannot be used by its customer if it is still in a development environment, isn't approved to be deployed, can't be bought, only solves half a problem or the users aren't trained or authorised to use it.

This manifests in several ways. When there are separate development, testing and deployment teams, it is common for the development team to think they are finished when the development is passed onto the test team. Unfortunately, the customer doesn't have value yet and, worse still, when the test team find problems, they may not be passed to the development team until the next iteration. This can mean a delay of two iterations or more, as shown in Figure 4.4. In contrast, a cross-functional Agile team (see Chapter 7) delivers complete features each iteration (see Figure 4.5).

Cross-functional teams delivering every iteration isn't always enough. Many teams use multiple environments to avoid development versions of the product causing problems in a production environment. When a team deploys a solution to one of these non-customer locations, it cannot be working for the customer since the customer cannot access it themselves for their real job.

Access to live data can also be a challenge for some teams, particularly in highly regulated or secure environments or where the product hasn't launched to market yet. This is another example where it cannot properly 'work'. Although the impact can be mitigated a little through test or synthetic data, it is always better to deploy a live product to live customers, even when there is more development to do.

Delaying deployment   Sometimes teams could deploy their product but choose not to. This is often because the increment only includes a subset of the solution or just one aspect is ready. The team or the customer suggests it would be better to wait until it is more complete before allowing it to be used.

Figure 4.4 Deployment cycle for separate development and test teams

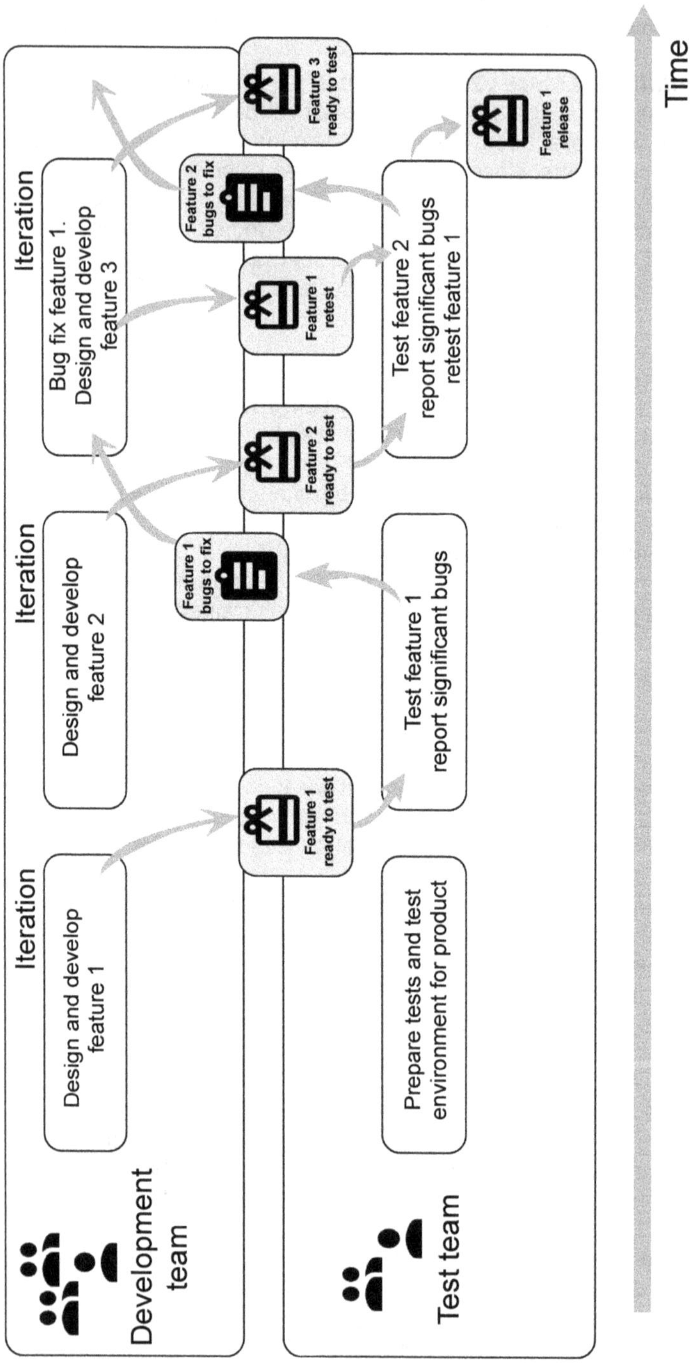

Figure 4.5 Deployment cycle for cross-functional Agile teams

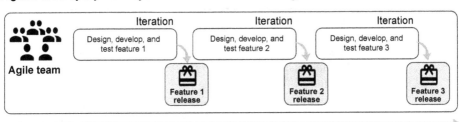

This misses the fundamental point of Agile approaches: deliver value early to the customer so that you can validate your solution and gather feedback on how well it is meeting the user need. The more frequently we do this, the quicker we get feedback on what is good and bad about our product, and the quicker we can respond to change. If the customer has changed what they need, we will know about it faster and can pivot, reprioritise or even stop the delivery.

Delaying this will not only delay any value to the customer but, more importantly, delay any feedback that we may be on the wrong track. And when that feedback does come, it will be longer and more expensive to fix. We often see this in organisations that value perfection when, ironically, delaying release until the product is perfect increases the likelihood that it will not be perfect.

Wherever possible, we should deploy the version of the product that we have, and that deployment should be to help real customers do their real job. We should ensure that our customers can use each increment of our product by knowing the criteria for use; split the work into small, user-value centric goals rather than components of the solution; and have all the skills, approvals and authorities needed to take the product live within the team or within easy reach.

Anti-patterns
Table 4.2 shows some of the anti-patterns and problems we have observed when trying to value working software or avoid over-valuing comprehensive documentation.

It is hard to overstate the importance of this value and the frequency with which it is ignored, even in teams who are trying hard to be Agile. We see teams create a backlog and earnestly work their way through it. Each iteration they make some progress, but don't have a version of the product that customers can use. Reviews focus on stories closed rather than on demonstrating the product or getting feedback from it being used by customers. Months pass before a version is presented that the customers can use, and inevitably it doesn't quite do what they need it to.

However, this is also the simplest value to do well and to improve. Simply focusing on having a working version of your solution available at each iteration is enough; preferably one that your customer will use. And that's a simple thing to test and measure.

Table 4.2 Anti-patterns for valuing working software over comprehensive documentation

Because they asked us for it	Other parts of the organisation often say they require additional documentation or reporting. Sometimes this is necessary, but not always. We often observe teams struggling with producing additional reports and documents for others without any clear justification of why.
	Understanding why the information is required can often allow you to either use existing team data or find an easier way to meet the need.
Copy and paste documentation	When teams are copying and pasting between systems they can introduce inconsistencies and are creating extra maintenance work for themselves.
	Try to keep everything in one place, preferably where the development is already happening.
Write once documentation	Documentation is something that should evolve and iterate along with the product. Refactoring applies just as much to documentation as it does to code or designs. Expecting to get it right first time can cost more time and result in a poorer quality product.
Write-only documentation	This refers to creating documentation that nobody will read. If we don't know who will read it, why and when, we shouldn't write it (or shouldn't write it yet).
We will need this later	Documenting in detail for future iterations – for example, elaborating backlog items we don't expect to prioritise for several iterations or detailed planning of several iterations into the future – is waste and risks the details being incorrect by the time work starts on the item, or, worse, results in wasted effort if the backlog item becomes redundant.
Documentation as collaboration	The most effective way to collaborate is face to face. Relying on documentation to take the place of conversations and interactions – for instance in review comments or job tickets – is counter to the Agile values and will result in poorer quality results.
Documentation specialists	Ideally the whole team works on documentation. If we have specialists (such as business analysts, architects, technical authors), they should not be the only people involved in the documentation.
Lack of authority to deploy	If the team can't release without marketing sign-off or approval from security, operations or anyone else, then they cannot create working products.
	This includes knowing all the criteria to safely deploy to a live environment. This can be a surprisingly long and varied list, which should be understood as early as you can. Definitions of done and good acceptance criteria help.

(Continued)

Table 4.2 (Continued)

Leaving stuff until the end	Delaying things such as documentation, accessibility, online help, performance testing, multi-lingual support, business change and so on until the end will inhibit your ability to deploy. All these things should be delivered incrementally.
Not having users in place	You can't deliver value if there is nobody available to use your product. Make sure that you have customers who are willing to use early versions of your product. Are they aware of the product and do they want it? What business change or advertising is necessary?
The wrong customer	Who is the product for? It isn't good enough that the product works for the development team or the Product Owner. It must work for the intended customer – and with their data and context.
Finished doesn't mean it is working	Completing the tasks doesn't mean the story is complete.
	We often break down a user story or high-level requirement into smaller tasks. Once all those tasks are completed, it is important to test the acceptance criteria of the original story, epic, use case or requirement. That's where the value is, not in the tasks. Even if all the tasks are complete, the acceptance criteria may not be met; and sometimes the story can be complete without needing all the sub-tasks.

Customer collaboration over contract negotiation

This value is all about people, the power of talking and face-to-face communications over written agreements (see Figure 4.6). It also returns to the theme of assuming that we can't know everything we would like to in advance.

By definition, a contract negotiation has a point when it is finished: when both parties sign. That implies that neither party expects it to change after this point. Contracting for something requires 100 per cent certainty, yet we know that 100 per cent certainty isn't possible in a VUCA world and it would be foolish to assume otherwise. We know that, in reality, very little is absolutely clear – most things aren't a binary yes or no and we expect frequent change. In order to navigate high change and low certainty situations, collaboration is critical and the best people to talk to will usually be our customers: high change requires high collaboration.

This value only has four significant words, and each one carries nuance and detail that is worth exploring.

Who are our customers?
The first question is what do we mean by the word 'customer'? For commercial products that might be quite simple: they are the people who will purchase and use the product. It isn't as clear-cut for internal products or services, where the person funding the work may be different from the person using the product. At least, internal customers are usually easy to identify; potential purchasers of a product that isn't yet on the market are less visible.

Figure 4.6 Customer collaboration over contract negotiation

The customers with whom we should collaborate are many and varied. If someone has (or should have) a stake or an interest in the product, they should probably be regarded as a customer. That includes other internal departments, such as audit, marketing, assurance or sales, who may not be direct users of the product but are still interested in it. This is because their perspectives or requirements could significantly affect how the product needs to behave, and it's important to know whether this is the case or not.

Collaboration is more than just talking

To collaborate we must work together. It implies an equal relationship and a shared goal. It isn't just keeping someone informed or asking them to keep you updated. It is a partnership.

Having a common goal that both the development team and the customers are striving for is important. It helps keep everyone aligned and honest. Agile teams don't create products or software; they solve their customers' problems. They don't build a feature; they know why that feature is needed and what impact it will have. Getting that insight requires teams and customers to work together throughout the product development. It requires them to truly collaborate.

While we can collaborate asynchronously and using written documents, we will be much more successful in achieving a shared goal when that collaboration is in person. Trust is easier to build when we have as many paths of communication open as possible. Conversation is often richer than text and less likely to be misunderstood.

Non-verbal communication is also important for the message to be understood properly. There is a widely quoted statistic,[34] based on research by Albert Mehrabian,[35] that only 7 per cent of communication is verbal. Even if 7 per cent feels too low, there is still a significant contribution to the message that comes from the non-verbal elements.

---

34 The 7 per cent statistic also has its critics: Yaffe, P. (2011) The 7% rule: fact, fiction or misunderstanding. *Ubiquity* (October), 1–5. https://ubiquity.acm.org/article.cfm?id=2043156.

35 Mehrabian, A. (1981) *Silent Messages: Implicit Communication of Emotions and Attitudes.* Wadsworth, Belmont, CA.

Non-verbal communication is particularly valuable when establishing trust. We can use it to show interest, agreement, confusion and many other emotions that are hard to convey as quickly or powerfully in written exchanges. This means that where teams are working remotely, or have fewer face-to-face meetings, they need to find other ways to build the trust necessary for effective collaboration.

There are lots of different types of contract

The second part to this value is often dismissed without much thought, especially when people assume the contract in question is the legal type of contract that not all teams have. The contract, however, does not need to be a legal agreement. Instead, think of a contract as any agreement that we make and will be held to account for by another party.

These include commercial or legal contracts, but they also include anything that has been signed off, such as requirements specifications, non-functional requirements catalogues, definitions of done and ready, test specifications, interface definitions, product features, performance figures, marketing plans, build schedules, communications plans and many, many more. Each one of these is an opportunity to over-value the agreement and undervalue the collaboration with the other parties.

But teams do need some contracts, and they need to adhere to them. Ideally, these are contracts that they also have a stake in creating and maintaining. Examples of beneficial 'contracts' include:

- definitions of done and ready;
- acceptance criteria for deliverables, features or stories;
- quality, security and assurance thresholds or standards;
- accessibility standards, and documentation formats and standards.

Even with these, we still want to keep options open to change them in the future. The more locked down and harder to change our 'contracts' become, the harder it is to be Agile.

This is similar to 'processes' in the first value. Agreeing things in advance can bring consistency that may be valuable to many teams, especially those in large organisations; however, there must be a balance. For anything fixed, it is important to know the criteria for changing it. Each time a standard or process is invoked is potentially an opportunity to improve (or remove) it. This means that if we treat them as contracts, then we must know when we can renegotiate those contracts. This is also true for agreements that are wider than one team, and that requires collaboration.

Negotiation implies winners and losers

The final word of this value – negotiation – is another interesting choice. Negotiation implies that the two parties start from different standpoints and that some give and take will be required to reach an agreement. This is because negotiation also implies that both parties have different goals. If we didn't have different goals, we wouldn't need to negotiate. That's not what we want in Agile teams. Agile teams and their customers should have the same goal. Agile teams collaborate with their stakeholders to get win–win outcomes; they don't negotiate with them to get to win–lose or lose–lose outcomes.

What makes this value hard to apply?
The biggest challenge of this value is getting the balance right – the balance between how much we collaborate with our customers, and how much we write down and agree.

Enough collaboration but not too much or too little   While collaboration with customers is a desirable thing, it is possible to have too much collaboration. Constantly asking your customer's opinion can leave them feeling that you aren't listening to them, or that you are asking them to do all your thinking for you.

> This can be a matter of perspective. When customers have been involved in setting the overall product direction at the start, they can have the impression that their involvement is over. They have explained everything they want.
>
> When the team repeatedly asks them for feedback on the product and asks for more details on what is next, it can feel like they are being asked the same questions again and again. This can be avoided by helping to ensure that your customers understand the Agile mindset as well as you do, and by structuring your collaboration to make it clear that each interaction brings unique information.

A challenge of too much collaboration is knowing when to stop. Particularly where there are differing opinions, teams still need to reach some consensus. Constantly revisiting the same topics without change or new information to justify it is damaging.

Everyone's opinion is important and should be listened to, but not everyone needs to agree with every decision. We see this sometimes in organisations where a team doesn't agree with the strategic direction of their product or its relationship with other products. In this situation, it is important to have your view heard, but then to commit to the decision even when you disagree with it. This practice is sometimes called 'disagree and commit'.

The converse of this is when there is too little collaboration – either too infrequent or too ineffective. This can lead to the team making too many decisions themselves and making assumptions about what the customer needs. We sometimes see this as the result of customers who are too busy for effective frequent collaboration. In these cases, getting the most value from the time you do have is critical, for instance by focusing their time on making decisions, presenting options for their consideration or encouraging them to delegate or get help from colleagues.

Too many customers   Another problem too much collaboration can cause is when accountability for product decisions is not clear. Agile teams have a single person who is accountable for deciding what the team should work on next, usually called the Product Owner, but they are rarely the only person with a view on the product. The level of engagement with those other stakeholders can be a struggle to get right. When there are lots of people interested in the product, we can see conflicting advice, confusion over who to listen to and assumptions on who has or has not been involved.

Sometimes, we see teams attempting to address this by creating additional governance. This can result in extra meetings or approvals processes to approve new requests, or requiring email confirmation from all stakeholders before a decision can be reached. These behaviours have the effect of creating additional process contracts and more documentation. A better approach is to focus on improving the collaboration and helping the Product Owner to be the single accountable role. Setting goals the right size can help – as big as possible without being too big for the team to deliver. Too big and additional clarification will be needed from the Product Owner; too small and creating them is a lot more work for the Product Owner.

Where is my customer? The opposite problem can also be a challenge – finding customers to collaborate with, especially when creating a new or innovative product or service. Startups have several techniques that can help, such as those discussed by Eric Ries in *The Lean Startup*,[36] Alex Osterwalder in *Value Proposition Design* and *Business Model Generation*[37] and Jake Knapp in *Sprint*.[38] If you don't know who your customers are, you must go and find them. Don't assume you know their needs better than they do. At the very least, test that assumption.

Treating 'requirements' as 'required' The Product Backlog is a critical artefact for Agile teams. It describes the work that could be done by the team to meet the product goals. However, it also looks like a list of product requirements. To stakeholders familiar with more traditional approaches, where requirements are agreed and committed to before work begins, this can be a problem – because the term implies that they are all **required**. They are not.

Once customers and teams think like this, it is easy to assume that the backlog won't change and must all be delivered. As each iteration is delivered, because there are still 'requirements' to do, it is tempting for the team to avoid releasing the increment until they are all complete. As the customer knows all the things they 'require' are not yet delivered, they are also not keen to have a version of the product to use – after all, it isn't finished. The effect of this is that the Product Backlog becomes regarded and treated as if it were a contract, which inhibits collaboration and inhibits change.

We frequently observe teams where their backlog is regarded as fixed – a contract – and there is even a form of change management process required to change it. This is common when the individuals in the Product Owner role have previously been senior users or principal users in traditional, linear approaches. There, their primary role was to decide what is in scope or out of scope. Once in scope it shall be delivered.

---

36 Ries, E. (2011) *The Lean Startup: How Constant Innovation Creates Radically Successful Businesses.* Portfolio Penguin, London and New York.

37 Osterwalder, A., Pigneur, Y., Bernarda, G., Smiorth, A. and Papadakos, T. (2014) *Value Proposition Design: How to Create Products and Services Customers Want.* John Wiley & Sons, Hoboken, NJ; Osterwalder, A. and Pigneur, Y. (2010) *Business Model Generation: A Handbook for Visionaries, Game Changers and Challengers.* John Wiley & Sons, Hoboken, NJ.

38 Knapp, J., Zeratsky, J. and Kowitz, B. (2016) *Sprint: How to Solve Big Problems and Test New Ideas in Just 5 Days.* Bantam Press, London and New York.

This is a completely opposing viewpoint from the Agile view, which assumes that everything not currently being delivered in an iteration is liable to change. Although the roles are similar – they are both focused on the users of the product – it is important to understand their differences and for the Product Owner to be well trained and supported.

To avoid this pitfall, consider the Product Backlog to be a list of options or ideas, not commitments. Refer to things the product may need to do as **items** on the Product Backlog and treat them as things that evolve over time, with some collaboration required each time. Do **not** refer to them as 'requirements'. This aspect is described in more detail in Chapter 10.

Seniority is valued over role Collaboration between the team and their customers requires respect for each other's opinions and equality. This can be a challenge in hierarchical organisations; it can be an issue when the Product Owner is relatively junior and has more senior stakeholders who think they can control the team or the backlog directly. This is not only a challenge for effective collaboration, but can also introduce implied or actual contracts that stakeholders expect to hold the team to account over.

A variant of this challenge is when the technical views of the team are disregarded by the Product Owner, perhaps favouring new feature development instead of infrastructure or architectural improvements. There is often a tension between technical excellence and rapid feature delivery. The Product Owner's job is to balance these, which means strong collaboration to help understand the value in the work and the impact or risk of deferring it. Deferring technical debt can lead to later increments not being deployable because they start failing quality thresholds.

Anti-patterns
Table 4.3 shows some of the anti-patterns and problems we have observed when trying to value customer collaboration or avoid over-valuing contract negotiation.

Table 4.3 Anti-patterns for valuing customer collaboration over contract negotiation

Detailed story descriptions	Overly detailed stories on the Product Backlog convey a false sense of completeness and certainty. Aim for stories to contain as little detail as possible – just enough to decide whether they can be prioritised for delivery. The time for detail is while they are being developed for implementation.
Sign-off or approvals processes	Over-bureaucracy of sign-off, approval, review or acceptance processes can turn conversations into agreements and contracts. Once a formal 'sign-off' is achieved, people perceive the previous stage to be finished.
	In Agile teams, we want to keep our options open, and possibly return to a decision if the situation changes. Examples where we see this include release plans, roadmaps, designs, component interfaces, application programming interfaces (APIs) and user experience (UX) designs.

(Continued)

Table 4.3 (Continued)

Company-wide standards	Consistency can be important, but sticking too rigidly to global standards, such as code review or documentation standards, without considering their suitability for a particular product can lead to longer lead times and even poorer quality products.
Fixed standards or processes	It is very unlikely that the authors of a standard could predict the future. For any standard you are using, it should be clear how you can challenge and evolve it.
Don't talk to the customer	This refers to discouraging the team from talking to the customers, perhaps because the story is assumed to contain all the detail necessary, or because another person has already talked to them.
	Direct communication between the people developing the solution and the people who will use it is critical. Even a short conversation can be extremely valuable.
Restricting who can talk to the customer	Customer collaboration being restricted to specific people or roles is especially damaging when those people are outside the team. Anyone in the team should be able to talk to the customer to help them develop a better solution.
Customer not present	The easiest way to collaborate is to be sitting beside the person you wish to collaborate with. Any other situation makes it harder, from being out of earshot across the room through to being thousands of miles and several time zones apart. Identifying what inhibits collaboration can help us to solve it.
One-time discussions	Collaboration enables iterative and increment development. It is highly unlikely that only one conversation is necessary to fully understand a story or feature. If it is, perhaps the stories are too small?
Lacking collaboration skills	There is a reason there are diplomas and training for business analysis, user experience and customer discovery; they are skills that not everyone has. If the team doesn't have these skills, then it will be harder for them to collaborate effectively. Delegating that job to others is also an anti-pattern. Instead, try to provide training or pairing with experts.
Not considering cultural difference	What we mean to convey isn't always how it is perceived, and this is magnified when collaborating across different cultures. Politeness, local idioms, slang, different body language and whether we are communicating in our first language can all have an effect.
Not considering accessibility and diversity	We don't all communicate the same way. Some of us have disabilities that make it harder or impossible to communicate, some of which are not obvious disabilities. For effective collaboration, we need to know how each of us communicate most effectively.

Responding to change over following a plan

Of all the values, this is probably the one people remember the quickest and relate most to Agile (see Figure 4.7). This is probably a good thing as it is the one that speaks most directly to the reasons why Agile emerged. It describes a direct outcome of Agile approaches – the ability to respond to change – that is more tangible than the other values.

It is also the most challenging and controversial when comparing Agile with more traditional delivery approaches – it downplays the significance of having a plan. This leads to two major responses, depending on your perspective:

- that planning is not important for Agile teams and they don't need to create plans;
- that the Manifesto says we still value the things on the right, so Agile teams still need to have a plan.

Both perspectives are right; and both are wrong.

In a VUCA world we know that plans, especially detailed plans, are usually wrong. But the activity of planning, especially collaboratively, can be hugely useful.

Figure 4.7 Responding to change over following a plan

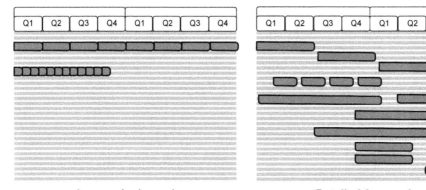

**Approach planned,
detail can change**

Detailed 2-year plan

All plans are lies – they almost never describe what will happen
The single thing that causes most projects to fail is that something happened that the project manager and the team didn't expect. In fact, it is usually lots of things. This means that it is not just difficult to come up with an accurate plan for a complex delivery, it's impossible. In a meeting with Scott Ambler, co-developer of Disciplined Agile,[39] he said something to us that describes this situation well:

---

39 Disciplined Agile is the framework of the Project Management Institute and is described in Chapter 11.

When somebody asks you for a plan, they are asking you to lie to them. You will be lying about the scope, the schedule or the cost. Or all three. You won't know what you are lying about at the time, but you will definitely be lying to them.

We know this is true, otherwise we wouldn't need change management processes and expect to use them frequently. We know that we are bad at predicting the future and this includes our ability to predict what features or requirements we will need.

The half-life of requirements is the amount of time it takes 50 per cent of your requirements to become obsolete – wrong, superfluous or missing. In an article from May 2011,[40] Susan Atkinson and Gabrielle Benefield explain that requirements' half-life is reducing drastically: from five years or more in the 1980s, to two to three years in 2000, to just six months in 2011. Given that we know the pace of change has continued to increase, we can expect it to be even shorter today. As Figure 4.8 shows, for projects longer than a few weeks the impact of this is stark.

Figure 4.8 Requirement obsolescence with a six-month half-life

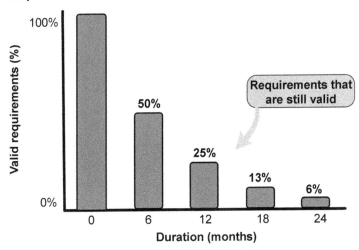

The impact of this is that we need to assume that unless we spoke to the customers today, there is a growing probability that what they told us is no longer correct. These are precisely the opposite conditions we need for accurate planning. Without input data we can trust, we cannot plan. Traditionally we try to overcome this by requiring 'sign-off' to validate that the requirements are right and transfer responsibility (or blame) to the customer if they are not, but, arguably, that is an unreasonable thing to ask of our customers.

We can make accurate plans – when they are short term or high level
If we can't predict the future well enough to be able to produce a plan we can trust, what can we do? There are two elements to the solution:

---

40 Atkinson, S. and Benefield, G. (2011) The curse of the change control mechanism. InfoQ. https://www.infoq.com/articles/the-curse-of-the-change-control-mechanism/.

- plan in detail only for a timescale we can be confident in;
- plan longer term by increasing the levels of abstraction until we can trust them.

In Agile teams we set our iterations to be small enough so that we can commit to work that we know will be valuable and highly unlikely to change – usually one to four weeks. Within this timeframe, we fix the work and don't accept change. Because the time is short, the requirements' half-life problem doesn't arise, and we can be quite sure that our customers need the things they are asking for; especially when they will be using the solution once the iteration completes.

Most products are not complete in a few weeks – some will take months or years to be complete – so we need a way to describe the purpose of the product without trying to describe the detailed features or capabilities. We can be confident that things such as a product vision or a high-level roadmap won't change, and if they do, there are probably bigger problems.

Our roadmaps contain the goals and user needs that we would like the product to deliver against, but don't need to be very detailed. If keeping the goals high level works for the team, then that's what we do. Otherwise, we break our big goals into smaller goals; we don't break big goals down into big plans. This is explained in more detail in Chapter 10.

The level of abstraction should be just enough to be able to describe the product, and give confidence to stakeholders or investors that the product should be developed, but not so detailed that the details are likely to turn out to be wrong. As the product develops, planning for each iteration uncovers a little more detail and, because it is done just before implementation, we can be confident it is correct. This multi-level planning is shown in Figure 4.9 and described in more detail in Chapter 10.

Deciding the detail incrementally just before we implement it means that it is easy to respond to change. This same principle applies with scaled approaches – agree the detail as late as possible, keeping as many options as possible. For instance, roadmaps don't need to position features against dates – Now, Next and Later are just as useful, but far more likely to be true, more honest. In this way, we can have a high-level plan, be able to respond to change and reduce the lies we are asked to tell our stakeholders.

Incrementally develop everything

Developing our solutions incrementally doesn't just apply to the finished product, it also applies to its design, architecture, interfaces, marketing, testing – in fact everything. Yet this isn't the natural way to develop some of these. Take architecture, for example. Traditionally, we understand our requirements and constraints in depth and then develop an architecture and design that takes them all into account and provides confidence that our product will be able to meet them all.

That won't work with Agile products, and attempting to do so introduces more risks than it mitigates. It risks locking in assumptions made early in the product development and inhibiting the ability of the product to respond to the changes in requirements that we expect will emerge in time. Instead, we apply the same incremental approach to architecture and design as we do to product goals and features – we do just enough architecture necessary to allow an increment of the product to deliver value to its users. Each iteration of the product is an opportunity to revisit those architecture and design decisions, each time armed with more information, and evolve it for the next iteration.

Figure 4.9 Using roadmaps to plan iterations

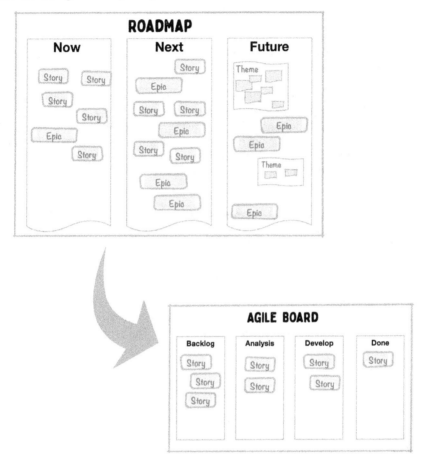

Repeatedly revisiting (or 'refactoring') the architecture and design each iteration isn't as wasteful as it may sound. By doing just enough design for each iteration we don't include things 'just in case' or create complex structures because 'we will need to use them later'. We keep things simple and only add complexity when we know for certain it is required. This increases quality by making the product simpler and less likely to break, and each time we revisit that part of our solution, we have another opportunity to spot any errors and correct them.

In this way we apply the 'responding to change' value to our architecture and all other elements of the product just as we do to the user needs.

What makes this value hard to apply?
By far the biggest challenge with this value is managing the expectations of stakeholders who think they need a greater level of planning detail and accuracy.

People like knowing what to expect   Our brain craves certainty. As David Rock explains in his paper 'SCARF: a brain based model for collaborating with and influencing others',[41] there are five domains of human social experience that are capable of inducing the same stress response we evolved to respond to life-or-death situations. One of those is 'certainty'.[42] When we are faced with uncertainty, our brain invokes the fight or flight response. Conversely, having a feeling of certainty or familiarity can trigger the reward response and cause us to feel good.

The lack of such certainty with Agile teams can be profoundly unsettling, especially when people are used to the perceived certainty of detailed plans. Many stakeholders of Agile teams believe they have experienced success with traditional delivery approaches that are very plan driven. Both the lack of certainty with Agile teams and the stark contrast with their prior experiences induce stress. Worse, because this stress originates in our primitive, limbic system in the brain, it overpowers our logical brain, making it harder to overcome.

This assumption that an accurate plan exists for this problem – we just need to find it – is flawed. As we explained earlier, an unfortunate artefact of this volatile, uncertain, complex and ambiguous world is that hindsight tends to remove the complexity. In other words, the problems look simpler once we have finished. We can look back at what happened, rationalise and justify it, and decide what we could have done better.

This gives a false sense of confidence about future work – and a false assumption that we just need to learn from previous deliveries, analyse more thoroughly and we will be able to come up with a plan that will definitely succeed. The problem is that this ignores the fact that at the point of planning and making decisions, the information we had at the time was very different from the information we have months later.

It is like the requirements' half-life discussion. When we are making decisions in a VUCA world, the information we have is a mix of correct, incorrect, misleading and missing data. With hindsight, we know which category every data point fits into – but at the time we don't. This is the fundamental problem with relying on plans, and why Agile approaches work better for complex problems.

External pressure to produce detailed plans   Sometimes external artefacts require more detailed plans than we would like. Business case templates often expect plans, milestones and detailed lists of features. Contracts with suppliers may wish to detail the 'outcomes' in terms of features or seek to specify the work at a level of detail that we can't provide without up-front analysis and planning. Ideally, we can recast these requests into things that we can be more certain of, perhaps higher-level features, or we can use outcomes that we can be confident are unlikely to change.

The Endowment Effect causes us to resist change   In psychology and behavioural economics, the 'Endowment Effect'[43] describes the observation that people demand more to give up an object than they would be willing to pay to acquire it. In other words, we think that things we already have are more valuable than they are. We see this with

---

41 Rock, D. (2008) SCARF: A brain-based model for collaborating with and influencing others. *NeuroLeadership*, 1, 44–57.

42 The other domains in the SCARF Model are described in Chapter 9.

43 Thaler, R. (1980) Toward a positive theory of consumer choice. *J. Economic Behavior Organiz.*, 1, 39–60.

systems that won't be decommissioned, yet if they didn't exist we would never prioritise creating them. We also see it with items on backlogs, roadmaps or project plans. Once we have put something on a plan, we attach more value to it than it deserves.

This leads to prioritising the completion of existing work over adding new stories, and a reluctance to remove items from a backlog. The easiest way to avoid the Endowment Effect is to have as little as possible on your backlog and to avoid describing backlog items as 'requirements'.

Sadlines and deadlines   A common challenge of plans is that they often contain deadlines that the work is expected to be organised around. People who like plans love deadlines. They create urgency, importance and certainty.

However, not all deadlines are equal. Agile consultant Liz Keogh[44] takes the word **dead**line literally: if nothing dies as a result of missing the date, then it's not a deadline. Often, all that will happen is somebody will become a little bit sad. So, she coined the word 'sadline'.[45] Genuine deadlines are important to know about and factor into our work, but we should first be confident they aren't really a sadline.

Anti-patterns
Table 4.4 shows some of the anti-patterns and problems we have observed when trying to value responding to change or avoid over-valuing following a plan.

Table 4.4 Anti-patterns valuing responding to change over following a plan

The tool makes us plan	Even tools that are marketed to Agile teams can encourage planful behaviours. Just because a tool allows detailed release planning, precise estimates or breaking work into detailed tasks doesn't mean you need to use all those features.
Focus on the tasks not the value	We often break a story down into tasks and assume that completing those tasks will mean the story is complete. This is an emphasis on planning. It may be possible to deliver the story without completing the tasks, and sometimes necessary tasks are omitted. The bigger the story, the more this is magnified.
Big backlogs	Big backlogs means there is a lot of work described that will probably take a long time to deliver. The requirements' half-life means much of it will be obsolete by the time we get around to starting it. Try to avoid them.
Dates on the roadmap	Writing down dates encourages stakeholders to treat them as commitments. When teams then assign features to releases on the roadmap, the association of the feature with the roadmap date can be treated as a plan.

(Continued)

---

[44] https://lizkeogh.com.

[45] https://twitter.com/lunivore/status/301007423106322434.

Table 4.4 (Continued)

Sign-off processes	Processes that require sign-off or approval can encourage too much effort up front and inhibit those artefacts being able to change easily later if they need to.
Expectations of detailed planning	External governance processes can assume greater levels of detailed planning than the team needs. This also includes contracts that describe outcomes in terms of detailed deliverables.
Long iterations	The shorter the iteration, the more frequent the opportunity to change. The iteration that matters is the one that results in release of value to the customer.
	If the team is Agile but delivers into a slower iteration, then the ability to respond to change will be determined by the slower iteration.
	We see this effect when an Agile team is included in other governance processes with longer cadence. A common example is with poorly implemented scaled Agile approaches – if releases only occur every five iterations, then the iteration length is really 10 weeks, not two (for two-week team iterations).
Inappropriate use of 'scaled Agile' approaches	This refers to using a 'scaled' approach when we don't need to, for instance when the scaled approach is to satisfy a governance need rather than a complex single product need. Chapter 11 discusses how to avoid the need to scale in the first place.
Small stories on the backlog	Lots of small stories are usually the result of too much analysis and the problem being broken down too much in advance.
Specialist roles in the team	Teams with specialist architects, business analysts or other roles that focus on analysis and early design can lead to too much work being done up front, inhibiting change and making it harder when you do decide to change.
	The case for specialists is covered in Chapter 11, but we often see specialist roles or teams when they are not necessary.
Iterations planned in advance	Beyond the current iteration, anything could change. So planning several iterations in advance means that the likelihood of them being correct will decrease.

SUMMARY

The four value statements of the Manifesto for Agile Software Development are short and concise. Yet, beneath their surface lies complexity, nuance, risk and temptation that are easy to overlook. Whenever we see Agile teams run into trouble or hear claims that 'Agile isn't working', we invariably also see the Manifesto values not being adhered to – we see the items on the right valued highly, and the items on the left being neglected or downplayed.

When we investigate the values in more depth, we can see why this is the case. Our organisations and our default behaviours have been conditioned through history to value the items on the right and find those on the left unsettling. Understanding this is the first step to overcoming it.

Agile values people and collaboration more highly than repeatable processes, consistency and certainty. Rather than fight against change through detailed analysis, planning and sign-offs, we expect and embrace change, aiming to do just enough to deliver some value and get feedback on what we can change – because we know it is highly unlikely we will have got everything right this time around.

This inevitably leads to higher levels of uncertainty than we are used to from traditional project approaches, and this is uncomfortable for many people. We can overcome this by seeking certainty in other ways: planning at higher levels of abstraction, using short iterations focused on small goals, expecting to refactor designs and architectures frequently, bringing our customers on the journey with us and measuring progress by seeing customers get value from using our product throughout its development.

Understanding this is the first step to being Agile, and is a strong foundation for successful application of any Agile approach.

5   UNDERSTANDING THE AGILE PRINCIPLES

The principles are the details of what it means to 'be agile'; seemingly straightforward, yet challenging to master

The second page of the Agile Manifesto[46] lists the 12 'Principles behind the Agile Manifesto'. Each principle stands alone as good advice, and together they show how the values on the first page can be applied.

Although several include the word 'software', there is little that is unique to software teams. The principles describe the behaviours and mindset that allow any project or product development to succeed.

It is common for people new to Agile to skip past the principles, particularly when their first introduction to Agile is learning an Agile framework or method. However, the principles so comprehensively address the essence of an Agile mindset that they deserve far greater attention and consideration.

This chapter will help you understand the principles. It will explain:

- What each principle is really about.
- What you can do to reinforce each principle.
- How to identify some of the traps and anti-patterns that can distract you from each principle.

THE 12 PRINCIPLES BEHIND THE AGILE MANIFESTO

Like much with Agile, the principles seem simple and common sense, but they are difficult to apply in practice and challenging to master completely. They are not presented with any narrative or explanation, which means that each person will apply their personal spin to them. Unfortunately, this can lead to differing understanding of what they mean, and differing implementations of them. In our experience, even where the principles are considered, it is common to pick principles, or aspects of principles, that suit and ignore the rest.

This ambiguity over what the principles mean can lead to confusion. In the following sections, we share our understanding of their meaning and what makes them powerful, based on our experience over many years of applying them with various teams.

---

[46] https://agilemanifesto.org/principles.html.

When the principles were first published in 2001, they were split into three sections based on who they were 'slanted towards': customers, managers or the team. Although they are no longer described as such, we think it is still a useful way to present them.

PRINCIPLES SLANTED TOWARDS CUSTOMERS

Figure 5.1 lists the four principles relating to customers and we discuss each one in detail below.

Figure 5.1 Principles slanted towards customers

Slanted toward customers

1 Our highest priority is to satisfy the customer through early and continuous delivery of valuable software

2 Welcome changing requirements, even late in development. Agile processes harness change for the customer's competitive advantage

3 Deliver working software frequently, from a couple of weeks to a couple of months, with a preference to the shorter timescale

4 Business people and developers must work together daily throughout the project

Principle 1: Our highest priority is to satisfy the customer through early and continuous delivery of valuable software

This principle really sums up the Agile approach with several key words and phrases:

- **Early ... delivery** – The sooner we can deliver something of value the better. This requires early feedback that provides confidence that we are heading in the right direction.

- **Continuous delivery** – Delivery is continuous. During the life cycle of the product or delivery, there will be lots of versions of the solution, not just one or two.

- **Valuable** – The thing we continuously deliver (and it doesn't need to be software) must be valuable. This means we need to know and be able to express **why** it is valuable. Often this means it must be able to be used in a real situation by the customer, but this isn't always possible (for example with some hardware products or where data aren't available). Another source of value is knowledge or learning. Sometimes the value is in proving a concept, running an experiment or learning something.

- **Satisfy the customer** – The person we need to satisfy is the customer. That means their views on value are most important; not the team's, not the testers', not the project manager's.

Taken together, this is a powerful principle and Agile teams will demonstrate **all** elements of it. This is where it becomes challenging. Traditional development approaches tend not to favour continuous delivery and often don't provide value to the customer until near the end of the delivery.

To reinforce this principle, consider the following things:

- Can you describe what value is being delivered in each iteration of your product?
- Is the value in this iteration valuable to the customer? If not, why not? Why should they care about this iteration?
- How quickly can you get a version of your solution deployed that your customer finds valuable? Why not faster?
- How frequently can you add value with new releases or iterations? Why not faster?

Watch out for the traps and anti-patterns given in Table 5.1 that can divert your focus from this principle.

Table 5.1 Anti-patterns for Principle 1

Deferred release	A version of the solution could be released, but it isn't. The customer wants to wait until more features are implemented.
Proxy customers	The solution is available, but is not being used by the end customer. Or, the team are not talking to the real customer, but proxies such as business analysts, architects, project managers, etc.
Infrequent releases	'Continuous' can mean multiple times a day. Frequent releases of small changes are easier to manage, lower risk and easier to fix if there are problems. They don't need to be available to all users to still have value.

Principle 2: Welcome changing requirements, even late in development. Agile processes harness change for the customer's competitive advantage

The most challenging word for most people in this principle is 'Welcome'. We are not conditioned to welcome change. On the contrary, most alternative approaches and much of human nature seeks to minimise change. However, that is also the power of this principle. When we expect and welcome change, we are quicker to spot it, quicker to respond to it and quicker to reach new stability. The second sentence explains why: by doing this, we can be more competitive.

The second challenging aspect of this principle is also in the first sentence: we welcome change 'even late in development'. Again, this isn't natural. It is common for teams to push on with the original plans, particularly the closer we get to the finish line. We are conditioned to changes being a sign of weakness – a 'U-turn', an 'exception'. A change late in development could threaten the viability of the whole endeavour and cause promises we have made to be broken. Of course, that's exactly why this is important;

when things change we ought to respond as quickly as we can or we risk not delivering the maximum value to our customers. Most traditional approaches inhibit change by making it difficult, time-consuming and expensive to respond to. This makes it easier to ignore and press on with the original plan. Agile teams that welcome and expect change are always accepting of it. Many of the other principles explain how we do this.

This flexibility doesn't mean that we can't have a clear vision, plans and roadmaps. It just means that we should expect them to change, and to welcome that change when it happens. And because we expect them to change, we should put as little effort into them as we can – just enough to make them valuable.

To reinforce this principle, consider the following things:

- Where do you expect change to come from? How will you know it is happening? Monitor these sources and keep your eyes open.
- What were the drivers for the work being started? Are these still true? Is the strategy still the same? Have market conditions changed? Are there any new competitors or customers?
- Use short iterations. Make short-term commitments. Avoid promising details months ahead.
- Keep backlogs short and high-level; go into detail only when you need to.

Watch out for the traps and anti-patterns given in Table 5.2 that can divert your focus from this principle.

Table 5.2 Anti-patterns for Principle 2

Roadmaps as commitments	Roadmaps and backlogs are guesses about what we think will be included in the solution in the future. They are not commitments or confirmed plans (even if there are indicative dates) and shouldn't be treated as if they are.
When will I get it?	This refers to customers wanting to know when specific features will be delivered, particularly when there are lots of features. The only feature the team can be certain of delivering is the one they are currently working on. Anything else might change.
	A better way to manage customer expectations is to focus the conversations on priority of features rather than dates.
Language and processes that imply change is 'bad'	Use of language like 'scope creep' assumes change is bad. Change management processes that are hard to engage with or describe an 'exception' process do similar.
	Scope should evolve, so changing scope is more likely to be a sign of a healthy team than one that is out of control.

(Continued)

Table 5.2 (Continued)

Sign-off, approvals, acceptance gates	Any form of 'sign-off' or other completion stage on artefacts that are likely to change (e.g. requirements, design, architecture, acceptance tests) implies these things can't, won't and shouldn't change.
	Where organisations need more certainty, try to use a higher level of abstraction that is less likely to change. Describe the vision or user benefits rather than detailed features. Better still, involve those asking for clarity in the prioritisation of the product so that they don't need to ask.
Planful governance processes	Governance processes may monitor progress against some expected state, such as milestones or plans. It is better to talk about what value has been delivered and whether to continue investing in the project.
	Governance is built into Agile through continuous planning and early and frequent release of value. Additional governance isn't always (or often) necessary, although frequently expected.

Principle 3: Deliver working software frequently, from a couple of weeks to a couple of months, with a preference to the shorter timescale

The principles reinforce one another and emphasise important points several times. This principle is an example – it focuses again on early and frequent delivery of a **working solution**. As we discussed in Chapter 4, the word 'working' is important here because a solution isn't working for the customer if they can't use it to solve some problem for them. It doesn't have to solve their entire problem, but it does need to solve some part of it.

The second part of the sentence makes it even clearer: not only should we deliver frequently, but we should also aim to release new working versions of our solution every couple of weeks and no longer than every couple of months. The more frequently we have customers using our solution, the more feedback we get and the more we learn about the problem and the solution. Each opportunity for feedback is an opportunity to reduce risk and increase our understanding. The earlier we start this process, the better.

This might sound extreme or implausible for some teams, but it's not. It just requires us to think differently about what constitutes value and how we organise our backlog. We discuss techniques for this in Chapter 10.

To reinforce this principle, consider the following things:

- Set short iterations.
- Split big goals into smaller goals, not into big plans. Check that the smaller goals deliver independent value. Could you stop after this goal and still have a valuable product?

- Are manual processes slowing you down? Invest in automation and continuous delivery tools to make releasing easier.
- Help your customers to understand why you want to work this way, perhaps with training or coaching.
- Do you know what 'working' means in your context?
- Does each iteration have a customer-centric goal?

Watch out for the traps and anti-patterns given in Table 5.3 that can divert your focus from this principle.

Table 5.3 Anti-patterns for Principle 3

Poor excuses for not releasing	The threshold for preventing release of an increment should be high. It's almost always better to release and get feedback than to hold back until later. Some poor excuses we hear frequently include: 'Users need more features', 'It doesn't perform as well as system X', 'We need more time to evaluate the system before you change it', 'We don't have time to keep dealing with new versions'.
Longer iterations	Avoid responding to problems by increasing the iteration length – always consider decreasing it first to see if that helps (tip: it often does).
Releasing on the longest cadence	This refers to when a longer cadence exists (e.g. in scaled approaches or when governed by another process) and only releasing on that rhythm. You can and should release versions between planning boundaries, even releasing multiple times a day. When something is ready, it can be released.
Delaying the first release	Release something as early as you can, even if it is just a small benefit to a few users, rather than waiting a long time before releasing the first version.

Principle 4: Business people and developers must work together daily throughout the project

For such a simple statement, it is surprisingly rare to see teams do this; yet it is such an important factor, as emphasised by the word 'must'. Working together is not optional.

The theory is simple: when we make it easy to ask questions, get feedback and clarify language, then communication improves. When we need information, we can access it quickly. We stop relying on formal meetings or reports for updates because everyone knows what's going on or can find out quickly. We spot mistakes quicker and make decisions quicker.

This increased collaboration helps to build stronger relationships and creates psychological safety in our teams. Psychological safety is one of the most critical things required to build high-performing teams, as we discuss in Chapter 9.

The easiest way to achieve this principle is for the team, their customers and the important business stakeholders to work in the same room. But that's not the only way – with remote or geographically distributed teams, we can always find ways to work better together and to achieve the same benefits. Working together reduces the need to communicate in more formal ways. It can reduce the amount of detail needed in digital tools and the amount of information we need to collate in advance, 'just in case we need it'. By creating an environment where we can overhear conversations between others, we increase our general awareness of the product and are able to contribute when we have something to add. This builds consistency in our 'tacit knowledge'[47] – the things that we implicitly know but would find difficult to write down or describe.

The word 'daily' is an interesting one in this principle. We aim for short cycles and frequent releases, so it follows that there should usually be something to talk about each day. This means the word serves two purposes:

- Business people and developers should be available every day to talk about the work.

- If there's nothing to talk about, perhaps this is a sign that the work is the wrong shape; perhaps too much detail is agreed up front, or the increments of work are too big.

To reinforce this principle, consider the following things:

- If you can co-locate the team and their business stakeholders, then do that. If you can't, could you co-locate some of the people, or for some of the time?

- How easy is it for the team and their business stakeholders to talk? Help them get to know each other early in the project and create frequent opportunities for them to talk. Choose meeting times and locations to maximise attendance and adapt these if you need to.

- Use digital channels such as Slack or Teams and invite business people and developers to the groups.

- Don't allow significant detail to be stored in requirements or stories. Leave them high level and vague to force clarifying conversations to happen once the team starts work on them. A definition of ready (DoR)[48] can help.

- How transparent are you? Can your stakeholders see the same information as the team? If not, why not? Try to encourage your stakeholders to look at the team's information and interact with it.

Watch out for the traps and anti-patterns given in Table 5.4 that can divert your focus from this principle.

---

47 The term 'tacit knowledge' is attributed to Michael Polanyi in his 1958 book *Personal Knowledge*, republished with new foreword by Mary Jo Nye in 2015. Polanyi, M. and Nye, M. J. (2015) *Personal Knowledge: Towards a Post-Critical Philosophy*. University of Chicago Press, Chicago, IL.

48 A definition of ready defines the criteria that work must meet before the team can commit to delivering it. This can include too much detail as well as not enough. See Chapter 10 for more details.

Table 5.4 Anti-patterns for Principle 4

Out of sight, out of mind	It is easy to forget stakeholders when you don't see them often. If your business stakeholders are not nearby, try to find ways to enable frequent or immediate communication.
Product Owner as queen or king	The Product Owner is a critical stakeholder, but not the only one and often not the right person to answer detailed questions on the specifics of a product feature or requirement. Avoid over-reliance on them for all stakeholder communications and relationships.
Over-reliance on meetings	Assuming that meetings or reports are sufficient. Meetings and documents are formal communications that often don't convey the richness necessary for good collaborative work. Attendance and interest can often decline as the delivery proceeds, exacerbating this anti-pattern.
Write only documentation	Writing a comment in a tool or sending an email is no replacement for face-to-face communication (see Principle 6). Don't assume that sharing information with someone means they have read or understood it.
Too much detail	Up-front analysis can be so thorough that the team don't think they need to talk to the users. Not only does the detail run the risk of being out of date before the team starts, but they are also missing the opportunity to get a deeper understanding of the customer's needs.
	High levels of detail can dissuade the team from asking questions because they assume the answer must be in the documentation somewhere.
Mismatched expectations	Ensure that the business people expect to be engaged throughout the work – many may be used to traditional projects where they state their requirements and wait for the finished product to arrive.
No time or too busy	Frequent communication takes time and effort. It is important that the business is constantly involved, and this time needs to be prioritised. If they don't or can't, it may be an indication that this work is not as important to them as you think.

PRINCIPLES SLANTED TOWARDS MANAGERS

Figure 5.2 lists the four principles relating to managers and we discuss each one in detail below.

Figure 5.2 Principles slanted towards managers

Slanted toward managers

5 Build projects around motivated individuals. Give them the environment and support they need, and trust them to get the job done

6 The most efficient and effective method of conveying information to and within a development team is face-to-face conversation

7 Working software is the primary measure of progress

8 Agile processes promote sustainable development. The sponsors, developers, and users should be able to maintain a constant pace indefinitely

Principle 5: Build projects around motivated individuals. Give them the environment and support they need, and trust them to get the job done

This principle captures what is required of management and leadership in Agile teams and organisations. We cover Agile leadership in detail in Chapter 9. Much of the advice and guidance there will directly reinforce this principle.

It can seem this is about autonomy – removing management and letting the team get on with it – but there is a lot more going on here, and a lot more to Agile leadership than just empowering the team. Let's start with building projects around 'motivated individuals'. This sounds simple, but it isn't. Not every individual in the team will be motivated in the same way, nor be demotivated by the same things. Motivation is not static, and individuals can become more or less motivated all the time. As we explore in detail in Chapter 9, the science and psychology of motivation and leadership is evolving, and much of the current theory aligns very well with the Agile values and principles.

To create and sustain motivated individuals, the environment and support around them must reinforce the Agile values and principles and remove factors that promote the wrong behaviours. That's exactly what this chapter and Chapter 4 will help you do.

We tend to think of 'support' as being things like training budget, development opportunities or mentoring and coaching. These things are important, but support is also about helping align the team with the organisational vision and strategy, identifying and mitigating external pressures on the team and creating opportunities for feedback and improvement.

One area that can cause problems with this principle is management processes. Real world Agile teams often exist within a larger organisation. They are required to follow management and governance processes that are rarely well suited to an Agile environment. Such an environment can impact individual motivation and impair team performance. Some examples are annualised processes, individual-focused reward (especially where employees are pitched against one another for bonuses) and a culture of fearing feedback because it only comes during appraisals.

This is why Agile principles and values are not just for software teams. HR, finance, procurement and other functions must also change if an organisation is to become truly Agile. There are many opportunities to do that. We discuss some in Chapter 9 (expense policies for instance), but by applying a principles lens to management processes, we have found many other examples.

THE TROUBLE WITH BONUS PROGRAMMES

Agile teams work collaboratively, but management processes can sometimes incentivise the wrong things. Bonus programmes that seek to reward individuals for 'exceptional' performance are one good (and common) example. The problem with exceptional performance is that for one person to be exceptional, it follows that their colleagues are not. So, each person is incentivised not just to perform at their personal best, but for their colleagues to perform more poorly. In this environment, you are not incentivised to help poorer performing colleagues to improve, suggest improvements that benefit the whole team, share your knowledge or skill with colleagues or make it easy for others to help you.

To get around this, perhaps don't have bonus programmes – they sometimes cause more problems than they solve, for example at Wells Fargo,[49] where sales targets for opening accounts led to employees opening bank accounts without customers' knowledge or permission. There is also evidence that bonus programmes can harm the gender pay gap, harm product quality and create tension within teams.[50]

Alternatively, empower teams to reward themselves. To create a more employee-led bonus programme, one UK software company gives each team member a number of votes proportional to the other members of their team.[51] They are then asked to distribute the votes to their colleagues to determine their bonus. If everyone contributed equally, the bonus distribution is equal, but sometimes one or two people are particularly valued by their colleagues, so they get a little more. The company found this worked best when half the bonus allocation was shared equally and the remaining amount allocated by the votes. When the votes were used for the whole bonus budget, people were too worried about some people getting nothing that they all shared their votes equally.

---

49 Koren, J. R. (2017) Wells Fargo overhauls pay plan for branch employees following fake-accounts scandal. *Los Angeles Times*, 10 January. https://www.latimes.com/business/la-fi-wells-fargo-pay-20170110-story.html.

50 Boué, G. and Corradino, D. M. (2019) Does incentive pay work? SHRM. https://www.shrm.org/hr-today/news/hr-magazine/summer2019/pages/does-incentive-pay-work.aspx.

51 Information from a conversation one of us had with the chief technical officer (CTO) of the company.

The final directive in this principle – 'trust' – is also easy to erode with poor management or leadership. Agile team members need to trust one another and have the trust of their stakeholders. Creating this trust can be hard because many organisations and processes assume the opposite – they assume people cannot be trusted. This means their processes and culture can inhibit the creation of trust, for instance multiple oversight or approvals processes or detailed tasking and micromanagement.

Agile organisations assume people are acting with noble intent. We assume people and teams can be trusted and do not need high levels of oversight and control. We use high levels of transparency and frequent feedback to prevent the kinds of misdemeanours or poor performance that require formal intervention from arising in the first place. For example, the focus on frequent feedback and continuous improvement means that Agile teams will often identify problems within their team themselves. If someone is beginning to struggle, the team will realise and can provide additional support, training or refactoring of the work. This can happen immediately and be revised frequently without waiting for a HR process to trigger an assessment.

Agile processes are designed for exceptions, and we only deploy them when those exceptions occur. There will still be processes to manage underperformance that can result in dismissal, but they are invoked only when necessary, not built into the processes used by the majority of good performers.

To reinforce this principle, consider the following things:

- What can the team make decisions about? What can't they? Is everything out of their control reasonable? Even if they don't have absolute control, could they be more involved in the decision making?

- Do they understand the purpose of their work? Autonomy requires connecting the team with its purpose (see Chapter 9).

- Do you involve (or invite) everyone in strategic decision making and setting strategic direction? If not, why not?

- Assume people are acting with noble intent (unless proven otherwise).

- Don't micromanage; encourage curiosity, asking questions and seeking advice. Encourage teams and individuals to ask for help when they need it. Listen more than you speak.

- Allow teams to work on challenging problems. Help them to increase the challenge as their skill improves, perhaps by adjusting the size and complexity of the stories.

- Use coaching to help the team develop and grow. This can be with dedicated Agile coaches, by using coaching skills in existing management processes, or both.

- Keep the faith. Things will go wrong; expect that to happen. Inspect and adapt to continually improve. It will be tempting to revert to a more command and control management style, so try to resist.

Watch out for the traps and anti-patterns given in Table 5.5 that can divert your focus from this principle.

Table 5.5 Anti-patterns for Principle 5

One size fits all	This refers to assuming all teams and people are the same and need the same levels of autonomy and the same kinds of leadership and management. The environment and support needed to motivate one person may not be the same as a different person (or team) requires.
Running before you can walk	Don't try to move too fast, for example by transitioning a micromanaged team to one with full autonomy and Agile leadership in one step. Help them to progress gradually.
Ignoring the environment	This refers to applying Agile approaches within non-Agile business processes and assuming they will 'just work'. Unless you can opt out of the existing processes, they need consideration to ensure they don't undermine the Agile practices. Adapt the processes if you can, and if you can't, understand how they negatively affect the team and try to mitigate their impact.
External checks and approvals	Review processes or approvals that assume the team's work needs to be checked. Separated out functions, such as test or quality assurance, are unhelpful; it is better to bring them into the team.
Leaders being too distant	Even with high autonomy, teams still need support from leadership and need to know how to get that support. Having visible leaders is as important as having accessible customers.
Chasing the metrics	Reporting and governance can drive the wrong behaviours. Being measured can drive changes in behaviour; measuring unhelpful things can drive unhelpful behaviours. For example, measuring teams on the number of bugs fixed, lines of code written or adherence to initial estimates can lead to teams gaming the measures so that they are met even if the product is in a poorer state as a result.

Principle 6: The most efficient and effective method of conveying information to and within a development team is face-to-face conversation

This is another principle about how people interact. Face-to-face conversations, particularly when they take place just when the information is needed, will be up to date and can reduce the ambiguity that might arise from written exchanges or voice-only calls.

When we use written means to communicate there is a lag between the information being written and it being read, meaning it may be out of date. There is also more opportunity for confusion and misunderstanding.

Email read receipts on one system at the Australian Department of Defence used to include the statement:[52] 'The message has been displayed on the recipient's screen. It does not mean that it has been read or understood.'

Face-to-face communication can be harder as it causes interruptions and breaks the flow of concentration when you are working on specific tasks. Lack of availability of the people you need to talk to can also introduce delays and can lead to single points of failure. However, we can look at these disadvantages as opportunities to operate in a more Agile way. For example:

- Interruptions can cause breaks in concentration when working on specific tasks. An Agile team should strive to work together on the most valuable stories, thereby creating an environment for collaboration. This should not be seen as interruption.

- Sometimes too many interruptions can be caused by there being too many people in the team. This could be an indication that the work should be split into smaller independent and autonomous teams.

Key individuals may not be available when they are needed. An Agile team encourages co-location of a team (physically or digitally), and key individuals should be part of that team. When this occurs, conversations are more ad hoc and frequent, so scheduling time to get answers to key questions shouldn't be a problem. When we are used to regular collaboration and communication with the team, each conversation will be shorter, since they happen more frequently, and we know we can go back for clarification if we need to. Also, the impact of key individuals is limited when teams are working together on the same stories. There is likely to be more than one person who can answer the question. Similarly, when we work directly with the users (rather than through a proxy), there is often more than one person we can ask.

The point of this principle is that development benefits from face-to-face communication. It doesn't mean that written communications are not also valuable, it just acknowledges that when we want to convey many types of information, face-to-face communication is better. However, there must be clear guidance on what **does** need to be documented and what does not. For example, technical constraints, system-wide non-functional requirements, anything contractual, changes to service level agreements and so on will probably need to be documented. Clarification on the detail of a story, opinions on a user interface (UI) layout or agreeing the agenda for a service launch probably won't.

To reinforce this principle, consider the following things:

- Are the team used to talking to one another? If not, work on building trust and psychological safety in the team.

- How will you know who to talk to? Build a network among the stakeholders and customers. Get to know who you can talk to for particular topics.

---

52 Personal experience from working there from 2001 to 2005.

- Consider accessibility, for example technology assistance (such as live subtitling in video conferencing software) can help with some disabilities. Not everyone prefers face-to-face conversation, so create adjustments if necessary.

- When you are not co-located, consider using video and phone calls in preference to email and messages.

- Create opportunities for ad hoc conversations to happen.

- Encourage sharing of knowledge to remove single points of failure. One good way to do this is to work together more in pairs or groups.

- If you must have reviews or approvals, try to have them in person rather than comments on a document.

Watch out for the traps and anti-patterns given in Table 5.6 that can divert your focus from this principle.

Table 5.6 Anti-patterns for Principle 6

Blinded by rank	Seniority, job title or grade shouldn't get in the way of two people talking. Bring the people with the information together, regardless of their place in a hierarchy. Be careful of the highest paid person's opinion (HiPPO) dominating decisions when they shouldn't.
Non-essential documentation	Before you write something down to store or publish it, think about who is likely to read it and what they will use it for. Don't document 'just in case'.
	Only document a conversation or decision if you need to.
The tool asked for the detail	IT systems can encourage over-documentation. Just because a field is available in an IT system, doesn't mean it has to be completed.
Just message me	Today many teams make great use of social and collaboration tools such as Slack, WhatsApp and Teams. Be careful not to let them replace conversations. It is easy to lose detail and context in text messages. We have even seen teams sitting in the same room chat over text rather than turn around and speak.

Principle 7: Working software is the primary measure of progress

This principle seems obvious, but like much in Agile it is not followed (or followed well) often enough. All too often teams measure progress by time elapsed, money spent or arbitrary milestones passed. While these things may be interesting, they are not good measures of progress towards our goal. A better measure is the extent to which we are confident our solution is meeting the needs of our customer, and the best way to do that is to let them use it and provide feedback.

As we discussed in Chapter 4, **working** software means that the solution (and it might not be a software solution) is performing the job it was intended to. It is helping customers with their real-life problems and their real-life data. It isn't working if it is in a reference environment, operating on dummy data, demonstrated by the development team or an idea on paper.

Only when a customer can use the product for real – even if it just meets a tiny slice of their overall needs – can they provide feedback on whether it is working for them. Only with this feedback can we have a genuine indication of progress. We refer to this as 'value in use', as it is only by using it that the customer can say whether it is valuable.

In Chapter 8 we discuss how Agile teams measure success, and why leading measures are better indicators than lagging measures. Working software, and the feedback it brings, is an ideal leading measure as it builds confidence that the goal will be met. Time and cost are lagging measures, as they can only be measured after they have occurred and are not good indicators that you will meet the goal.

To reinforce this principle, consider the following things:

- Do you have a clear understanding of what 'working software' means for your product? Does your customer agree?
- Are you being asked for other measures of progress? Have you challenged this?
- Do your iteration goals represent something of value to your customer? Could they use it for 'work'? Ensure you set iteration goals that are small slices of real value to the user (see Chapter 10).
- Set acceptance criteria that ensure the goal is met (or the story complete) and is being used in a real scenario.
- Describe progress in terms of customer value, rather than in terms of percentage complete or tasks finished. Try adding 'so that' to the end of tasks when describing them; for example: 'Check Balance on mobile app **so that** customers can see their points balance while in the store and decide whether to redeem points.'
- Use DevOps practices and deploy stories to production as soon as they are complete.

Watch out for the traps and anti-patterns given in Table 5.7 that can divert your focus from this principle.

Principle 8: Agile processes promote sustainable development. The sponsors, developers, and users should be able to maintain a constant pace indefinitely

The word 'sustainable' here means that the team should be able to sustain the pace. Today, sustainability is often assumed to mean sustainable from an environmental perspective. This is also very important for teams to consider, but is not the point of this principle. Certain things can achieve both, such as automation.

Table 5.7 Anti-patterns for Principle 7

Multiple deployment environments	Having multiple deployment environments (such as development, staging, production) can increase lead time and tempt teams to consider a story finished when it hits the first of them. If the product is ready to be deployed to the first one, it should be ready for the final one. Otherwise, it isn't finished yet.
One release per iteration	Avoid waiting until the end of the iteration before releasing all the changes made. Get them live as soon as you can. The released product should be additive – each iteration is the product of the previous iteration plus the new work. This can happen multiple times each iteration. An added benefit is that if things go wrong there are fewer things that have changed, so the problem is easier to find.
What is measured matters	Measuring something leads to the team valuing that thing over other things, sometimes to the detriment of what the team ought to care about. Be sure that the things that matter to you are measured, not the things that don't.
I want it all	Some customers want to wait until all the features are available before using the product. The longer they wait, the more problems they will find. Aim for early and frequent feedback and find combinations of features that will provide value for customers in early releases.

One of the benefits of traditional, linear development is that it can be relatively calm for most of the delivery. Often, it isn't until the end that stress levels rise, deadlines get closer and testing throws up problems that require urgent attention. Customers and other stakeholders are generally quite happy during the early stages, content to trust the Gantt chart and believe the final product will meet all their needs – only to find that features get descoped to meet deadlines, costs start to rise and expected release dates get further away. This is not the pattern in Agile teams. With each increment of the product ideally being used by customers, teams can feel the stress and urgency to get a working version ready every single iteration. It can all feel a bit relentless, and that's why this principle is so important.

Because Agile teams work in frequent, short cycles, it is critical that they don't burn themselves out. If every week is release week, we mustn't spend every release week working until midnight to get the release out. The team needs to find a pace that suits them and that they could continue with indefinitely. It needs to accommodate taking leave, personal and professional development, and any corporate processes. While there may be times when additional effort is called for, this should be the exception rather than the norm.

For large pieces of work that may run for many months, or even years, it is important to ensure the work doesn't become monotonous. Using short- to medium-term product goals or releases can provide opportunities to reflect on progress and celebrate the team's accomplishments even though the work is not yet finished.

To reinforce this principle, consider the following things:

- How is your team feeling? Do you know if anyone is struggling? How would you know? Good psychological safety and approaches such as daily Check-In Core Protocol[53] can help, or consider using part of a daily stand-up as a mental health check-in.
- Set clear, achievable goals for your iteration. We cover prioritising and setting goals in Chapters 8 and 10.
- Account for other essential activities (such as training, corporate meetings, annual leave, etc.) when planning iterations.
- Use release planning and longer-term goals to set direction and manage expectations.

Watch out for the traps and anti-patterns given in Table 5.8 that can divert your focus from this principle.

Table 5.8 Anti-patterns for Principle 8

Big Bang delivery	This refers to customers who want to wait until a product is finished before using it. When we don't get feedback during development it can lead to lots of unforeseen issues and defects arising at the end.
Planning 'hardening' iterations	Often perceived as good practice because they provide time to ensure product quality is maintained, in practice 'fallow iterations' or 'hardening sprints' inevitably turn into dumping grounds for technical debt and quality enhancements that ought to have been done when the feature was first implemented.
	They can also be seen as a safety net for delays that get filled up with stories that got carried over from previous iterations. Refactoring, improving quality and reducing technical debt are part of the product development and should be part of regular iterations, not deferred until later.
Catching up masquerading as innovation	Scheduling time for innovation, particularly in large or long deliveries is a great idea. However, be careful they don't turn into time to fix the technical debt from prior iterations, as described above.
Velocity as a performance measure	Velocity is a measure of the amount of work a team completes in an iteration. Avoid using it as a performance measure, especially if it is linked to reward. It inevitably ends up being gamed and losing any value it started with.
	Estimates must be owned by the team; when those same estimates are used to measure the team's performance, we shouldn't be surprised when they evolve in the team's favour.
	Velocity can be a good internal metric that helps the team to improve their planning. It is not a measure of performance.

---

53 https://thecoreprotocols.org. The Core Protocols are a set of techniques for high performing teams developed by Jim McCarthy and Michele McCarthy and are an open source resource. They are also described by Richard Kasperowski: Kasperowski, R. (2015) *The Core Protocols: A Guide to Greatness*. With Great People Publications.

PRINCIPLES SLANTED TOWARDS THE TEAM

Figure 5.3 lists the four principles relating to the team and we discuss each one in detail below.

Figure 5.3 Principles slanted towards the team

Slanted toward the team

9 Continuous attention to technical excellence and good design enhances agility

10 Simplicity – the art of maximizing the amount of work not done – is essential

11 The best architectures, requirements, and designs emerge from self-organizing teams

12 At regular intervals, the team reflects on how to become more effective, then tunes and adjusts its behavior accordingly

Principle 9: Continuous attention to technical excellence and good design enhances agility

A common criticism of Agile teams is that their focus on short timeframes leads to sloppy implementations, short-cuts and poor-quality solutions. Teams start implementing straight away without thinking about design, and the result is a mess. This principle states that if this were happening, those teams would not be Agile at all.

Technical excellence and good design are not just 'nice to have', they are essential enablers for incremental and iterative delivery and of being Agile. It is a helpful first principle in this section. Together with the following two principles, this principle describes how and why Agile is not an excuse to hack together a solution without following good practice. Designing with change in mind, expecting to refactor and evolve both your solution **and** your design, and keeping the solution simple are all important considerations for any team, but they are especially important for Agile teams since these practices make it easier for them to be Agile.

The first word in this principle is important: 'continuous'. It isn't enough to have a design that you follow. To enhance agility, the design and technical excellence will evolve and change as the team learns more about the problem and solution, but 'continuous' also means they are present from the start. The team starts with a design and attention to technical excellence and expects them to change and evolve. Good design expects and enables change.

To reinforce this principle, consider the following things:

- Iterate your design. Do just enough at the start to know where to begin. Don't be afraid to refactor. Just because you know the final product will include a database with a million records, doesn't mean the first iteration needs it – perhaps a text file would be good enough?

- Don't neglect non-functional requirements such as performance, security or accessibility. Design these in from the start, especially if they are challenging and failure to meet them would cause the product to fail.

- Include quality in your acceptance criteria or definitions of done. If you can, automate quality testing. For software products, this could be in your continuous integration/continuous deployment (CI/CD) pipeline.

- Automation, version control and loosely coupled architecture are examples of technical excellence practices that enhance agility.

- Minimise coupling with other systems or teams. The more interfaces that need to be agreed, the greater the impact if they need to change. Where you do need to agree interfaces, make them as simple and as generic as you can.

Watch out for the traps and anti-patterns given in Table 5.9 that can divert your focus from this principle.

Table 5.9 Anti-patterns for Principle 9

Over-complicating things	Do just enough design to support this iteration. Be aware of what might be coming later in the backlog, but don't anticipate too much or try to future-proof everything; after all, it might never be prioritised into an iteration.
Sign-off processes	The presence of sign-off processes usually means that people or the organisation are not comfortable responding to change. They assume that a design can be complete and 'signed-off' – frequently before allowing implementation to begin. In a VUCA world, we know this is illogical at best, if not delusional.
	Where a sign-off process is essential, set checklists or criteria that define the start point for implementation and that expect iteration. Set policies or rules that explain what circumstances would require the sign-off to be repeated or are clear about what the team can decide themselves.
Assuming design decisions are final	Whether or not there is a sign-off process, design decisions and technology choices are only finalised when the development stops – not when they are first made. There may be a better answer that you won't realise until later, or a simple design will do for now but will need to be replaced later.

Principle 10: Simplicity – the art of maximizing the amount of work not done – is essential

This rather clumsily worded principle is probably one of the most important, and one that describes the essence of what Agile is. It is applied in all aspects of Agile and should be the first consideration before any action:

- How can I make this as simple as possible?
- What can I do without and yet still ensure the delivery is valuable?

We also like to capture this principle with the phrase 'just enough, just in time'.

This principle is the reason that Agile can claim to deliver quicker than traditional, linear approaches. It isn't because Agile teams build the solution faster than non-Agile teams, it is because, by following this principle, Agile solutions do less, reduce waste caused by over-engineering solutions and don't implement features that aren't needed.

Traditional projects tend to build all the 'must have' requirements listed, even when those requirements are very large (feature sized) and contain many smaller stories. These smaller stories seldom carry the same priority. Some will turn out to be neither necessary nor a priority, yet will still be built. Agile deliveries only build the user stories needed. They do this by simplifying – delivering just what is essential in small usable increments of the solution iteratively. As customers use these early versions, they realise what they do and, more importantly, **do not** need.

This focus on simplicity isn't just on the stories we include in our iteration, it is also about how complete we make the solution, how comprehensive we make our documentation or training, how we test to ensure the solution meets the customer needs and even how much time we spend meeting those needs. It isn't about cutting corners or making compromises – it is about being ruthless about what is necessary and what is not.

To reinforce this principle, consider the following things:

- Always ask yourself and the team: Could this be simpler? What could we remove and still deliver the value?
- Use reviews and retrospectives to challenge each other and identify ways to simplify.
- Use techniques such as 'Good-Better-Best' or 'story mapping' (see Chapter 10) to simplify stories, goals or releases to deliver them earlier.
- Apply this principle to all aspects of work, including backlog generation, roadmaps, architecture, design, communications, reporting and documentation.

Watch out for the traps and anti-patterns given in Table 5.10 that can divert your focus from this principle.

Table 5.10 Anti-patterns for Principle 10

Taking this principle too far	Don't cut things that are necessary. Remember, just enough often means we still do some work, not do nothing.
'Just in case' development	It is tempting to set things up for later features when you don't really need to. This is over-engineering and can introduce waste and technical debt into the development process.
Over-governance	This refers to governance and reporting processes that result in multiple requests for similar information in different forms. Consider report automation or a pull process where requesters can get the information themselves.
Neglecting the essentials	Don't neglect essential areas such as accessibility, information assurance, policy requirements, audit or reporting. These should be built in from the start, not added on at the end.
	With accessibility in particular, making a system accessible will often improve the user experience for everybody, not just those who need better accessibility.

Principle 11: The best architectures, requirements, and designs emerge from self-organizing teams

This principle covers two important practices – emergent artefacts and self-organising teams – yet people tend to focus solely on the second. This is probably because it is easier to understand, although still difficult to master in practice. However, the notion that important artefacts such as architecture, user needs and design emerge from teams is arguably more important to the Agile mindset.

The word 'emerge' is an interesting choice. It implies something that is becoming known. It isn't necessarily arriving fully formed, but emerging bit by bit. The word supports the previous ideas that architectures, user needs and designs are also things that are iterating, just as the overall product is. Furthermore, those artefacts are emerging **from** the team and their collaborations – they are not given to them or imposed on them. This is a really important point – the job of the team is to iteratively and incrementally develop architectures, design and their understanding of the customer needs. It is no accident that these three things are mentioned explicitly. They are all important aspects of successful product development and if they are neglected the value of the product to the customer can be severely compromised. They are also things that are hard to create accurately up front.

Much like the 'technical excellence' Principle 9, this principle reinforces that Agile teams need to consider all aspects of development. An Agile team is collectively responsible for **all** the work needed to achieve the working software. They don't receive requirements from a requirements team, implement what the architects hand them or handover their work to a testing team. These patterns are common in a traditional, linear development project, but are not how Agile teams operate.

This brings us to the other part of this principle: self-organising teams. There are two elements to this.

Self-organising teams have all the skills, knowledge and authority necessary to create a product increment the customer can use

As we have just discussed, the team is collectively responsible for developing the architectures, user needs and designs. This means they need the right skills, training, tools and authority to be able to do that. The same is true for anything else that is required to create 'working solutions' – versions of the product that the customer can use to solve their real problems with real data.

Depending on their context, that may mean the team also needs to have some expertise in other areas, such as marketing, information security, policy, user training, technical writing, change management or a whole host of other areas. Even for software products, the development team need to know a lot more than just how to code. This creates a problem. Historically, many of these areas have been covered by specialist roles and jobs; many organisations are structured in ways that make these areas specialised, with specialist teams that are distanced from development teams, which can impede collaboration.

In a self-organising team there is no room for dedicated specialists. They create handoffs, with some of the team creating parts of the solution and others doing the rest. This adds waste, cost, risk and time. It also makes it hard for the team to always be concentrating on the most valuable work unless the most valuable work happens to match the specialist skills mix of the team. This isn't how to adhere to the manifesto values and principles; and it isn't being Agile.

We discuss this topic further in later chapters, including discussing situations where specialists **can** be required.

Self-organising teams are empowered to organise themselves

The second element to self-organising teams is the most obvious: they must be able to organise themselves. This isn't as simple as it sounds and can be made even harder when the nature of the problem means that there is lots of specialist knowledge or skill required.

The primary goal of every Agile iteration is to maximise the amount of value to a customer within the iteration. To achieve this, we need everyone on the team to be contributing to that value. This can be tricky when there are specialists. After all, if I am a security architect and there isn't much security work involved in this story, then what can I do? I usually have three choices:

- Find some other security work to do, perhaps on a story that might be prioritised in a later iteration or at a lower priority in this one.

- Go and do some work for a different team.

- Find some non-security tasks to do that will help the team deliver the highest priority story earlier.

The correct choice is obviously the last one, yet we frequently see people choose one of the other options; sometimes because of a misguided notion that they are not valuable unless applying their specialist skill, but sometimes because they don't want to do other work or think it is beneath them.

Organising the team to focus on maximising the value they can deliver means that they must be motivated, competent and empowered to work that way, as shown in Figure 5.4 and discussed in Table 5.11.

Figure 5.4 Attributes of a self-organising team

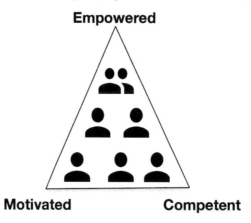

Table 5.11 Pre-conditions for self-organising teams

Motivated	Team members need to want to do whatever is necessary to deliver the value even where it isn't their favourite thing. This also means they need to be motivated to learn the skills the team needs, which may mean learning from more junior team members.
Competent	To be able to switch focus to the work needing to be done, team members must have enough skill and competence to be able to help. This doesn't mean they must all be experts in everything, but they do need at least some competence in all elements of the solution.
Empowered	The organisation must support self-organisation by encouraging and rewarding team-centric behaviour. This also means discouraging individual incentivisation such as individual performance bonuses or skill-centric policies that discourage people from working outside their skill area.

Creating the conditions for intrinsic motivation and empowerment requires strong leadership, as we discuss more in Chapter 9.

To reinforce this principle, consider the following things:

- Can the team get the product live? Can they take it to a point where the customer can use it for their work? If not, what is missing? Is it people, skills, authority, business process?

- Can the product operate on the right data? Are real users available to use the product?

- Minimise external handoffs, reviews or approvals. If possible, bring the authority into the team.

- Create 'T-shaped' team members (see Chapter 7) where people augment primary skills with other skills, perhaps at a lower skill level. Only use dedicated specialists where you really need deep expertise and experience.

- Set goals for the team; let them work out how to meet them (see Chapter 9).

- Set expectations for supporting artefacts such as architecture, design and roadmaps and include them in acceptance criteria or definitions of done. Expect them to iterate and evolve.

Watch out for the traps and anti-patterns given in Table 5.12 that can divert your focus from this principle.

Table 5.12 Anti-patterns for Principle 11

Governance imposing review gates	Sometimes external governance processes impose external reviews, approvals or sign-off on the team. Identify and challenge these if you can, or understand the business drivers behind them to ensure you are doing 'just enough' governance.
Passing the buck	This refers to assuming that the work of the team is complete when passed to the 'next stage'. Where possible, bring those 'next stage' responsibilities into the team. We shouldn't be happy unless we see our solution in use.
One size fits all	Teams will have different levels of self-organisation and empowerment that work for them. They may not be at the same level. All three factors in Figure 5.4 need to be balanced.
'Best practice' that isn't	Corporate 'best practice' isn't always the best advice for all teams and isn't always kept up to date. Be careful, particularly if it's not clear when it was last reviewed, or what the triggers for a review are.
Management focus on individuals	If management or performance processes focus on the individual rather than the team, then you can expect team performance to be degraded as a result. What's best for each individual to impress their manager is rarely the best for the team.
Skill assessments	Career paths or skill validation processes can encourage developing deep specialism over delivering customer value, particularly if they discourage or penalise people from working in other skill areas or from collaborating with colleagues. Watch for assumptions that a single person will be 'responsible' for technical decisions; this can inhibit collaboration and sharing of knowledge.

Principle 12: At regular intervals, the team reflects on how to become more effective, then tunes and adjusts its behavior accordingly

This principle encapsulates perhaps the most widely recognised and powerful element of Agile, that of continuous improvement through reflection. It acknowledges that teams can always improve (adjust), and states that these reflections should be regular events.

The most common way that teams do this overtly is with a retrospective: a regular meeting where the team considers how it can improve and agrees actions to make changes to how they behave. This is the 'inspection' and 'adaptation' pillars in action. The term 'retrospective' originated around the same time as the Agile Manifesto, in Norm Kerth's book, *Project Retrospectives*,[54] and a Sprint Retrospective is a critical part of the Scrum framework.[55] When teams diverge from other good Agile practices, they often retain retrospectives. Retrospectives are described in more detail in Chapter 7 and in the book *Agile Retrospectives* by Esther Derby and Diana Larsen.[56]

Although seemingly simple, there are pitfalls that can make retrospectives less effective. They need honesty and trust within the team, a willingness to accept there will be ways the team can improve and a desire to make those changes. These elements can be affected in various ways, as discussed below.

Trust and honesty
We previously mentioned the importance of psychological safety to team performance, and it is particularly important when teams are trying to become more effective. In teams with good psychological safety, there is no blame culture and everyone acts with noble intent. Everyone in the team makes decisions that they honestly believe are the right ones given the information they have at that time. Often, we later realise that a different decision may have been better, but we are reaching that conclusion at a different point in time and with different information.

In a psychologically safe team, suggestions of things to do differently or ways to improve do not imply blame or that previous decisions were wrong. This is quite a difficult leap for some teams to take, particularly where there is a management culture that expects perfect performance and assumes that changing your mind is bad.

The primary value of retrospectives is to the team, so it should just be the team who participate and just the team who share the results. Don't include additional stakeholders in a team retrospective, especially if any of them have a performance management relationship with the team.

Of course a retrospective doesn't have to be a single event. We can have several retrospectives with different audiences, focusing on different things to improve. For example, conducting a retrospective with other teams you work with or with wider stakeholders can be a powerful way to improve.

---

54 Kerth, N. L. (2001) *Project Retrospectives: A Handbook for Team Reviews.* Dorset House Publishing Co Inc., New York.

55 https://scrumguides.org/scrum-guide.html.

56 Derby, E. and Larsen, D. (2006) *Agile Retrospectives: Making Good Teams Great.* Pragmatic Bookshelf, Dallas, TX and Raleigh, NC.

For retrospectives to be useful, two aspects need to be embraced:

- **Acceptance that we can improve.** Even high-performing teams can improve, and this needs to be understood and accepted. Every change is an experiment; we think it will make us better, but we don't really know until we try. Agile teams are constantly finding different things to try to see if they can improve.

    There are always changes that can be tried. In his book, *Black Box Thinking*,[57] Matthew Syed describes how small changes that result in marginal gains can amplify to help teams and organisations make radical leaps forward. The Japanese concept of *kaizen*, which means 'change for the better', also advocates small frequent changes and these concepts should be embraced by the team.

- **Willingness and ability to make changes.** Even with teams who **can** identify things to change, they still need the willingness and ability to make those changes. Very often, this will take some effort and must be factored into the other work of the team. The team's stakeholders, leadership and management need to be committed to the team's investment in themselves too, even if it impacts the product.

    Teams frequently identify great actions from their retrospectives, but consistently de-prioritise them and never find the time to make the change. These actions and problems then arise at future retrospectives and are a sign that teams are not investing in their continuous improvement. This may be because the problems are too big for the team to solve.

    Teams need to ensure proposed changes are realistic. A common trap is for teams to think broadly in their retrospective but over-emphasise problems beyond their control. Problems are easy to identify, but unless they can also identify realistic actions that they can achieve themselves, they won't be able to enact any actual change. In this situation, the team needs to refocus their attention to identifying problems they **can** solve and find other ways to address their higher order issues.

To reinforce this principle, consider the following things:

- Ensure teams have regular retrospectives that are properly facilitated.
- Include improvement goals alongside product goals and give them priority.
- Celebrate failures as opportunities to learn.
- Have a future-facing mindset. Focus on the future and use your knowledge of the past to improve that future. Previous behaviours are just information and data that can help you to improve in the future, they are not mistakes.

Watch out for these traps and anti-patterns given in Table 5.13 that can divert your focus from this principle:

---

57 Syed, M. (2015) *Black Box Thinking*. John Murray, London.

Table 5.13 Anti-patterns for Principle 12

Groundhog day retrospectives	This refers to using the same format for every retrospective.
	Asking the same questions can result in the same answers. Frequently changing the format of the retrospective can bring fresh perspectives and insights. There are lots of online resources and tools that can give you some ideas.[58]
Too much change	Don't try to make lots of change at once; it is better to make one or two small changes stick than to start 10 things and not complete any of them.
Being too ambitious	The bigger the improvement, the harder it will be to implement. Identify small changes you can implement quickly and see whether they work. Then iterate and continue.
Not involving the whole team	The whole team should be engaged in the identification and implementation of the changes.

SUMMARY

The principles of the Agile Manifesto are 12 relatively simple statements. However, there are two key factors that are important to remember:

- The principles may appear common sense, but are not common practice in many teams. There are systemic behaviours and practices that undermine or directly oppose the principles in many organisations and teams.

- Although short, there are hidden depths and nuance within the principles that aren't always obvious when they are first encountered.

Understanding the principles in depth and understanding what lies beneath them is critical to being able to harness their full potential for yourself or your team.

---

58 Some examples: https://retromat.org; https://www.tastycupcakes.org; https://www.liberatingstructures.com; https://www.retrium.com; https://www.mural.co/; https://miro.com/guides/retrospectives/ideas-games.

6   FUNDAMENTAL CONCEPTS IN AGILE

Several core concepts emerge from the values and principles; understanding and applying them is crucial

When considering the manifesto values and principles, we can identify a number of key themes and fundamental concepts that run through them. This chapter introduces and explains those fundamental concepts that we will frequently refer back to throughout the book. They are:

- empiricism;
- the three pillars of transparency, inspection and adaptation;
- continuous improvement and feedback;
- Lean approaches and the wastes of Lean;
- incremental and iterative delivery;
- customer centricity;
- self-organising, empowered teams.

This chapter will help you to understand these fundamental concepts that, together with a deep understanding of the principles and values, are the foundations for a successful Agile mindset.

FUNDAMENTAL CONCEPTS OF AGILE

While the manifesto values and principles define what we mean by 'Agile', there are also several fundamental concepts and ideas that are entwined throughout. Understanding and applying the following concepts will help you to understand and apply the values and principles in the Agile Manifesto, and vice versa.

These three things – the values, principles and fundamental concepts – are the foundations of an Agile mindset.

Empiricism

Empiricism is an unusual word that isn't commonly used, but it captures perfectly what Agile is all about.

Empiricism is a noun defined by the *Oxford English Dictionary* as 'the theory that all knowledge is based on experience derived from the senses'.[59] In other words, we only know something because we have sensed it in some way. Therefore, to learn new things we must find ways to sense them. Given that Agile is about finding solutions to new problems, particularly in a changing environment, we won't have experienced these things already, so won't have the knowledge. Creating short experiments and learning from them is therefore essential if we want to learn quickly.

The three pillars

Scrum is one of the most dominant, popular and influential Agile approaches. It is a framework described in a short document called the Scrum Guide.[60] Scrum is founded on empiricism and Lean Thinking, and it implements what it describes as the 'Three Empirical Scrum Pillars'. These pillars are **transparency**, **inspection** and **adaptation** (see Figure 6.1), and between them they cover pretty much everything the manifesto mentions. Despite being introduced in the Scrum Guide, they apply to any Agile approach, which is why we mention them here.

Figure 6.1 The three pillars

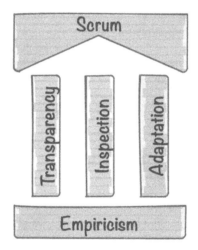

When we talk about Agile to new people, the two most important things we want them to remember – and the two things that will be of most value to them – are the Manifesto values and the three pillars described here.

Transparency

Transparency is a key driver for psychological safety, empowerment and self-organising teams. It is also the first step towards continuous improvement; if we all know what's happening, it is more likely we can identify ways to improve.

---

59 https://www.lexico.com/definition/empiricism.

60 https://scrumguides.org.

Agile teams are transparent by default. They are open about what they are doing through their backlogs, with each other and with their stakeholders. This may be visualised through an Agile board in their workspace that shows what is being worked on and by whom. It may be having open invitations to iteration reviews or inviting review of their work and feedback from others in the organisation.

Most importantly, Agile teams are transparent with themselves. This transparency builds trust within the team and with their stakeholders.

Inspection

The natural counterpart to transparency is inspection. There is no point in transparency if nobody is taking in the information you are being transparent about and doing something with it – that's what inspection and adaptation are all about.

Inspection is being curious about anything and everything that could affect the work, and applying critical evaluation to that information. Really understanding it and putting yourself in a position where you can use that information should you need to is crucial.

Good inspection is about ensuring that you have any and all of the data or information you may need. It's a bit like an insurance policy against change. If (or more likely when) a change happens, not only will a culture of inspection mean that you will know it has happened, but you will also have the information you need to make an informed decision about what to do.

There are many ways that Agile teams can create a culture of inspection. One is through frequent use of feedback (as we discuss later). Another is adopting an enquiring mindset to team interactions: active listening, asking questions, testing assumptions, clarifying intentions and ensuring coherence. This requires a culture of psychological safety (see Chapter 9) and for people to act with noble intent and kindness to ensure that a question is not perceived as an implied criticism.

The most important thing is that the team takes every opportunity to share, learn and understand their work. This collective consciousness is what helps Agile teams to focus on the most important work items. It requires transparency to ensure the right information, and adaptation to respond to the information and make changes.

Adaptation

The final pillar is adaptation: the changes we make because of the inspection. Inspection is useless without a culture where the team is willing, able and empowered to make changes when the information warrants. Adaptation is key to the Agile team's ability to 'respond to change' mentioned in the Agile Manifesto values. It isn't enough to notice change, we must be able to do something about it.

This could be changes to a backlog as a result of stakeholder feedback at a review session, or perhaps the offer of help one team member gives another when they learn they are struggling with something. If we don't expect to adapt in the face of new information, we are not being Agile and the efforts of transparency and inspection are fruitless.

Agile teams constantly use the inspection and adaptation cycle to maximise the value they are creating for their customers and to improve the way they work. This is empiricism in action and can be observed in virtually all the Agile practices we discuss in Chapters 7 and 8.

Continuous improvement

Agile teams never believe they are perfect. We believe that there are always things that can be improved, and this is reinforced throughout the 12 principles, particularly Principle 12, which states 'At regular intervals, the team reflects on how to become more effective, then tunes and adjusts its behavior accordingly.' That doesn't imply we are doing things wrong; rather, it implies that we are constantly learning and there are always new things that we could try that may make us better.

Feedback

Without feedback the whole concept of Agile falls apart. Soliciting and listening to feedback allows us to experience a wider range of opinions and perspectives than we can provide ourselves. This additional information is invaluable to help improve our product and ways of working. That is why Agile teams use short cycles – they bring more opportunities for feedback, and they make the feedback more directed towards a smaller set of actions or features. In a VUCA world, the more information we have, the more likely the chance we will make good decisions. Feedback helps us to keep doing things that are helpful, and change things that are not.

The problem with feedback is that it has become toxic in many organisations, especially large organisations. It gets conflated with other activities, such as performance management, bonuses or promotions, and its true value gets lost. When feedback stops being about additional insights to help us improve and becomes an input to a different decision, such as promotion, it loses its value. It can become backwards-focused, dwelling on what a person should have done differently rather than being the rich source of insights and information it should be.

We mention this because an organisation's relationship with feedback can be a barrier to Agile adoption, especially when feedback has become synonymous with receiving bad news and defending historic decisions. Expecting teams to embrace more feedback can be a hard sell. To test how hard, try asking your team what words or feelings are evoked when someone offers them feedback.

Lean approaches and the seven wastes

Taiichi Ohno was chief engineer at Toyota when he developed the original seven wastes (*Muda*) as part of the Toyota Production System,[61] the approach that influenced not only Agile, but also led to Lean Thinking, Six Sigma and many manufacturing processes today. He identified seven wastes that should be recognised and minimised (or removed) in order to speed work through a system. They are set out in Table 6.1.

---

[61] https://global.toyota/en/company/vision-and-philosophy/production-system/.

Table 6.1 The original seven Lean wastes

Transportation	Waste resulting in the movement of resources (materials) that doesn't add value to the product. Excessive movement of materials can be costly, damage quality and result in additional costs for time, space and machinery.
Inventory	The result of a company holding more stock than is needed 'just in case'. Excessive inventories are waste because they don't add value or contribute to customer value, but instead increase storage and depreciation costs. They also risk becoming obsolete and needing to be replaced.
Motion	The movement of employees (or machinery) that complicates or unnecessarily extends production time. Motion should be minimised as much as possible to ensure efficiency in completing jobs. While you are moving, you are not creating value.
Waiting	Waste caused by goods or tasks not moving. Easily identifiable because lost time is the most obvious thing to detect. For example, goods waiting to be delivered, parts waiting for the next machine to become available or a document waiting for approval.
Overproduction	Producing more than you need to meet customer demand. Overproduction triggers the other six wastes to appear too, in that excess products or tasks require additional transportation, excessive motion, greater waiting time and so on.
Over-processing	This type of waste usually reflects in doing additional work that doesn't bring additional value. This includes things such as adding extra features to a given product. This increases costs, but not the price customers are willing to pay.
Defects	Defects are waste as they cause rework, which costs valuable time.

Later, in the 1980s, an eighth waste was added[62] – unused talent – which occurs if the front-line workers are not consulted or involved in making improvements/adjustments, as they are closest to the work and will have valuable insights. Not utilising this talent is a form of waste, and this talent is also the source of solutions to the other wastes.

These wastes are also often present in Agile teams, even when they are not building cars or weaving looms like Toyota. The Lean wastes are important because they are reflected in the Agile values in several ways, such as:

- Valuing comprehensive documentation such as too much detail in requirements, design or test specifications can lead to unnecessary work being done (overproduction) or work being done before it is needed (inventory).

---

62 It is not clear where the eighth waste originated, or from whom. It is commonly included by Lean practitioners, although you can argue that it is more often the solution to minimising the other wastes so its absence is a different type of waste from the others.

- Valuing contract negotiation by doing detailed work up front increases the risk of it being wrong (defects) or not being necessary (overproduction).

- Not being able to deliver working software by having all the skills and authority within the team means handing some work to others (transportation) or requiring approvals (waiting).

Lean software development principles

In 2003 Mary and Tom Poppendiek took this one step further for software teams by creating an explicit mapping between the Lean wastes and how they manifest themselves in software teams.[63] These are set out in Table 6.2.

Table 6.2 The seven Lean wastes of software development

Inventory	Partially done work that cannot be used by the customer. Including things that are complete but not able to be used (such as awaiting security or legal sign-off).
Overproduction	Features or documentation that are not needed or do more than the customer requires (including delivering things that may be required later but not now).
Extra processing	Relearning things that are already known (i.e. through not sharing information or components).
Transportation	Handoffs between teams (e.g. having separate development and test teams).
Waiting	Delays of any kind.
Motion	Context switching (e.g. by working on multiple things at once or being called away for support tasks frequently).
Defects	Defects.

This helps teams to identify where they may have inefficiencies in their ways of working and areas where they can improve. This Lean software development approach describes seven Lean principles and a toolkit of 22 tools that teams can use to help adhere to the principles. They align very well with the Agile values and principles, and are set out in Table 6.3.

Incremental and iterative

Agile approaches apply an incremental and iterative approach to delivering customer value, but what this means can be confusing and teams can think they are being incremental and iterative when they are not.

---

63 Poppendiek, M. and Poppendiek T. (2003) *Lean Software Development: A Toolkit*. Addison-Wesley, Boston, MA.

Table 6.3 Lean software development principles and toolkit

Lean principle	Lean software tool
Eliminate Waste	Seeing Waste
	Value Stream Mapping
Amplify Learning	Feedback
	Iterations
	Synchronisation
	Set-based Development
Decide As Late As Possible	Options Thinking
	The Last Possible Moment
	Making Decisions
Deliver As Fast As Possible	Pull Systems
	Queuing Theory
	Cost of Delay
Empower The Team	Self-determination
	Motivation
	Leadership
	Expertise
Build Integrity In	Perceived Integrity
	Conceptual Integrity
	Refactoring
	Testing
See The Whole	Measurements
	Contracts

Agile is **incremental** because there are many versions of the solution, with each version improving on the last. Crucially, each increment is a version of the solution that works and can be used by the customer. It won't do everything the customer wants, but it will do some of what they need.

Agile is **iterative** because value is delivered in a series of small time-bound chunks – iterations. It takes many iterations to complete the solution.

It is possible to be iterative without being incremental and this is a mistake that many 'Agile' teams make. Consider the example of a store loyalty card that we use throughout this book. We could imagine we would deliver the initial solution in a series of iterations like this:

1. Design the card and submit it for manufacture. Design the back-end database systems that will hold customer details and purchase information.

2. Design the user-facing systems for the customers and the sales points in the stores.

3. Implement the database and UIs (perhaps over a few iterations).

4. When the cards arrive, launch the programme in a small number of stores to test the processes and the system.

5. Update the systems based on feedback and roll out to more stores.

This feels like it meets many of the conditions of Agile. We are delivering small iterations frequently; each iteration has a goal; we can't launch the programme until the cards are manufactured, so early iterations are about learning; we learn from an initial small set of users before rolling out to the whole network. However, we don't see any customer interaction until the end, and we are making quite a lot of potentially critical decisions early (see Figure 6.2).

Figure 6.2 Splitting delivery by component

| Design cards | UIs | Implement store systems | Launch in pilot stores | Roll out and add features |

Here is an alternative implementation:

1. Design the card and submit it for manufacture. Launch pilot programme for customers in one store to register for the programme via a simple website. Capture basic customer details in a database or even just a spreadsheet.

2. Implement changes to the sales points to allow the customers' total bill amount to be linked with their loyalty account via manually entering their customer number. (This could be changing the till software or implementing an alternative solution such as a separate IT system or a paper-based solution.)

3. Iterate the sales point solution and database system to transfer more information about the customers' purchases and store it. Get feedback from staff and customers on the usability of the system. Get feedback from marketing on what information is useful to store and analyse.

4. When the cards arrive, implement the card scanning functionality and issue cards to initial customers.

5. Update the systems based on feedback and roll out to more stores.

This is similar, but we are getting early feedback, even though we don't have the physical cards yet (see Figure 6.3). The first database is very basic, as is the initial data gathering process. We know the database needs to have more detail, but it doesn't need it **yet**. When all we have is total purchase amount, that is all the database needs to hold. We can add the extra fields when we are able to gather those data.

Figure 6.3 Splitting delivery for early value

| Design cards, simple sign-up process | Launch in 1 store, manual processes required | Iterate store and customer apps | Launch cards and increase functionality | Roll out and add features |

In this way, we get genuine user feedback from customers, staff and marketing very early in the delivery. This gives us confidence that we are going in the right direction; and if we are not, we can change direction quickly and cheaply.

Customer-centric

The customer is key in Agile. Everything is geared around the customer: understanding what they need, delivering value as early as possible, seeking their opinion and feedback often, expecting change to occur and providing transparency so they can see what we are doing is all part of being customer-centric. Agile teams only exist because there is a customer with a problem they are able to solve.

However, it's not usually the case that there is one single customer. Sometimes there are several; sometimes, for instance with new product development, there are none or at least none yet. There are also stakeholders and users who may not be customers. This distinction is covered in more detail in Chapter 10 along with guidance on how to manage them. The customer-centric nature of Agile development means that teams focus on **value** for the users of the product or to the business, no matter how those users are described.

This focus on the customer may sound obvious, and in many respects it is; however, it is common for teams to lose sight of this and for someone or something else to dominate. For instance, we see teams focus on an architecture, a project plan, a delivery date, local manager requests or the completion of a sub-component instead of the customer and their needs.

This problem becomes more of an issue when there are more layers of hierarchy between the customer and the team; and with more teams working to the same customer. That's why Agile teams should be able to have as much direct contact with the end users as possible and be working on discrete solutions that have direct customer value rather than components of highly coupled solutions.

Self-organising, empowered teams

Agile teams are self-contained units that are able to deliver value to their customers without requiring help from anyone else. Furthermore, within those teams, the mix of skills will always be able to deliver the work that delivers maximum value to the customer.

While that sounds simple, it can be helpful to explore what Agile teams are **not**, since it can sometimes be easier to avoid negative traits than introduce positive ones. Agile teams are not teams that:

- are given tasks to implement;
- follow other people's detailed designs (although they may follow high-level architectural direction);
- wait to be told what to do;
- hand their work onto others to continue or complete;
- work in skill silos, with team members specialising in particular skills that their colleagues don't have.

Teams that are self-organising are empowered to decide for themselves what is the best way to do their work. Empowerment isn't just given – it must also be accepted. This means that the teams must want to be empowered and must be comfortable organising themselves. This isn't always the case, as we discuss further in Chapter 9.

An aspect of self-organisation is self-management, where the team internally decides who does what and when. In fact, this aspect is so important that in 2020 the Scrum Guide changed its guidance that Scrum teams are self-organising to require them to be self-managing. This was to reinforce that the team is accountable for the delivery of the product and shouldn't have external interference. In most real teams, however, there are organisational management constraints that make truly self-managing teams hard to create. Nevertheless, the closer teams can get to self-organising and self-managing the better.

This is important as it helps the team to focus on value. When a team can complete all the work themselves, the only thing that stops them delivering value to the customer is themselves. This means they can have stronger customer focus and, by working more closely with the customer, will understand their needs better.

This customer centricity is eroded when other people talk to the customer and hand requirements into the team, or when other people conduct testing and work with the customer to deploy the product. It also adds delay, waste, complexity and risk. The more work is passed around between people, the higher the risk that it is miscommunicated and the wrong things are done.

As we discuss in Chapter 9, having autonomy is an important driver of intrinsic motivation and high-performing teams. Autonomy implies that the team is making important decisions themselves rather than others making decisions for the team. It also means they are likely to be making decisions later and at a time when they have the most up to date and accurate information to support that decision. Moving decision making to where the information is requires trust in the team and good leadership, but it is an important factor for successful Agile teams.

SUMMARY

There are several common themes that cut across the Agile Manifesto and all Agile approaches. These fundamental concepts are core to an Agile mindset and can be a helpful summary of Agile in their own right.

The most critical things to understand and recall are the Agile values and the three pillars of empiricism. With these mastered, you will be well equipped in understanding and applying an Agile mindset.

7 AGILE DELIVERY

Agile delivery is different from traditional approaches, with different language and different assumptions

The previous three chapters have focused on the foundational elements of all Agile approaches. It is important to understand these well before trying to apply them. However, most people have their first experience of Agile in the context of one of the Agile frameworks or methods. When looking at these frameworks (and there are several), they tend to share much in common, even though they may be described in different language.

This chapter looks at the core activities and decisions that are part of any Agile endeavour and uses a loyalty card scenario to provide some tangible examples that will help you to understand:

- the core elements in Agile deliveries and how they work;
- how they reinforce and apply the core Agile concepts discussed previously;
- how you can be successful in applying them.

By now, it should come as no surprise to learn that these things are frequently misunderstood and/or applied badly, and that this leads to poor results and Agile teams struggling to get the benefits they expect. We will help you avoid those problems.

We will describe some of the ways that Agile teams behave throughout the delivery life cycle, including how we deliver value early, how teams improve and the common roles in Agile teams.

HOW DOES AGILE DELIVERY WORK?

Agile deliveries look very similar to non-Agile deliveries in many respects:

- A problem worth solving is identified.
- A team is formed and charged with solving the problem.
- The team spends some time delivering a solution.
- Finally the problem is solved or the business decides to stop investing in it.

For any given problem, the skills required in the team are the same in Agile and non-Agile approaches; for instance, our loyalty card example will require design, marketing and software engineering skills. What is different is who has those skills, how they are employed and how the solution evolves during its development.

Agile deliveries have a single team developing the entire solution iteratively and incrementally. The team collectively has all the skills, knowledge and authority to deliver the solution to the customer, and the customer can start using versions of the solution from very early on.

An example timeline

Figure 7.1 shows one possible timeline for our loyalty card example. We say **one possible timeline** because the nature of an Agile delivery is that we expect things to change and we try to keep our options open as much as possible. We could have drawn a dozen different examples of this timeline and they would all have been valid.

This example illustrates several important attributes of Agile deliveries that are not always present in traditional projects. The detail in later months is intentionally vague. We don't know whether an iteration sees updates to each element of the solution or not. Perhaps, in some iterations, the team focuses on the data analytics and doesn't make many changes to the customer's app. Perhaps, in other iterations, the opposite is true (see Table 7.1).

Table 7.1 Attributes of Agile delivery

We can stop the delivery early	There are many opportunities to stop the delivery early based on information we learn during the development:
	• If the reaction of the customers is not favourable.
	• If the data we gather don't help us make better decisions than stores without the data.
	• If we don't see the business value in rolling out to more stores.
	• And once live, we can stop at any point if the value of further iterations is not worth their cost.
There is early use by customers	Customers can use the loyalty programme after just a few weeks; the business can see the data and make decisions based on them shortly afterwards.
Early versions can be low quality	The early versions require manual processes from customers and staff, even though we ideally want it to be automated.
Solution elements may be temporary	The Cashier app allows early time to market, but once there is integration with the store IT systems it isn't necessary and can be discarded.
Long lead items can be scheduled at risk	Marketing materials and physical cards may take some time to be manufactured, so they are ordered as soon as we can be confident the delivery is likely to continue (i.e. as soon as we know the data are valuable).
Frequent updates	Solution elements are updated frequently (every two weeks) based on feedback from users and the business. This will include bug fixes and additional functionality that increases business value.

Figure 7.1 An example timeline for an Agile delivery

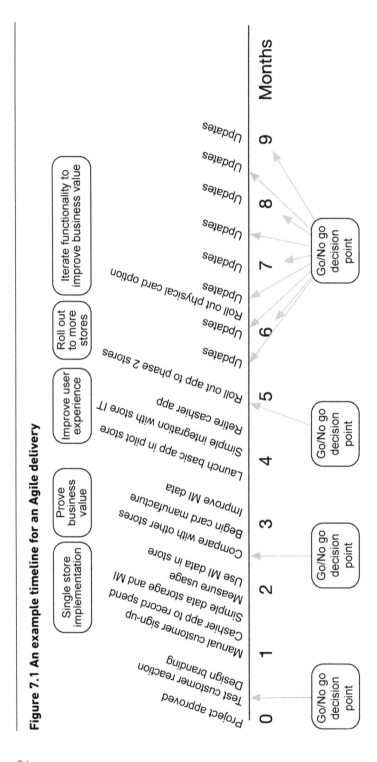

Months

This Agile team will have the skills and knowledge to work on anything that delivers the maximum business value – whether that is front-end UI design, back-end data architecture and analytics or designing marketing materials to support the rollout to new stores.

In practice, teams are not always as multi-skilled as we would prefer and aren't always as willing to do the work that is needed. It is common to see developers who prefer UI work find things to fix on a perfectly adequate web page when there is critical work elsewhere that is not being done – and vice versa.

The discipline required, from both the team and the stakeholders, to release very early versions of a solution can be a challenge. It is easier to wait until the solution is more complete. In this example, waiting until later may have meant that we missed an opportunity to maximise sales of a promotion, or invested lots of time and money in a data analytics solution that didn't help store managers make better decisions.

GETTING STARTED

Most Agile approaches assume that you already know what you are going to produce and that your initial 'backlog' of work exists. In fact, that is rarely the case, and creating this starting point can be challenging for many teams.

Traditionally, a project manager would be appointed to lead any new endeavour. They would begin by creating a business case or project proposal to secure resources (people[64] and/or money). To do this, they would usually come up with a project plan that was detailed enough to identify all the factors necessary to deliver the project successfully; usually, this means detailed costing, delivery milestones, resource plans, dependencies and risks. Only with this level of detail could the project manager come up with numbers that they could trust and be held to account for, and only once the proposal was accepted could the team be assembled and work commence. Very often, this process would take some time, as meetings need to be arranged, estimates approved and documents drafted.

There are many problems with this approach, particularly given that we are in a VUCA world where assumptions are likely to be wrong, change is certain to occur and stakeholder guesses and opinions will change. It also relies heavily on one person and their wisdom, experience and knowledge: the project manager.

How do Agile deliveries differ?

If we reflect on the Agile Manifesto, starting an Agile endeavour ought to be very different indeed:

- We rely more on people and collaboration than on plans and detailed agreements.

---

64 There is a terrible trend of using the word 'resource' to describe people. If you mean people, say people. Resources are money, pens, fuel and so on. We won't use the word this way in the book again, and we hope you won't either.

- We expect customers using early versions of the solution to be a better source of product requirements than detailed analysis done in advance.

- We expect change, including changes in the detail of the problem we are solving and in our intended solution.

This means that an ideal Agile delivery starts by identifying a problem to be solved (or opportunity to be pursued) and immediately assembling a team to begin working on it. At this point, the detail of the problem and solution isn't that clear, so the team needs to have the skills, knowledge and authority to cope with a variety of different ways forward. They will probably each be multi-skilled and comfortable learning new skills and technologies any time they need to. We will discuss this type of team – of generalising-specialists – later in this chapter.

Once the team is assembled, they focus on two things:

- understanding the problem (and business context) well enough;

- identifying the quickest and most valuable version of a solution to deliver first.

For small startups this can be relatively simple – just get some people together, perhaps with an external investor or some startup capital, and get on with it – but in larger or more bureaucratic organisations, this is so different from what they are used to that it can cause problems. How can I fund something when I don't know how long it will take? When will I have a version I can sell? How will you mitigate your risks?

There are still plans in Agile

The first stage – understanding the problem – is where we address 'planning'. For any endeavour, there are elements that are clear and unlikely to change, and there are elements that are not. The problem of traditional project management is the assumption that most things don't change.

However, a criticism of Agile is the opposite – that Agile teams never commit to anything. This is wrong. In Agile delivery, the overall solution goal or vision will be stable. How that goal is met may change, but the business need will not. If it were to change, then the whole delivery should stop and we should reconsider whether the new situation still requires our effort.

So, the first thing an Agile team does is to agree the overarching vision and goal of the work. Very often, it will become obvious how much effort or time will be required, even if that estimate is vague. For example, developing a loyalty card programme will probably take a few quarters; we won't be able to complete it in a month, and it's not likely to take several years. We can also guess at the types of people we will need, for instance we need a software team that can deliver both user-facing systems (an app, data dashboard) and crunch numbers for management information. We will also need some marketing, branding and communications experience.

This level of information – a rough idea of the type of solution, the types of people we will need and a ballpark schedule – should be enough detail to start an Agile delivery. Figure 7.2 shows an example.

Figure 7.2 Simple Agile business case

AG STORES
Loyalty card business case

Vision:
     A customer loyalty programme that increases
     average spend per customer and supports
     better strategic decision making

Investment:
     – Team of 7 people with software, marketing
       and design skills
     – For up to 12 months
     – Up to £1m

Results:
     Initial version available in less than 2 months
     Iterate based on feedback and business
     impact

The information necessary to make a business decision is still there and the team will have done some initial analysis of the problem, the business context and the possible solutions in order to come up with it. That analysis could have been very lightweight – perhaps just a couple of hours – or it could have taken a few weeks.

Inception Deck and Agile chartering This 'pre-delivery' work is sometimes called Sprint 0, because it describes the time before the first iteration that teams using Scrum would call Sprint 1.

In *The Agile Samurai*,[65] Jonathan Rasmusson describes a technique called the Inception Deck, which teams use at the very start of an Agile delivery to capture their assumptions and share their intentions with their stakeholders. It is a simple set of slides, with each slide conveying an element of the work being proposed. For instance, solution vision, stakeholder map, candidate architecture, ballpark costs and so on. Over the past few years we have used this approach many times and evolved our own version.[66]

Another powerful approach to putting just enough work up front is Agile chartering. This is an approach described superbly in the book *Liftoff* by Diana Larsen and Ainsley Nies.[67] In Agile chartering the team focuses on analysing the problem from three perspectives before starting an endeavour, or to realign a team. The key is to do just enough analysis to align the team with the work, each other and their environment. Spending a day or two on this, a 'Liftoff'[68] can make them much more likely to succeed. The three core perspectives are:

---

65 Rasmusson, J. (2017) *The Agile Samurai: How Agile Masters Deliver Great Software.* Pragmatic Bookshelf, Dallas, TX.

66 https://www.linkedin.com/pulse/navigating-inception-deck-simon-girvan/.

67 Larsen, D. and Nies, A. (2016) *Liftoff: Start and Sustain Successful Agile Teams* (2nd edn). Pragmatic Bookshelf, Dallas, TX.

68 We sometimes call this a 'Liftoff' after the book, or sometimes a 'kickstart', 'project refresh' or 'realignment'.

- **Purpose** – Focusing on the work. Know why this is important and to whom; take ownership and accountability for the outcomes.

- **Alignment** – Focusing on the team. Know each other at a slightly deeper level. Appreciate our strengths and development needs, our similarities and differences. Teams cannot self-organise well without understanding one another.

- **Context** – Focusing on the environment around the team. It's rare for a team to be 100 per cent responsible for all their outcomes. Understanding the wider context, the boundaries of their responsibility and the resources[69] they require is important to their success.

Spending time on an Inception Deck and Agile chartering can be a powerful way to instil confidence in your stakeholders, particularly when they are involved in the activities themselves. It can make them much more content with a proposal like the one in Figure 7.2 compared to the multi-page documents they may be used to.

Measuring progress
Once the delivery is underway, we are presented with another problem: without a project plan with milestones and dates, how do we know whether the delivery is on track?

The Agile Manifesto is clear on this point: it says that 'Working software is the primary measure of progress' (principle 7)[70] so that's what we do. As early as possible, we produce versions of the solution (whether software or not) that can be used by customers. Their feedback will be a powerful measure of how well we are doing. Inviting stakeholders to witness and, better still, experience the work completed in each iteration is a better way for them to gauge progress than green ticks on a Gantt chart.

Measurements are discussed further in Chapter 8.

Innovation Accounting
Stakeholders, particularly those supplying the budget, can often be uneasy at the apparent open-ended nature of Agile delivery. With no milestones or firm dates and improved versions of the product arriving every couple of weeks, it can be difficult to know when to stop investing. That's where Innovation Accounting comes in. The term was introduced by Eric Ries in *The Lean Startup*.[71] Innovation Accounting works well with Agile teams because it places responsibilities both on the team and the investors.

- The team is encouraged to make tangible progress each period and is more likely to do that through usable versions of their product rather than deferring release until the end.

- The investors are encouraged to focus on the value being created by the team right now, rather than adherence to a plan generated months ago.

---

[69] Here we mean resources in the paper, software licences, desks and money sense, not people.

[70] https://agilemanifesto.org/principles.html.

[71] Ries, E. (2011) *The Lean Startup: How Constant Innovation Creates Radically Successful Businesses.* Portfolio Penguin, London and New York.

With Innovation Accounting, the investors decide how long (or how much) to invest in a team (or product) before they want to see some results and decide whether to continue funding. This could be as frequently as weekly or monthly.

This differs from traditional project accounting because a traditional project assumes that the project will last for the duration planned, and, while it can be stopped early, this would be an exception activity and regarded as a failure. As we explained in Chapter 3, even the use of the word 'project' leads people to assume it will last (at least) as long as initially planned.

In contrast, in an Agile delivery, even where we expect it to take a couple of years, our assumption is that change is likely to happen and that we might want to change direction or even stop it. This would not be regarded as an absolute failure; instead, it would just tell us that an assumption we had was wrong, or an experiment we tried had failed.

So, in an Agile delivery using Innovation Accounting, we may expect a full year's investment but begin with just a month's money to begin proving that our ideas have merit. After a month, the investors would look at our results and decide whether we should persevere (continue as expected), pivot (still aim for the same vision, but try a different approach) or fail (the vision is not likely to be met or would be too expensive).

Creating the backlog

The final thing that the team needs to have in place before they can start is a backlog of work to start doing. Preferably one that is in priority order with high priority items estimated in enough detail that they know whether they can complete an item in one iteration.

Some of the things that teams can do to create a backlog include:

- Stakeholder workshops to elicit user needs and problems.

- Value stream mapping, a Lean technique to walk through all the end-to-end steps that need to happen to realise value for the customer, including identifying where there are pain points, waste, delays or other opportunities to optimise the flow.

- User story mapping,[72] a technique (and book) developed by Jeff Patton that allows large and complex products to be visualised in a map and prioritised to break the work down into small releases of value.

- Impact mapping,[73] a technique developed by Gojko Adzic where you start with the goal and work backwards to identify the behaviour changes necessary and then the activities or tasks required to make those changes.

Chapter 10 covers this in much more detail, including more guidance on some of these topics.

---

72 Patton, J. (2014) *User Story Mapping: Discover the Whole Story, Build the Right Product*. O'Reilly Media, Sebastopol, CA.

73 https://www.impactmapping.org.

THE FIRST DELIVERY

We know that Agile teams aim to deliver early and frequently, but this can be a challenge when the solution is inherently large or complex. Sometimes it can seem impossible to begin delivering something of value in a few weeks. That could be the case with our loyalty card example. The final solution includes (at least):

- An app that customers use to sign up and track their progress.
- An analytics method to sift through the data and generate information that supports operational and strategic business decisions.
- Integration with the existing store systems and tills to connect customer purchases to the new system.

Figure 7.3 shows a candidate architecture that the team could have created as part of their Inception Deck.

Figure 7.3 Candidate architecture for loyalty card programme

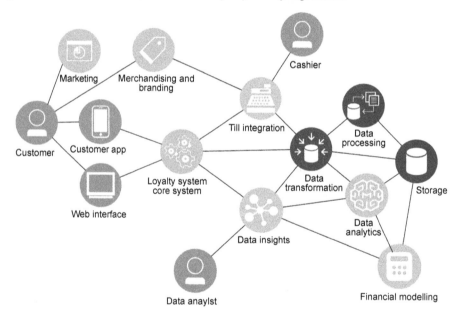

This architecture looks like it could be pretty complex and might take several weeks to build enough that it could be used. So how can the team deliver earlier? This is where the minimum viable product (MVP) comes in.

Minimum viable product

The term 'minimum viable product' (MVP) was popularised by Eric Ries' book, *The Lean Startup*,[74] where MVPs are critical to the Build–Measure–Learn cycle and an important way for entrepreneurs to test that their ideas have merit.

Put simply, an MVP is the quickest, cheapest version of the solution that will allow you to test your hypotheses and assumptions. It doesn't need to demonstrate all of your product's functionality, but it does need to have an outcome that you can measure in order to decide whether you are on the right track.

> Tesla's first car wasn't really much of a Tesla – it was a Lotus Esprit body with a battery powered engine. It was quick to produce and allowed Tesla to test their hypothesis that people would buy a high-end expensive electric car.

> When Nick Swinmurn thought about selling shoes online, he didn't build a complex website and sign deals with shoe manufacturers. He went to a local shoe shop, took photos of all their shoes, and put them on his website. When somebody bought a pair, he would go to the store, buy the shoes, and post them to the customer. It wasn't a scalable or sustainable solution, but it proved that people were comfortable buying shoes online and Zappos was founded.

An MVP ought to be a **viable** product – it should be able to be used by the end user to solve a specific problem. However, some people extend the definition of MVP to include products that test a market but don't actually provide value. When Buffer launched their first 'product' it was just a web page asking if people were interested in purchasing a product that would schedule their social media posts. The interest received was enough to justify further investment, but at that time there wasn't actually a product that existed and it wasn't possible to generate any customer value.

When this definition of MVP is used, the first version of the product that **does** provide value is sometimes called the minimum marketable product (MMP). In either case, the important thing is that the product is the cheapest and quickest way to complete a learning cycle. The knowledge you gain from the MVP helps you to decide whether to continue and what to prioritise next. Figure 7.4 shows how the loyalty card example uses MVPs.

While the concept of an MVP is relatively simple, like many things in Agile it is easily and frequently misunderstood and abused. The earlier discussion on whether a marketing test (as Buffer used) is an MVP or not is one example, but the more common problems we see are MVPs that don't test a clear hypothesis, don't have measurement and learning built into them or don't provide any value to the customer.

---

74 Ries, E. (2011) *The Lean Startup: How Constant Innovation Creates Radically Successful Businesses*. Portfolio Penguin, London and New York.

Figure 7.4 Product evolution of the loyalty card with MVPs

Evolution of the Loyalty Card Product

Minimum viable product (or marketing test)

A manual survey of customers to ask them about their attitude towards a loyalty card for this store. This is testing our assumption that a loyalty card will be used by customers.

Enthusiastic customers are offered an Early Adopter bonus where their purchases will be worth more points when the programme launches.

Minimum viable product (or minimum marketable product)

A functional loyalty card programme with manual sign-up, paper cards, a simple app for cashiers to correlate a customer card ID with their shopping and manual data extraction, processing and analysis.

This version may undergo several iterations but will ultimately be superseded by new components and discarded.

Final system

An automated and integrated system with online sign-up, self-service account management, integration with store tills and back end systems and complex data processing capability.

This version will undergo several iterations.

Some examples where the term MVP is misused include:

- proof of concepts, wireframes, models or non-functional prototypes;
- early versions of products that don't include enough functionality to meet the users' needs, for example not operating on real data, not being approved for business use or only partially solving the problem;
- products that customers cannot use, for instance products created to demonstrate features that the customer can't use themselves.

That isn't to say that an MVP needs to do everything – far from it. An MVP exists early in product development when there are many more features to add and improve. But it does need to solve enough of the customer's needs to provide them with some value, which could be a very small slice of value. Breaking down big problems into small goals is described in Chapter 10.

CONTINUOUS IMPROVEMENT

One of the reasons an MVP is useful in early development is that it provides a start point from which continuous improvement can commence. Getting actionable feedback from customers early increases the chance that our product will deliver the value and quality to the customer.

Continuous improvement is a fundamental aspect of anything Agile. It isn't an add-on to delivery, it is a fundamental component of how Agile teams deliver value for their customers. It has its own principle in the Agile Manifesto and is integrated throughout Agile practices, methods and frameworks. Agile teams always believe there is opportunity to improve, and actively seek out those opportunities. The most obvious way this happens is through a retrospective.

Agile retrospectives

Agile retrospectives are held frequently, usually each iteration. They are also useful for looking back over longer periods such as funding cycles or product releases/increments. Retrospectives involve the whole team reflecting on what has happened in an honest and non-judgemental way and taking decisions about things to change or improve.

In their book *Agile Retrospectives*,[75] Esther Derby and Diana Larsen set out this agenda:

- Set the stage.
- Gather data.
- Generate insights.
- Decide what to do.
- Close the retrospective.

Each stage is a facilitated session and there are dozens of different techniques you can use to keep the event fresh and generate powerful insights from the teams.

This open and honest approach to finding ways to improve is very powerful, but it isn't how many people are used to working. To some people, finding a potential improvement means admitting that things have been done wrongly until now. Reflecting on progress and identifying areas to improve can become an opportunity to highlight failure and attribute blame. The retrospective can become an adversarial and unpleasant place to be.

Potential changes don't need to be big things. The Japanese word for continuous improvement or 'change for the better' is *kaizen*. In the Toyota Production System, team members propose thousands of *kaizen* a year. They could be something as simple as moving a waste bin closer to a machine to see if it makes the operator more effective, or moving it back if it doesn't. When Agile teams are self-organising and empowered there should be lots of things about their work that they can change and lots of opportunities to improve.

We often see the opposite problem, where teams identify big things that could improve, but which they are not empowered to change themselves, for example unwieldy

---

75 Derby, E. and Larsen, D. (2006) *Agile Retrospectives: Making Good Teams Great.* Pragmatic Bookshelf, Dallas, TX and Raleigh, NC.

corporate processes, lack of people or slow procurement. It is important that the changes identified can happen and that the team commits to the changes.

THE ITERATION

Agile delivery focuses on iterative and incremental delivery of a product. This usually means that the team chooses a regular cadence to regulate their work, such as two or three weeks. Although different Agile methods use different language, there are certain things that are common across most approaches, whether teams are using Scrum, a scaled approach or an in-house method. The elements in a generic iteration are set out in Figure 7.5 and discussed in Table 7.2.

Figure 7.5 A generic iteration

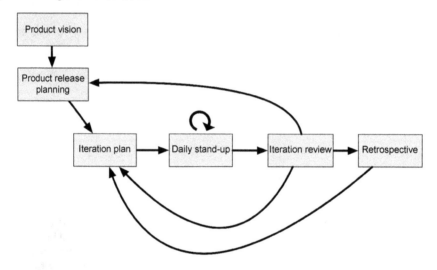

Table 7.2 Common elements in an Agile iteration

Product vision	The high-level vision for the product that describes the problem being solved or the value being proposed. This should not change over the life of the delivery. If it does, this should trigger the delivery to be re-evaluated and potentially cancelled.
Product release planning	High-level release planning that gives an idea of how we think the product will evolve over the delivery period. We should expect this to change and evolve based on the feedback we will get from each iteration. There may be several artefacts that describe this plan, such as roadmaps, story maps or a release plan. There will usually be a high-level set of prioritised features or outcomes in some form of backlog.

(Continued)

Table 7.2 (Continued)

Iteration plan	An iteration is generally a short period of time (often two or three weeks). The team should be able to commit to the work with a reasonable degree of certainty. Often an iteration is focused on achieving a specific goal.
	The iteration planning is usually done in collaboration with a business stakeholder such as the Product Owner. It involves deciding whether the highest priority work can be done in the time available. If so, the team commits to doing that work, and may spend time analysing the work to understand it better and identify lower-level tasks that are required. For large or multiple teams, they may need to do further analysis to identify dependencies or conduct more in-depth planning.
	They then consider the next highest priority work and decide whether they can also do that work in this iteration.
	When the work being considered is too big, the team will break it down into smaller goals and decide which of these smaller goals can be delivered.
Daily stand-up	The team get together frequently (usually daily) to share with each other what they have been doing, whether there are any blockers and what they intend to do next. This is often a short, time-boxed meeting, perhaps 15 minutes.
	This is demonstrating the Agile pillars of transparency, inspection and adaptation discussed in Chapter 6. It is not a 'progress update'. It is an opportunity for the team to check that what they intend to do will be the most valuable thing that helps them to meet the iteration's goals. Often, hearing from other team members will prompt someone to change what they will do today.
Iteration review	The point of an iteration is to deliver a version (or increment) of your product that customers can use. The review is where that increment is reviewed by the stakeholders. Ideally, this is through the customer actually using the new version and proving that it delivers the value intended. It shouldn't really be the team demonstrating to the customers.
	The review is also an important opportunity to involve wider stakeholders and to elicit feedback to improve future iterations and evolve the backlogs.
Retrospective	Manifesto Principle 12[76] states: 'At regular intervals, the team reflects on how to become more effective, then tunes and adjusts its behaviour accordingly.' The retrospective is where that happens, with the team reflecting on the prior iteration and committing to actions that will improve future iterations. The actions should have a high priority when planning the next iteration.

(Continued)

---

[76] https://agilemanifesto.org/principles.html.

Table 7.2 (Continued)

Feedback	There are multiple feedback opportunities, reinforcing the empirical nature of Agile delivery.
	The high-level product planning is an ongoing activity that relies on feedback from iteration reviews to ensure it evolves as things change and we learn new information. It may result in updates to the backlog(s).
	Iteration planning not only considers the higher-level backlogs but also stakeholder feedback from the review, team feedback and improvement actions from the retrospective.

Iteration length

We know that Agile is biased towards change being inevitable. One of the ways to cope with this is through iterative delivery. Delivering without any plan is stressful and challenging, so we still want to have some planning and certainty in an Agile delivery. The iteration is how we do that. As we have shown, the iteration is a simple plan with a few events and artefacts.

The secret to being able to respond to change is to have short iterations. The longer into the future we try to predict, the more likely we are to be wrong. I can tell you with high certainty what the weather will be like two minutes from now, and I can have a fairly accurate guess about an hour away and even a day. If I try to predict the detailed weather in 10 weeks' time, I am much less likely to be correct. It's the same with iterations. Iterations work best when we have a clear and certain goal that we are working towards, with a team we can depend on being available to work towards it, and when we know the customer will benefit when it is delivered. The longer the iteration, the less likely these things are to be true.

In Scrum, an iteration length of no more than four weeks is mandated. Other approaches have different guidance, or none at all. Two weeks seems to work well for many teams. The iteration events should all scale depending on the iteration length – so the planning and reviews for a one-week iteration should be three times shorter than for a three-week iteration.

The iteration length is one factor the team has within their control and can adjust as part of their continuous improvement actions. Generally, we always advise: the shorter the better. Teams struggling to deliver on time often want to increase their iteration length when often this just exacerbates the problem. Try a short iteration first – the short timeframe requires smaller, simpler goals that take less effort to meet.

AGILE BACKLOGS

In Chapter 3 we introduced backlogs and explained their importance to Agile teams. Agile teams don't have the same requirements artefacts that we find in traditional project delivery, and a backlog is very different thing from a requirements specification. The main difference is that we tend to assume that a requirement in a catalogue or in a requirements document is **required**. In other words, we expect to meet that requirement with our product and the product will not be complete otherwise.

In contrast, most backlogs contain items that **may** be included in our product, but also **may not** be. This is because we assume things might change and we might change our mind about a feature we thought we wanted at the start of the endeavour. The only exception is where the work for an iteration is described in a backlog, as happens in Scrum. Because iterations are short, we can be confident that the work planned won't change and we can treat a Sprint backlog as something we have committed to.

Because backlog items might not be implemented, particularly those lower in priority, it is important not to put too much effort into them. Similarly, it can be wasteful to create lots of backlog items that you know are not likely to be implemented for a long time. It is better to wait until the team is close to being able to work on them.

Figure 7.6 shows an example Product Backlog for the loyalty card. The items at the top are the things we want to prioritise for the next iteration. Some of these are solution elements that we revisit many times to improve them, for instance the dashboard doesn't need to have rich functionality right at the start because there aren't many data to analyse. As the delivery progresses and we get more data in the system, there will be many more backlog items describing how that part of the system needs to change.

As we move further down the backlog, the descriptions get more vague. As the delivery progresses, those items will need further analysis, which will result in new, more specific items to be added to the backlog and prioritised. This is an ongoing process that is driven by feedback and by the need for the items at the top of the backlog to be detailed enough for the team to be able to consider them for the next iteration – too vague, then the team cannot possibly judge whether they can complete them in the next iteration or not.

Backlogs should have a 1:1 relationship with products. However, sometimes there are several backlogs (for instance in some scaled Agile approaches). This can be because there are different stakeholders involved in the backlog refinement and reviewing or because the teams are organised in a way that makes it hard for them to work from one backlog. Where there are multiple backlogs there is a higher risk of confusion, and it can be harder to be confident that everyone is working on the most valuable items.

Backlogs do not include everything that would be described as a requirement in a traditional approach. Things like non-functional requirements are managed in other ways, such as via acceptance criteria or definitions of done. Chapter 10 discusses in more detail how Agile 'requirements' are managed.

AGILE TEAM BEHAVIOURS

Perhaps the greatest difference between Agile and traditional teams is how they behave. Focusing on the left-hand side of the Agile Manifesto and following the pillars of transparency, inspection and adaptation requires a different mindset and behaviours.

Figure 7.6 A Product Backlog example

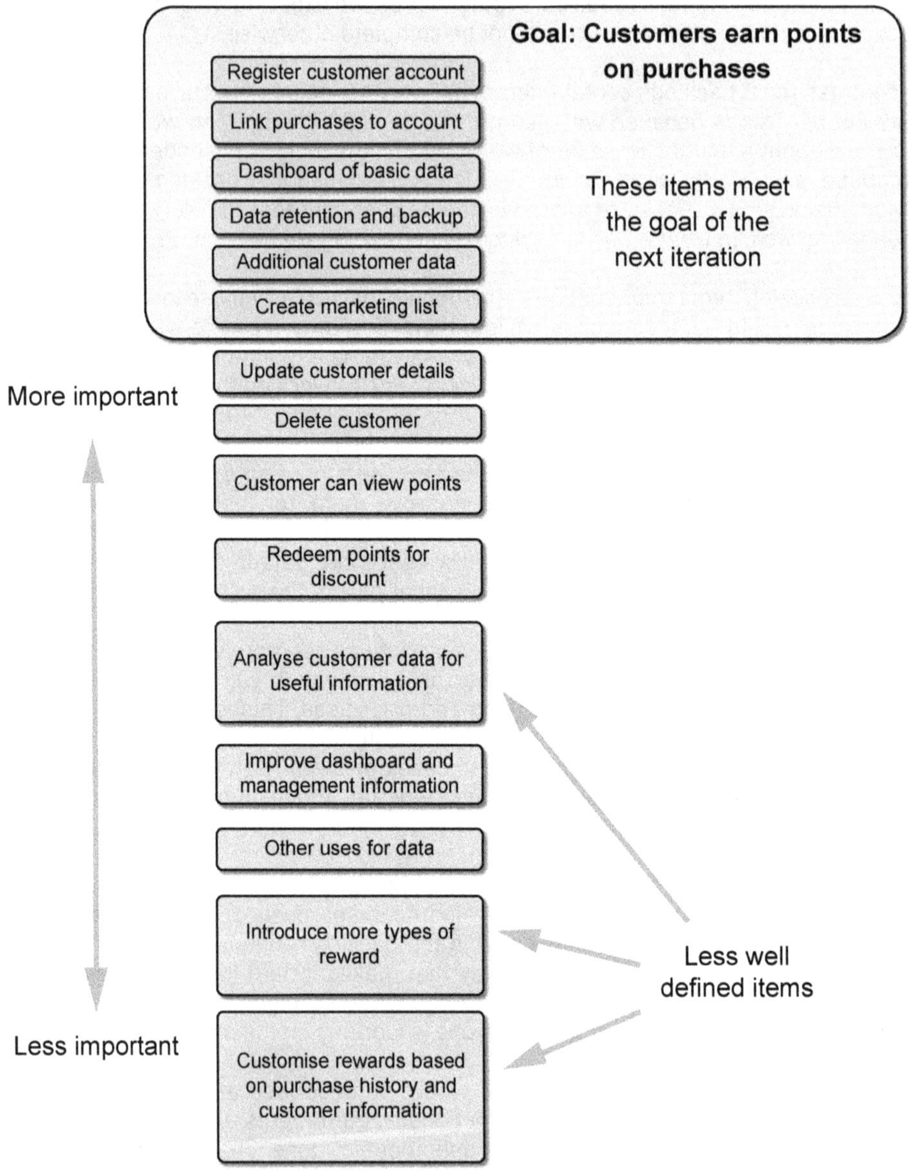

Goal: Customers earn points on purchases

Register customer account
Link purchases to account
Dashboard of basic data
Data retention and backup
Additional customer data
Create marketing list

These items meet the goal of the next iteration

More important

Update customer details
Delete customer
Customer can view points
Redeem points for discount
Analyse customer data for useful information
Improve dashboard and management information
Other uses for data
Introduce more types of reward

Less well defined items

Less important

Customise rewards based on purchase history and customer information

The main pivot in mindset is from individual accountability to team accountability. Agile teams are collectively responsible for their outcomes. The team focuses on doing the most valuable work and working together to meet the goals they have committed to. That means helping one another, identifying opportunities to improve, changing plans to respond to events and doing the work that needs to be done, even when you would prefer to do something else.

High levels of collaboration

In an Agile team, while individual working is sometimes necessary, it is the exception rather than the norm. Working as a team allows for better decisions to be made – because there are more brains engaged on the problem and more perspectives shared – and creates higher quality products. When we work collaboratively, we get quality reviews and design improvements for free. This is why pair programming and mob programming are so effective.

Pair and mob programming are when two or more people sit around a single keyboard and monitor and work on creating a product. The conversations, challenges, discussions, explanations and experiments that result mean that the subsequent artefact has already had several rounds of review and several opportunities for problems to be found and improvements made. This also works for creating documents or other non-software artefacts. It sounds counter-intuitive – how can five people doing a job one person could do be more efficient? Yet, in practice, they can.

Some companies, such as Menlo Innovations,[77] believe this so strongly that all their work is done in pairs, as co-founder and chief storyteller Rich Sheridan describes in his book *Joy Inc*.[78]

Customer focus

Menlo also demonstrate other core behaviours that we see in good Agile teams. They have a strong focus on the customer, including their 'High-Tech Anthropologists' who focus on gaining a deep understanding of who the customers are and uncovering their underlying needs, not just asking them what they think they want.

This customer discovery process is also a core part of the Lean Startup approach, and Alex Osterwalder's Strategyzer[79] series of books (such as *Value Proposition Design*[80]) contain many examples of how to do this.

People focus

It isn't just customers that Agile teams focus on; they also focus on themselves. As we describe more in Chapter 9, motivating people who do knowledge work is not the same as motivating people to do manual work. It requires more sophisticated leadership and creation of environments where people are challenged, supported, trusted and empowered.

---

77 https://menloinnovations.com/our-way/our-people.

78 Sheridan, R. (2013) *Joy Inc: How We Built a Workplace People Love*. Portfolio Penguin, New York.

79 https://www.strategyzer.com.

80 Osterwalder, A., Pigneur, Y., Bernarda, G., Smith, A. and Papadakos, T. (2014) *Value Proposition Design: How to Create Products and Services Customers Want*. John Wiley & Sons, Hoboken, NJ.

Agile teams recognise that people develop professional skills faster when the work they do provides the right balance of challenge against skill. This optimal state – where the challenge of the work matches the skills of the person, stretching them without leading to failure – is described as the state of 'flow' by psychologist Mihaly Csikszentmihalyi.[81] This is the state where we can lose track of time, stop worrying about other people's opinions and want to continue with the task for its own sake.

If the challenge becomes too great, we can get stressed, anxious, worried or give up; if the challenge is too simple, we can get bored, relaxed or go on auto-pilot. This can also lead to poor quality work, because being in a bored or relaxed state can lead to poorly performing the task, for example it's easy to do a poor job of cleaning the house, even when we know we can do it better.

The problem for many teams is that being in a balanced skill and challenge state will tend to increase our skill, but the challenge often doesn't change. This can lead to the dwindling performance of a team and its people becoming less motivated. To solve this problem requires one of two things to happen:

- Adjust the work to increase the challenge, perhaps by the team taking on bigger chunks of work that require more skill and effort to break down.

- Move the people around to give them more challenging work, perhaps by moving to a new team with different technologies, customers or challenges.

In both these cases there can be concerns over disruption to the team, particularly if there are unhelpful measures being applied, such as Story Points.[82] However, when this is a regular occurrence, as at Menlo, then teams are used to welcoming new members and adjusting to new types of work. The Tuckman cycle of 'forming, storming, norming and performing'[83] still happens around teams gelling together, but it completes much more quickly.

This type of dynamic Agile team is also better able to cope with other types of change than a stable, unchanging team – and we know from earlier chapters that change is the one thing that we can depend on in a VUCA environment.

Professional development

This focus on the person extends to personal and professional development. Agile teams find ways to help each other develop and they factor that into planning and continuous improvement actions.

---

[81] Csikszentmihalyi, M. (1990) *Flow: The Psychology of Optimal Experience.* Harper & Row, New York.

[82] Using Story Points to measure a team's performance is a bad idea for many reasons. In this context, it requires both the team and the work to be homogeneous and consistent. This means we can't change the team, the roles or the type of work without making the measure meaningless.

[83] Tuckman, B. W. (1965) Developmental sequence in small groups. *Psychological Bull.,* 63, 384–399.

One of the most valuable activities we use in the alignment part of Liftoff is to understand each other's aspirations for this delivery. For example, are there skills or technologies team members would like to learn, or skills they don't want to use? It's easy to see people as the product of their previous work (particularly when we also describe them as resources and define them by their CV) when it is better to see them as the potential for future work. This means that we want to include opportunities or training that help to develop the team as well as focus on delivering value for the customer. In this way an Agile team ensures that it is stronger and more capable after each cycle.

Formal training courses can help, and be scheduled and costed into the delivery, but there are many on the job opportunities that teams can choose to take to develop themselves. Some examples are:

- pairing with specific people;
- choosing work that challenges the person;
- setting specific development actions for each Sprint;
- regular knowledge sharing sessions;
- cross team collaboration, such as inviting other teams to design discussions or review sessions;
- open review sessions (and participating in those of other teams).

Continuous improvement

As we have mentioned previously, continuous improvement is a core principle of Agile teams and is woven throughout their practices and behaviours. Identifying something to improve is a positive thing with no implication of blame.

Success is not a binary attribute; we can succeed in meeting a goal and still find ways we could improve. Conversely, if we fail to meet a goal, we can still find things that worked well that we should do again.

Feedback
A primary driver of continuous improvement is feedback. Feedback in all its forms is a gift, whether it is systemic feedback from the results of a process or a personal comment from a colleague. The problem is that feedback is too often entwined with performance management.

To test this, ask yourself how you feel when a manager says to you: 'I'd like to give you some feedback on that task.' How does that make you feel? Are you intrigued to get their perspective on how it went and excited to learn something that can help you to improve? Or are you nervous about what they have spotted and dread hearing their criticism?

In many organisations, feedback is almost always negative and often conjoined with some other purpose, such as an annual review, a promotion application or an assessment. It is rarely given solely for the purpose of continuous improvement. This also means that it is often given after the event it concerns, perhaps long after, and frequently bundled with other people's feedback and anonymised. This makes it really hard to interpret and really easy to dismiss.

Agile teams have a much healthier relationship with feedback. It is both sought and given frequently, and it is always for the benefit of the recipient and given with kindness and respect – and it is often feedback on what went well; it's not always critical. A helpful mantra for feedback that we have used is that it should always be kind, specific and helpful, as in the feedback model at Table 7.3.

Table 7.3 A simple model for giving feedback

Kind	We give feedback to help others see what they are doing from another perspective. It is for the benefit of the recipient. It is not to help the giver feel (or look) better. It is given when we know it will be received well.
Specific	We can't act properly on feedback without being clear on the context. This is also why we should seek and provide feedback as soon after the event as possible, while it is fresh in our minds.
Helpful	There must be a reason for the feedback and something that the recipient can do with it. If is not helpful, perhaps it doesn't need to be said.

AGILE ROLES

There are a few common Agile roles found in many approaches and methods, and there are some that are specific to a particular method. This book will not attempt to describe all the possible roles, not least because the frameworks change and evolve frequently. The main roles are the most important to understand. In all cases the roles need not be full-time. Apart from the 'Developer' role, it is common for people to either work on more than one product or have additional responsibilities to their Agile role.

The Scrum roles

In the 2021 State of Agile[84] survey of more than 4000 people, over three-quarters of respondents were using Scrum or some variant of Scrum, so it is no surprise that the Scrum roles[85] have become synonymous with Agile. They are described in the Scrum Guide,[86] and there are three: Developer, Product Owner and Scrum Master (see Table 7.4).

---

[84] https://digital.ai/resource-center/analyst-reports/state-of-agile-report.

[85] The 2020 Scrum Guide uses the word 'accountability' not 'role' in order to prevent them being interpreted as 'job titles'. Roles are not meant to be synonymous with jobs. A job can entail many roles.

[86] https://scrumguides.org/index.html.

Table 7.4 Accountabilities in a Scrum team

Developer	Developers are the people in the team that are committed to creating any aspect of a usable increment in each iteration.
	Scrum does not use more specific job titles (such as software engineer, business analyst, tester, marketing, etc.) to reinforce the self-organising and collaborative nature of a good team.
Product Owner	The Product Owner is accountable for maximising the value of the product resulting from the work of the team.
Scrum Master	The Scrum Master is accountable for establishing Scrum as defined in the Scrum Guide. They do this by helping everyone understand Scrum theory and practice, within both the Scrum team and the organisation.

Other common roles

Most Agile approaches use the Scrum language, but some have additional roles. Even with Scrum teams, there are often responsibilities that fall outside the three accountabilities that need to be done. For example, Scrum doesn't talk about financial accounting, contract management or performance management of staff, yet these things are often still required, particularly in large organisations.

One solution is to assign those responsibilities to a Scrum role. However, when the Scrum Master is also your manager or responsible for your contract, human nature means you are less likely to be open and more likely to defer to their view. This is not conducive to self-organising and self-managing teams.

Another approach is to have other people involved, either as an individual role or as part of a support function. The support functions can also be useful where a person in a role doesn't have enough time to devote to it. In this case, it is really important that the support function doesn't become a 'proxy' for the accountable person.

There are a few additional roles that we commonly see, either when we are using one of the other Agile approaches, or when organisations have created their own version of Agile. These are listed in Table 7.5.

Table 7.5 Other roles commonly found in Agile teams

Business sponsor	Ideally, the Product Owner is solely accountable for the product. However, particularly with large organisations or complex products, there is often a business sponsor who is accountable for the money or is the main advocate for the product. Ideally, they would also be the Product Owner, but often they are not.
Coach	While the Scrum Master has coaching responsibilities, it is usually a good idea to have access to dedicated external coaches. They can provide a one-to-one coaching service for the Scrum Master or other team members, but can also bring a more objective external perspective that can be hard to see when you are working day to day with a team.
	They can also bring more experience and a wider range of perspectives that can help the team with their events and decision making.
Product manager	When there is a portfolio of related products, it can be useful to have a product manager who is accountable for the whole set. Each individual product should still have a Product Owner.
Scaled Scrum Master	Where there are several, related teams there can be a hierarchy of Scrum Masters. It isn't usually called a scaled Scrum Master, but this is a good generic description for roles such as service delivery manager, Scrum of Scrums Master, delivery manager, release train engineer, solution train engineer, etc.

Specific roles

Some Agile approaches have specific roles that are common enough to be worth us mentioning (see Table 7.6). The sources of these roles are: AgilePM,[87] SAFe,[88] LeSS,[89] Scrum@Scale,[90] Kanban[91] and UK Government Digital, Data and Technology (DDaT) Framework.[92]

---

87 https://agilepm.wiki.

88 https://www.scaledagileframework.com.

89 https://less.works.

90 https://www.scrumatscale.com.

91 https://resources.kanban.university/kanban-guide/.

92 https://www.gov.uk/guidance/delivery-manager.

Table 7.6 Specific roles in Agile approaches

Project manager	Most Agile approaches don't have a specific role for project manager, the main exception being AgilePM. However, Agile deliveries are often 'projects' from an organisational perspective and some additional artefacts may be required as a result. Therefore, it is quite common to see project managers around Agile teams, even when they are using Scrum.
	This can be a dangerous situation because the traditional responsibilities of a project manager overlap with all three of the Scrum accountabilities, so careful leadership and clarity on responsibilities and accountabilities is important.
Release train engineer	The Scaled Agile Framework (SAFe) is built around the concept of an Agile release train, which aligns multiple teams to a shared business and technology mission. The train has a fixed timetable and is aligned around value, with several teams contributing and integrating artefacts to each release. The release train engineer is the servant, leader and coach for the release train, much like a Scrum Master is for a Scrum team.
	There is a further level of hierarchy with the solution train and solution train engineer.
Architect	Some complex problems and scaled approaches require high-level architectural coherence and may have an architect role involved to ensure coherence and integrity. This can risk disempowering the technical experts within teams, but without them can lead to incoherent solutions, duplication of effort and difficult integration or interoperation. Getting this balance right can be tricky.
Delivery manager	The UK Government DDaT Framework describes roles in digital delivery, and specifically describes a family of delivery manager roles that are responsible for the Agile leadership and management of delivery teams.
Manager	Management is seldom mentioned in Agile approaches and is generally assumed to be happening naturally within the teams. However, large organisations often require some formal manager–staff relationship.
	In Agile teams, a manager does not task the team, nor dictate how the work is done. The manager role is more focused on professional development, creating the right culture and environment, and dealing with procedural issues such as approving expenses. However, they do need to know enough about the work to identify and deal with capability or poor performance issues.
	In practice, managers are often also involved in the leadership of the work at a higher level (perhaps as business sponsor) and must be careful not to undermine the Agile ethos of the team by exerting the positional authority they have as managers.

(Continued)

Table 7.6 (Continued)

Technical specialist	Where there are many teams in an organisation, it is common to have communities of practice for some technical skills. Within these communities there may be hierarchies, skill levels or other opportunities for members to demonstrate leadership and specialism.
	This is an important aspect to creating a culture of self-improvement and mastery within teams. However, caution is needed to ensure that this does not create a hierarchy within their development teams, as this can disempower other team members and impact the team.

T-SHAPED PROFESSIONALS

We have mentioned that Agile teams are self-organising and that they arrange themselves around the most valuable work necessary to meet their goal. However, we also know that there are roles, specialisms and careers that people either are in or aspire to be in. This apparent contradiction causes problems for many organisations. They desire to have specific career and skills paths for their staff, such as architecture, business analysis, testing or software engineering.

Often, we see that this segregation of skills finds its way into job titles and team membership, so that teams are not made up of 'team members', but of junior, senior and principal developers, analysts, testers, architects, technical writers, DevOps engineers and more. While this solves one problem, we have observed that it creates several more:

- Labelling people with specific skills leads them (and the rest of the team) to assume that they will be the people to do that type of work. This is also true of seniority labels. This leads to people only doing work of their 'type', even when it would benefit the team for them to help others (if their help would be accepted, which often it isn't).

- Unless the necessary work is evenly distributed across the skills (which it never is), this leads to some people running out of important work and busying themselves with less valuable tasks (creating 'inventory' waste) and others having too much to do and running out of time – which often results in the iteration goal not being met and work carried over to the next iteration.

- The presence of 'experts' leads others to abdicate themselves from responsibility for that skill. This means that, even when they see problems or errors, they are less likely to speak up about it and less likely to be listened to.

- The segregation of role type inhibits a team's ability to behave as one. In particular, seniority labels create an explicit hierarchy and pecking order.

- Individual desire to do particular work to achieve a skills assessment or promotion can mean work is hoarded by one person or things made more complicated than they need to be in order to get better 'evidence'.

- Single points of failure, sometimes called Towers of Knowledge, are more common. This is where an individual (or small group) is the only person with skill, knowledge or ability to do a particular type of work, often one that is critical to the team's success.

- Pairing and mob programming become harder to do (despite them being good ways to share knowledge and reduce risk).

Overall, these problems (and the many others we haven't listed) make it much harder for the team to achieve their main purpose – to always be working on the most valuable work that will deliver the goal for the customer.

A solution to this is to have a team of T-shaped professionals. This describes people who are competent in a range of skills, even though there are one or two areas where they have deep expertise. This is in contrast to people who have depth in a skill but no real breadth in other skills. Scott Ambler coined an alternative phrase – 'the generalizing specialist'[93] – since the person can reasonably call themselves a specialist but is still able to do more general tasks at a more basic level.

In an Agile team, the range of skills where we expect breadth are the range of skills necessary to deliver the product to the customer in a way that they can use it. For the loyalty card product, we have several customer-facing components, so we need some UI skill, but we also may have iterations where there is much more back-end data analytics to do; therefore, the T-shaped profile shown in Figure 7.7 could be a good fit for our team.

It isn't necessary for everyone to have the same breadth, but across the team we would expect to see all the necessary skills present in:

- at least one person;
- preferably more than one person;
- preferably at least one person with some depth.

The level of depth required will depend on the complexity of the product, and there is often more than one area that requires some depth. For our loyalty card example, we also need some marketing and branding skills. Perhaps people with depth in those areas could also bring some competence in user experience testing or business change. Our engineer in Figure 7.7 has some data architecture skill, but we would want to boost that with other team members with more depth in data science and data analysis.

Constructing a team in this way not only helps to ensure we have the skills we need for the job, but also presents more opportunities for our people to learn from one another to develop their own skills. It can be a powerful way to bring more diversity into the team.

---

93 www.agilemodeling.com/essays/generalizingSpecialists.htm.

Figure 7.7 T-shaped professional example

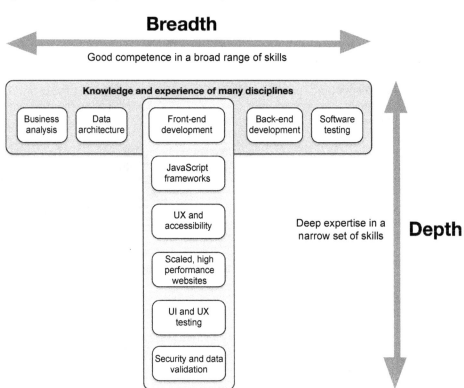

SUMMARY

While an Agile team starts with the same objective as a traditional project team – deliver a product that meets the customer's needs – they approach and meet that objective in a very different way.

Although there are several methods or frameworks used by Agile teams, they follow the same basic format and share more in common than they may care to admit. They are biased towards change and use early delivery of value, short iterations, frequent feedback and flexibility to be able to respond to that change when it happens.

While from the outside Agile delivery may appear just like any other project, look a little closer at a **good** Agile team and it will look and feel very different indeed. Agile teams have a strong focus on people and collaboration. They care about their customers and that their needs are understood and being met, and they care about their colleagues, factoring professional development into planning and aiming to keep the work challenging and interesting.

Continuous improvement runs throughout Agile delivery, from early versions of the product, such as a validated MVP, all the way through to actionable feedback from customers to allow the Product Backlog to evolve. Additionally, daily stand-ups and frequent retrospectives provide multiple opportunities for feedback, reflection and identification of improvements the team can make to their approach.

Conversely, a poorer Agile team can look quite like a traditional project team, with similar poorer outcomes. Each of the differences described above can be challenging to implement and to persist with. People are not always used to working in these ways and there are many opportunities to revert to traditional practices, particularly when things get challenging.

Achieving successful Agile delivery requires everyone involved in the endeavour to understand the Agile Manifesto and principles, to have them at the forefront of their minds and to be supported by strong Agile leadership (see Chapter 9).

8 AGILE PRACTICES

While the Manifesto tells us what we want to achieve, it doesn't tell us how to get there

The Agile Manifesto takes 68 words to describe the four values, and a further 186 for the principles behind them. While admirably simple, as we emphasise throughout this book it is hard to apply consistently and easy to misunderstand and misuse.

As Agile grew in popularity, a number of methods, frameworks, approaches and books that helped people put Agile into practice also grew in popularity. Many of these predate the Manifesto and some even influenced it. Over the following 20 years, more have emerged and evolved.

A method is simply a collection of practices, techniques and patterns packaged into something that is more approachable to learn and apply (and often more marketable). So, the success of any method is dependent on the practices it includes and how well those are applied by its followers.

This chapter describes some of the practices that are commonly used by Agile teams, grouped by themes such as leadership, ways of working and estimation. Given that some have entire books written about them, we shall not attempt to teach them all to you or describe them in detail. However, we shall try to help you realise how they can help you to adopt more of an Agile mindset, and guide you to further information.

WHAT DO WE MEAN BY 'PRACTICE'?

The noun 'practice' is defined by the *Oxford English Dictionary*[94] as 'the actual application or use of an idea, belief, or method, as opposed to theories relating to it' and 'the customary, habitual, or expected procedure or way of doing of something'. We will take a broad definition, and define an Agile practice to include anything that is a concrete, specific thing that Agile teams do that helps them with an Agile mindset. That includes things that other people may describe as a technique, approach, process, pattern, model, map and so on.

Given the roots of Agile, it should be no surprise that there are many practices that are common across several methods; as we saw in Chapter 7, the overall anatomy of an iteration is a common pattern. The same is true for many of the underlying practices. Other practices are present only in one approach; however, that doesn't mean that their value should be restricted to followers of that approach.

---

[94] https://www.lexico.com/definition/practice.

This chapter will describe a number of Agile practices in common use. These are agnostic of any method or framework. We will help you to understand why they are useful and how you can get the most value from them. Some are discussed in more detail elsewhere in this book, but we include them here in summary for completeness. The practices are in these broad categories:

- leadership;
- ways of working;
- requirements;
- estimation;
- prioritisation;
- software development;
- measuring success.

We will also briefly describe Scrum and Kanban, two commonly used approaches.

A TOOLKIT OF PRACTICES

For many people, their first introduction to Agile will be either a training course of some kind or joining a team that are practising Agile. This can be very helpful, as it provides an end-to-end view of the delivery, but it can also be confusing. There is often so much to understand and learn it can be overwhelming, and if you are just joining your first Agile team it can be hard to separate out what is 'Agile' from what is the method and what is a team's bespoke adaptation.

When teams have been established a while, we often observe that they develop some bad habits that compromise their ability to be Agile and sometimes even their ability to deliver. This is a particular issue when new people join that team, observe and copy their ways of working, and believe that this is good practice. Sadly, as any good Agile coach will tell you, just because something is common practice doesn't mean it is good practice.

The relationship between Agile, Agile methods and Agile practices

As we explored earlier, 'Agile' is defined in the Agile Manifesto[95] as a set of four values underpinned by 12 principles. While these tell us what Agile is, they don't tell us terribly much about how we can **be** Agile.

There are many Agile methods or frameworks that purport to help you be Agile if you follow their rules; some examples are Scrum, SAFe, Disciplined Agile and LeSS.[96] Each of these methods is composed of practices and patterns, with quite a lot of similarity and overlap. Ultimately, it is these practices that will determine whether you are being

---

[95] https://agilemanifesto.org.

[96] See Chapter 11 for brief descriptions of these and others, including references to further information.

Agile or not. All the method is really doing is helping you to decide which practices to use and when.

In addition to the practices found in the methods, there are many other techniques, approaches and practices that can be very useful and help to reinforce the Agile Manifesto. Some examples are story mapping, customer discovery, pair programming and Planning Poker.[97]

This relationship is shown in Figure 8.1, where you can see that, although each method looks different, there is in fact much in common. Plus, there are additional practices we can adopt that are not in any of the methods.

Figure 8.1 Relationship between Agile, Agile methods and Agile practices

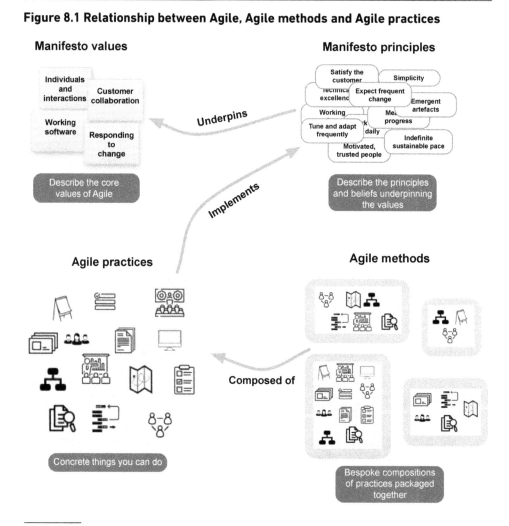

---

97 Planning Poker is a registered trademark of Mountain Goat Software. https://www.mountaingoatsoftware.com/agile/
planning-poker.

ESSENCE: A STANDARD FOR DEFINING METHODS AND PRACTICES

This focus on practices over methods is the thinking behind the OMG standard, Essence.[98] It describes the core elements that all software development requires and a language that is used to define the practices and methods that sit on top of that core.

There are a small number of 'things we always work with', such as opportunity, stakeholders and ways of working, and a small number of 'things we always do', such as 'explore possibilities', 'understand stakeholder needs' and 'prepare to do the work'. These things will always happen, whether the team is following a traditional approach or an Agile approach. Essence is similar to the Agile Manifesto in that it describes what we want to achieve, but not how.

This common language can be used to describe practices (for example Scrum, user story or DevOps) and because they are all described in the same way, it is easy to mix and match practices. For example, one team may use Scrum with user stories while another team prefers use cases.

Essence is growing in popularity, being taught in universities, being used in some Agile training courses and it complements Agile approaches well. Essence can be a good way to select the practices that a team wants to use, check that they provide coverage of the whole life cycle and combine Agile, traditional and bespoke practices that don't clash with each other.

LEADERSHIP

Agile leadership practices are arguably the most important to get right as, when neglected, they can have a devastating effect on everything the team is doing. We explore Agile leadership (including many of these practices) in much more detail in Chapter 9.

The behaviour of leaders is critical to creating the environment for Agile success. Leaders can be outside the team, of course, but there are also leaders within Agile teams. There are the obvious roles where people can lead – Scrum Master or Product Owner, for example – but leadership can come from anywhere in an Agile team. For example, the most experienced developer or the person who understands the customer best can also be great (or poor) leaders.

Servant leadership

The leader is servant first – their aim is to serve the needs of the team, not to further their own ambitions. This involves understanding the needs of the team first, knowing when and how to intervene (or not) and how much challenge and support to provide.

---

98 The Object Management Group (OMG) is an international, open membership, not-for-profit technology standards consortium. Information about Essence can be found here: https://www.omg.org/hot-topics/essence.htm.

Servant leadership is not always noticed by others, so leaders must also recognise when others are being good servant leaders and ensure that they are acknowledged and rewarded.

Empowering teams

Teams and individuals are trusted first. We assume they know what they are doing and are motivated to do good work. Teams are monitored lightly and are empowered to make decisions themselves. There are few or no approvals required, and teams don't need review processes.

Empowered teams must still follow the overall vision, but should be trusted to make every decision they can. In *The Art of Action*,[99] Stephen Bungay quotes a useful rule from German Field Marshal von Molkte: '... an order should contain all, but also only, what subordinates cannot determine for themselves'.

Creating self-organising teams

Agile teams are self-organising and self-managing, but this is often impossible without action from their leadership. Leaders need to learn to step back and avoid the temptation to task and allocate work. Instead, leaders set direction and vision. This helps teams to identify their boundaries and be trusted to work out for themselves how to reach the vision.

These high-level goals don't all need to be product related, for example having a goal or value about professional development, and asking teams to commit to it, can change how they behave. They will factor development into their work, pulling work that will help them to develop rather than choosing only tasks they can already do well.

Collaboration

In an Agile team, collaborative work is the default, individual work the exception. The quality of most knowledge work is enhanced when undertaken collaboratively by a diverse team. This includes collaboration with stakeholders and customers, inviting them to team events and having ongoing engagement with them throughout the delivery. Practices such as pair programming can remove the need for approval cycles or code reviews.

Transparency

Agile leaders aim for transparency by default, and secrecy by exception. When people are aligned to the overall vision (both project and organisation), it makes sense to share as much of the information with as much of the organisation as we can. That way, there are more opportunities for better ideas, spotting problems and being innovative. Where there is secrecy, and people are excluded, it is easy to perceive unfairness, which leads to disengagement and feelings of demotivation.

---

99 Bungay, S. (2011) *The Art of Action: How Leaders Close the Gaps Between Plans, Actions and Results.* Nicholas Brealey Publishing, Boston, MA, p. 62.

Good leaders open as much as they possibly can to the workforce. For example, shadow boards,[100] inviting observers to all management meetings, having flat hierarchies and avoiding the use of terms such as 'senior leadership team' can all boost transparency.

Coaching

Coaching practices help people to solve their own problems and are a great way to accelerate personal development. Topic-specific coaching, such as Agile or innovation coaching, combines coaching with mentoring and consultancy to both help coaches develop themselves and introduce them to new concepts and ideas.

Inclusive facilitation

Agile teams make frequent use of workshop style events such as retrospectives. Their success is heavily dependent on the quality of the facilitation, including how inclusive it is and how safe the participants feel. Good facilitation can turn these from being lectures that are endured into inclusive, collaborative events where everyone contributes.

Agile chartering

Agile chartering is a great way to increase strategic alignment and psychological safety. It is most commonly used at the start of an endeavour, but is also valuable during delivery, particularly if there are problems or changes in vision or team membership. Agile chartering is described more in Chapter 7.

WAYS OF WORKING

The ways that teams organise themselves and their work offer many opportunities to embody the Agile values and principles. Some of these practices are described within particular methods, and sometimes called different names. However, as we pointed out in the previous section, it is possible to extract a practice from a method and get value from it on its own.

Stand-up meetings

In stand-up meetings, the team share what they have been doing, what they intend to do and any blockers that are stopping them. These are not one-way updates; instead, they are a chance for the team to embody the three pillars of transparency, inspection and adaptation. The sharing is 'transparency'. Listening to what everyone else is saying is 'inspection'. Changing what you intend to do because of what you have heard is 'adaptation'.

Often held daily, stand-up meetings can be any frequency that makes sense for the team, but are often time-boxed to 15 minutes to keep them focused. In larger organisations, or when people are working on several projects, there may be more than one. However, trying to do too much work in parallel is an anti-pattern that should be avoided (see the subsection later in this chapter on limiting work in process).

---

100 A shadow board consists of members of the workforce who hold a 'shadow' board meeting, considering the same questions and seeing the same information as the main board. The main board take their feedback into account.

Agile boards

Another chance to demonstrate transparency, Agile boards are typically a public way to share the work of the team. They are often structured in a 'Kanban' style with columns representing the category of work and a ticket, card or sticky note representing the value being worked on.

They can be electronic (but make sure you haven't locked down access), but there's something special about physically moving a card on a board. Physically standing around the board while discussing the work can help to stimulate ideas and creativity; making the board visible to passers-by can help to foster collaboration.

The example shown in Figure 8.2 also shows who is working on each task and whether anything is currently blocked. Later in this chapter we will discuss the Kanban Method and explain why this is not a Kanban board, although they share some attributes.

Self-organising teams

The team needs to be trusted to organise their own work, but they also need to be disciplined enough to use that permission. The team collectively pulls work in and decides what they want to work on. This could be driven by their expertise, their personal development needs or just because they are interested in it.

The team will also decide its ways of working, organisation, rhythms, rules, working patterns and so on. Agile chartering (especially the alignment section) can be a useful way to do this. In fact, anything of significance should be within the control of the team.

This self-organising requires a responsibility to be aware of wider corporate or organisational initiatives and to consider them in team decisions. For example, there may be corporate standards to adhere to or work from other teams that could be reused if we choose to use the same technology. Agile teams are self-organising, not self-determining. They still need to achieve the goals that their employer requires.

Time boxing

Setting a time box for an activity is about responding to change. It is used when we cannot be certain of what is required to reach a goal, or we want to limit our planning to a time horizon within which we can be reasonably certain.

The best example of Agile time boxes are time-bound iterations. These are often two or three weeks (and we always favour shorter iterations over longer ones), but in some scaled approaches they can be as long as 12 weeks. Time boxing forces teams to limit their ambitions and not to try to deliver too much. Used properly, they force teams to split large items into many small slices of value that incrementally build into the complete product. They can also be used poorly; after all, we could consider a traditional 18-month project as 18 or 36 'iterations'.

Other common uses of time boxing include spikes – short, time-bound tasks in an iteration that are not critical to the iteration goal. They are often used for investigations, research or other exploratory activities that are necessary to be able to plan or understand future work. For example, we may have had an early spike in our loyalty card example to investigate two different database technologies to decide which one to use.

Figure 8.2 An example Agile board

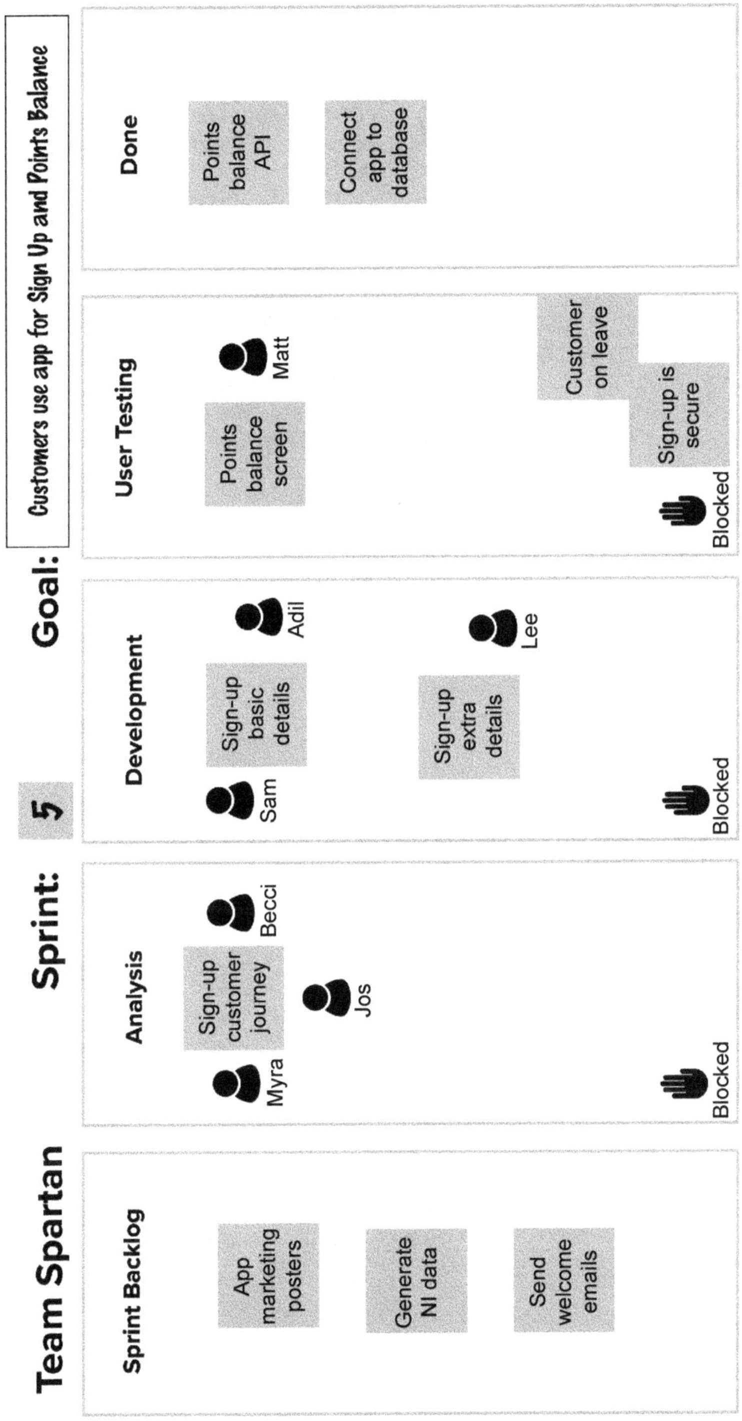

Team Spartan

Sprint: 5 **Goal:** Customers use app for Sign Up and Points Balance

Sprint Backlog

App marketing posters

Generate NI data

Send welcome emails

Analysis

Sign-up customer journey — Becci

Myra

Jos

Blocked

Development

Sign-up basic details — Adil

Sam

Sign-up extra details — Lee

Blocked

User Testing

Points balance screen — Matt

Customer on leave

Sign-up is secure

Blocked

Done

Points balance API

Connect app to database

We also use time boxing when a team has other responsibilities alongside developing the product, for example support of earlier versions or other corporate responsibilities. This makes it easier to predict what capacity is available for the development iteration.

Finally, events or meetings are often time-boxed. The framework Scrum is explicit about this – for instance, their stand-up meeting (called the Daily Scrum) is time-boxed to 15 minutes. Event time boxes are often scaled based on the iteration length, so an event that takes two hours in two-week iterations should just take one hour with one-week iterations.

Collaborative planning

Agile teams collaborate in everything that they do, and this includes planning. Problems are not broken down into tasks and assigned to the team by someone else; the team does this work themselves, together with the customers and other stakeholders. This has the major advantage that everyone gains a strong understanding of the work and where each task has come from. The collaborative nature brings review and challenge for free, and the team makes fewer assumptions and fewer misjudgements as a result.

When planning an iteration, the work being considered (from the top of the Product Backlog) should be in small enough chunks to complete in this iteration, but should still require some analysis and elaboration once the team commits to it. This means that the team sometimes needs to do some analysis of the work during planning in order to decide how and by whom the work can be done. To paraphrase Bungay,[101] stories on the Product Backlog 'should contain all, but also only, what the team cannot determine for themselves to deliver the goal'.

Big room planning

Agile teams value collaboration, and this is true for all Agile endeavours, not just those with small teams who can all sit around the same table. With multiple teams it is still valuable to collaborate for key events, particularly planning and reviews. In scaled approaches, these are often less frequent, for example in SAFe, their programme increments are 8–12 weeks long.

Ideally, we get everyone together in the same room and the planning works the same way that small team iteration planning works:

- Guided by the highest priority items on the backlog and the business stakeholders, the whole group agree the iteration goals.
- Teams pull work from the backlog into team backlogs that represent the things they can do to help meet the goal in this iteration.
- As they do so, they ensure that they understand the work and its acceptance criteria. This is done in collaboration with the customers and other teams.
- The teams may elaborate the work into more precise items as part of understanding it and being able to commit to it.

---

101 Bungay, S. (2011) *The Art of Action: How Leaders Close the Gaps Between Plans, Actions and Results*. Nicholas Brealey Publishing, Boston, MA, p. 62.

- Because the teams are all present, they are able to identify any dependencies or collaboration opportunities and agree how to work together.

In practice, this is an area we see many teams struggling with. It is hard to get everyone together, partly for logistical reasons but also because it feels like a waste of so many people's time. This often means the events are shortened and attendance limited to one or two people from each team (often not the actual developers). This is a false economy. It impedes collaboration and information sharing and increases risk. Teams are therefore more likely to take work they don't understand properly and are less likely to deliver on time. Because the people doing the work weren't part of the meeting, they not only feel less empowered, but they also know less context of the work and are less aligned with the overall goals for the iteration.

What's worse (and also sadly common) is for these events to turn into a tasking meeting, where team leaders turn up and are told what their teams must do by the management of the programme. This will typically be more work than they are realistically capable of doing (to provide 'stretch goals' and avoid them running out of work) and broken down to low levels of detail that is likely to be out of date before the team starts on it.

Backlog refinement

The Product Backlog is where we describe future work that we think may be required to meet the customer's goals. Because we expect frequent change, we don't expect the backlog to be correct. Periodically, the Product Backlog is reviewed so that we are confident that the backlog has the right amount of detail to allow us to plan the next iteration. This will usually involve some or all of the following activities:

- Split a backlog item to form two or more smaller, more precise items.
- Add new items.
- Delete items (really valuable, but surprisingly rarely done).
- Combine items into larger, less precise items.
- Reprioritise the items.
- Ensure the highest priority items have enough detail to be planned – refine and add detail if necessary.

The new backlog represents today's best idea of what work we should do next and later in order to meet our goals. In line with the simplicity principle, we do as little work on the Product Backlog as we can to ensure we don't waste time understanding and elaborating work items that may not be important.

Limiting work in process

Work in process (WiP) is a Lean term to describe the number of separate things that are being worked on at the same time. It originates from manufacturing, where it was the number of items currently still in the manufacturing process. It is sometimes called work in **progress**, for example in the Kanban Method. Agile teams aim to limit WiP as much as they can. Doing this results in more work being done, because:

- It is more efficient to work on one thing at a time rather than try to multi-task.

- Unfinished work is an example of inventory waste. It has cost time and money to get it this far, but it isn't bringing any value yet.

Limiting WiP forces teams to focus on finishing work, since we cannot start new work until the work already started has been completed. While this sounds logical, we frequently see teams doing the opposite. This is partly because starting a task gives us the illusion that it is closer to being complete. It's also because senior stakeholders can share this delusion.

In fact, the mathematical theorem Little's Law proves this. Little's Law states that the average number of items in a system (L) is defined by the arrival rate of the items (λ) multiplied by the average time they spend in the system (W).

$$L = \lambda W$$

We can consider the number of items in the system to be WiP, the arrival rate to be the throughput of the system and the average time to be the lead time. This means Little's Law becomes:

$$WiP = throughput \times lead\ time$$

Reorganising the equation for either throughput (WiP/lead time) or lead time (WiP/throughput), we can see that, in each case, reducing WiP has a beneficial effect on the other variables – we get quicker lead times and we can process more work items. This simple but counter-intuitive law proves that increasing WiP in our system will slow down delivery and restrict the number of items we can process.

The Kanban Method has a simple way to limit WiP. In each column of our Agile board, we set a limit to the number of items that can be in it. Since items can only leave a column by moving to the right (and move towards done), this encourages teams to pull work from the right. This also means that team members must be able to work across all of the columns, otherwise they risk sitting idle waiting for other people to create space in a column where they can work. Self-organising teams with T-shaped professionals can do this.

Small batch sizes

Large units of work will take longer to get through the system. This is not only because they require more work, but also because they will be inherently less certain and more likely to have unforeseen problems. There is also increased risk that the customer need isn't understood properly or has changed. Additionally, large batch sizes can result in longer iterations as teams compensate for the uncertainty by giving themselves more time.

Agile teams aim for small batch sizes. They split their big goals into smaller, simpler, more achievable goals, while still aiming for an increment of the product that brings value to the customer. Delivering small increments of value frequently is a great way to build customer trust in your team. Seeing tangible progress being made is also rewarding for the team, and the sense of satisfaction and pride when you see customers using your product helps to motivate and build engagement.

Chapter 10 discusses some ways we can reduce batch size of the work through goal and story splitting and managing the backlog.

Open reviews

The iteration review is an opportunity for the iteration work to be showcased to stakeholders and customers. Ideally, this is by the customer (perhaps the Product Owner) using the new version of the product to demonstrate that the goal has been met.

This is both a celebration and an opportunity for feedback, so it is a good idea to invite as wide as audience as you can – even making it an open meeting where anyone can drop in and see what has been going on. The review is an important event, and the team should regard it as such. This means that in iteration planning they should ensure they are confident that they will be able to deliver a working product.

Retrospectives

A retrospective is one of the most recognisable Agile practices and one also commonly used for non-Agile projects. The retrospective is a meeting in which the whole team reflects on the previous period and uses these reflections to continually improve ways of working. This is usually a combination of:

- Things that worked well and should be continued.
- Things that didn't go so well and should be stopped.
- Things we didn't do but should consider starting.
- Things to which we should consider making some changes.

To reach these conclusions, teams usually use a facilitated workshop, often following the pattern described in Chapter 7, Agile retrospectives. There are a number of formats in common use and there are many examples on the internet and in collaboration tools. It is also fun to make up your own. Keeping the format fresh is important, as following the same agenda each time can stifle creativity and limit the value.

Although often run at each iteration, retrospectives can also be valuable over longer time periods, such as a whole project, a major release or when a team experiences a particular upset or failure. Whenever held, it is really important that the retrospective is a positive, safe, open and honest event. Establishing psychological safety (see Chapter 9) and avoiding blame is critical. The actions that result must also be achievable. There is no point identifying things to change that the team has no control over, for example hiring new people or changing corporate processes.

REQUIREMENTS

A requirement is a feature or need that has been requested by a stakeholder. Requirements engineering is so important in systems development that an entire discipline has built up around its practices. However, despite stakeholders still requesting features and having needs, the word 'requirement' loses its relevance in the Agile world.

This is because, in traditional software engineering projects, requirements have been treated as a contractual obligation development teams should fulfil and implement. This is no longer the case in Agile development as collaboration and working software are valued more than requirements documents – yet the term 'requirement' somehow still persists. What does remain true is that customers and stakeholders still need to be identified and their needs understood. How and when this occurs is what differs. We should apply the Agile mindset to customer needs and wants, and only confirm something is required at the point we decide to implement and deliver it as part of an iteration. Figure 8.3 shows some of the more popular techniques that can be used to understand customers and their needs in an Agile context, and these are explained in more detail in Chapter 10.

Most of these practices allow teams to demonstrate all four Manifesto values, with customer collaboration and responding to change being particularly valuable. However, since people are used to capturing requirements artefacts as documents, the right-hand side aspects of comprehensive documentation, contract negotiation (especially signing off plans) and treating requirements as plans can easily result in teams behaving in a non-Agile way.

Instead of managing individual requirements, Agile teams and their stakeholders often find more value in managing at higher levels of abstraction. Therefore, managing the backlog is an important area to get right. A backlog may contain a mix of detailed requirements ready to be implemented, larger descriptions of things that will need breaking down further and future aspirations of product functionality. Effective management and refinement of the backlog is, therefore, arguably the most important Agile practice.

The most significant backlog is the Product Backlog, which contains the things that we think will be necessary to deliver the value to the customer. The work being done in the current iteration is also often described in a backlog, the iteration (or, often, Sprint) backlog. This backlog contains a lower level of detail – often down to task level – that the team uses to ensure they know what they need to do to meet the iteration goals. There may also be higher level, strategic backlogs with portfolio or programme level items, but generally speaking the fewer backlogs the better.

Backlogs are described in greater detail in Chapter 10, including guidance on creating and managing backlogs.

Release planning and roadmaps

Despite wanting to keep our options open and respond to change in our customers' requirements, we often need to have a longer-term plan or view on the development of our product. Because this spans a long period of time, we should expect it to change and evolve, so it is important to make release plans and roadmaps as simple as possible.

Some common planning tools allow high levels of detail to be devoted to long-term planning, so this is something to be cautious of, particularly when they are perceived as committed plans. Roadmaps should be as simple as possible, with just enough detail to be useful, and no more.

Figure 8.3 Some common requirements practices

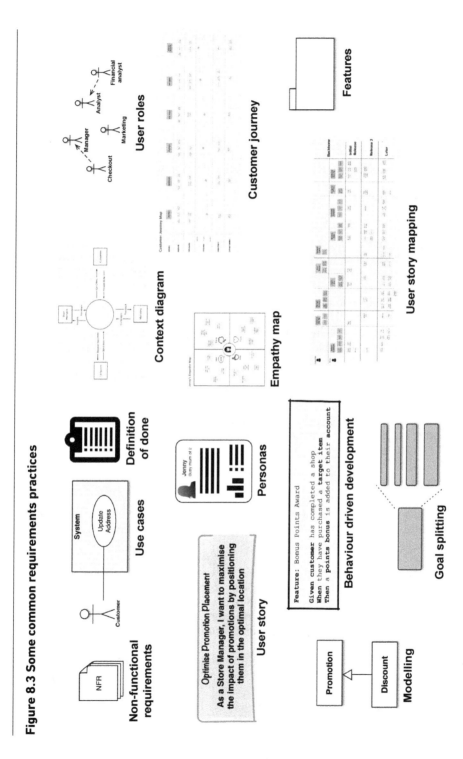

ESTIMATION

In linear development processes, estimation is a critically important process. Without precise, accurate estimates, we cannot create plans we can trust or give assurances to stakeholders. However, Agile teams working in a VUCA environment struggle with both precise and accurate estimates because so many of the data necessary to create them are uncertain. We can be accurate – between 6 and 18 months, or between £500,000 and £2 million – but that isn't precise enough for most stakeholders.

Agile teams do still estimate, but do so with data they can trust. There are many different ways to estimate Agile work, but they all tend to make use of two core concepts that both reinforce Agile concepts: relative sizing and Wideband Delphi, or wisdom of the crowds.

Accuracy and precision

Many approaches to estimation involve understanding the problem well, defining a solution and then breaking that solution down into small enough tasks that can be understood really well. At this point, each task is simple enough to estimate with precision. Then, we can add up all the estimates to get to an overall figure for the whole solution or feature.

This depends on being able to accurately break the whole problem down to very small elements and to be absolutely certain that we haven't forgotten or misunderstood anything. However, we know this is really hard to achieve – we make mistakes, misunderstand things and forget essential tasks. That makes our estimates less accurate.

Furthermore, to reach an estimate, we usually break it down to small parts, estimate each part and then add them up again. However, each element has its own tolerance, perhaps plus or minus one day. Adding the best and worst case tolerances ends up with a large range, which gives our estimates poor precision. This means that the usual ways of estimating are poor, both in accuracy and precision.

A NOTE OF CAUTION

Agile teams should resist the temptation (or request) to relate estimates to time. While there is a relationship (bigger things will take more time), humans are notoriously poor at estimating time.

When teams start to relate estimates to time, they tend to moderate the results, usually being more optimistic, and the power of relative sizing is lost because they are now comparing with two things: the reference item and time. Finally, teams can improve over time, perhaps achieving more units of work – but they cannot create additional hours or days by working better.

It also invites comparisons between teams and the gaming of the numbers to please managers or show improvement.

We consistently see better and more useful estimates from teams who do not use time as the measure.

Relative sizing

This problem with estimation can be overcome by recognising that there are some things we are very good at estimating. While our ability to estimate from scratch is poor, we are good at estimating relative sizes. When we know one thing, we can quite easily estimate something else compared to that known entity. For example, consider the jar in Figure 8.4 containing liquorice sweets. Can you estimate how much liquorice (weight or number of sweets) are in the jar?

Figure 8.4 Liquorice sweets in a jar

Now, if you know that a full jar of liquorice contains 400g or 85 sweets, do you find the estimation easier, and would you get closer to the right answer (202g and 42 sweets)? This is how relative estimation works. When we have a reference, we find it much easier to compare a different thing to that reference than we do to estimate it from scratch.

Agile teams use relative estimation by agreeing that a particular task has a specific value, for example they may agree that creating a simple web page and connecting it to a mongo database using Amazon Web Services has a value of 5. When estimating a different task, they can judge how similar, easier or harder it is in comparison and come up with an estimate.

This means that, over time, a team can build up knowledge of how they work and thus make their estimates more accurate, which can help them to predict how much work they can get through (see the subsection on velocity under Measuring Success later in this chapter) or when they might complete the items on the Product Backlog. Since this depends on the team and the work remaining consistent (and we know that things are likely to change) it must be done with caution.

Relative sizing can be made more effective when the set of answers is constrained. Limiting choice helps teams to avoid the trap of attempting to be very precise with their estimates and encourages just enough analysis to be useful. One common approach is to use a modified Fibonacci[102] sequence to restrict the estimates to a limited set of values, often

---

102 A Fibonacci number is a number in a list that is the sum of the two numbers preceding it. For example, 0, 1, 1, 2, 3, 5, 8, 13, 21, 34, 55, and so on.

this set: ?, 0, ½, 1, 2, 3, 5, 8, 13, 20, 40, 100, ∞.[103] These are commonly available in decks of cards for use in estimation games (see Planning Poker subsection later in this chapter).

The increasing gaps between the numbers may look odd, but it is intentional. As estimates increase, so too does the complexity and uncertainty of the item. The bigger gaps help to remind us to break these more complex items into several, simpler items that will be easier to implement correctly and less likely to change. Compared to an absolute estimate, this also means that we don't need to include tolerance or ranges, since they are built in. By definition, estimating 8 really means it is more than 5 but less than 13. As we move higher up the range, our certainty decreases, so our range or tolerance increases. Conversely, when we estimate a low number, we are a lot more certain – a 2 is more than 1 but less than 3. If you are asked to estimate using absolute numbers, then you should ensure you include tolerance or a range in your estimate; for example, 7±2 or 15 per cent.

Other common ways to limit choices include moving away from numbers completely with T-shirt sizing (e.g. small, medium, large) or other abstract units such as animals (mouse, cat, dog, cow, elephant).

Wideband Delphi

In the 1950s, the Rand Corporation developed the Delphi estimation technique,[104] which involved making an estimate, talking about it and then re-estimating it. This was further developed by Barry Boehm[105] and John Farquhar[106] in the 1970s as Wideband Delphi by increasing the collaboration. The process involves suitably qualified people discussing the problem and iteratively arriving at an estimate that they all agree with in this way:

- Discuss the problem as a group.
- Individually and anonymously come up with an estimate.
- The coordinator collates and summarises the (still anonymous) estimates.
- The group then discusses the results, focusing on the outliers.
- The experts fill out their estimation forms again.
- If necessary, this process iterates until all the estimates are similar enough to reach a result they can all agree on.

One of the reasons this works is that it benefits from James Surowiecki's *Wisdom of the Crowds* theory,[107] where estimates from lots of people will tend to result in an average that is more accurate than that of an expert, so bringing more people together ought to result in a more accurate answer. Bringing in more people also results in more diversity

103   This sequence of values is © Mountain Goat Software LLC, 2007.

104   https://www.rand.org/topics/delphi-method.html.

105   Boehm, B. (1981) *Software Engineering Economics*. Prentice Hall, Upper Saddle River, NJ.

106   Farquhar, J. A. (1970) A preliminary inquiry into the software estimation process. Rand Corporation: Santa Monica, CA.

107   Surowiecki, J. (2004) *The Wisdom of the Crowds: Why the Many are Smarter than the Few and How Collective Wisdom Shapes Business, Economies, Societies and Nations*. Doubleday Anchor Books, New York.

of opinions, experience and challenge, increasing the richness of the discussion and making the group more likely to take account of all the important factors.

This highly collaborative and iterative nature demonstrates Agile values, as does the anonymous element that removes hierarchy and bias from at least the initial estimates.

Planning Poker

Most Agile estimation approaches follow the basic premise of relative sizing and Wideband Delphi. As mentioned above, many are also based on Planning Poker, an Agile planning game developed by James Grenning[108] in 2002 and later popularised (and trademarked) by Mike Cohn with a slightly different set of numbers.[109] The game is played like this:

- Each team member has a deck of cards with the values ?, 0, ½, 1, 2, 3, 5, 8, 13, 20, 40, 100, ∞.
- The customer reads the item to be estimated.
- The whole team discusses the item.
- Each estimator privately chooses a card that represents their estimate.
- When the whole team has chosen, all the cards are revealed at the same time.
- If the cards are all the same, that's the estimate. No discussion is necessary.
- If the cards are not the same, the team discusses the estimates, focusing on the outlying values.
- Repeat until the estimates converge.
- There is also a break card (often a coffee cup) that can be played to propose the team takes a break.

Planning Poker is most commonly used for iteration planning, and it is important that the whole team is involved; this gives the best estimates and also ensures that everyone has been involved in discussing all the work. Usually, the estimate is the relative size of the item being estimated (i.e. how much work will it take to complete), but it can also be used to estimate other attributes such as value or complexity.

Played properly, the game exemplifies much of the Agile mindset, including customer collaboration, transparency, iterative decision making, responding to change, self-organising teams and more. Common ways that we see teams playing the game poorly include:

- Not involving the customer or the whole team.
- Deferring to the estimate of the most senior person rather than having an open discussion.
- Adding in extra values, even decimal points.
- Treating the numbers as representing time.

---

108 Grenning, J. W. (2002) *Planning Poker: Or How to Avoid Analysis Paralysis While Release Planning.* https://wingman-sw. com/papers/PlanningPoker-v1.1.pdf.

109 Cohn, M. (2005) *Agile Estimation and Planning.* Prentice Hall, Upper Saddle River, NJ.

Story Points

Many Agile teams describe the estimates from Planning Poker as Story Points and then use these individually or aggregated to help with planning, forecasting, contracting or other purposes. This can be very useful, but it can also be damaging, particularly when these secondary purposes become drivers away from the left-hand side of the Agile Manifesto.

Story Points are generally used as a proxy for the amount of time it will take to complete the story. Since they usually use a relative sizing estimation approach, this means that Story Points are unique to the team. One team may score a story as 5 where another team scores it as 3 or 8, even if they will complete it in the same amount of time. This also means that two teams scoring a story the same number of points may take different lengths of time to complete it, which makes it hard to use Story Points to compare teams. Some common ways to use Story Points include those listed in Table 8.1.

Table 8.1 Uses for Story Points

Iteration planning	This is probably the most common use for Story Points. The team arrives at a target number of points that they think they can achieve this iteration, usually based on how many points they have completed in previous iterations modified by availability, holidays, etc.
	The team pull in the highest priority stories from the backlog until the target number of points is reached.
Velocity	Team velocity is the average number of points a team can complete in one iteration. When everything else is constant, it can be an indication that a team is improving or struggling.
	However, if this were used to measure or reward a team, it is easily gamed.
Forecasting	The velocity can be used to provide a forecast of how much of the remaining backlog a team may get through in a given period of time. This requires the backlog to be estimated in points (which may be a lot of work) and the team to remain consistent.
	Sometimes, just counting the number of stories rather than points gives just as good a forecast (with much less work).
Contracting	Sometimes Story Points are used as a contractual method to describe the capacity expected of a team. They can also be used as a performance metric, with reduction in velocity sometimes resulting in penalties.
	For the reasons above, this is a very bad idea.
To convey complexity	Story Points, particularly when restricted to a Fibonacci type sequence, are a helpful addition to the language of the team. Describing a story as 'at least 20 points' provides a reference that the whole team will understand.
Managing capacity	The overall number of Story Points on a backlog can be viewed as the capacity of work that can be done, or has been agreed to or contracted for.
	If a stakeholder wants to add more work, then they can do so for the same cost or time, but only if they remove work of equal or greater number of points from the backlog.

WHY POINTS DON'T MAP TO UNITS OF TIME

If we can use Story Points as a proxy for time, then why not just treat them as units of time? We often see teams doing this, but there are several reasons why it isn't a good idea.

Estimating in time is harder and takes longer. To be accurate we need to understand a lot more about the problem and solution. This detailed analysis takes time and assumes things will not change or that the changes can be predicted. Relative sizing using points is fast and provides good enough precision.

People are not the same. A story that took Jill and Paul three days in one team may take Sam and Adil in another team more or less time. To estimate for time, we now need to know who specifically will be doing the work and factor their skill, competence, available time and so on into the estimate.

Effort and duration are not the same. Teams don't just focus 100 per cent of their time on the work. They have other meetings, take breaks, help one another, or work to improve team processes. These are hard to take into account in estimates. There may be essential tasks for the team that aren't in a story, and therefore not counted as points, things such as support tasks, stakeholder management, training, responding to user questions and so on.

Time can be mistaken for commitment. Estimates are not guarantees, they are estimates; expressing them in time units can lead to people treating them as commitments.

Time doesn't follow a Fibonacci sequence. Converting Story Points to time makes larger stories less accurate. While this encourages some teams to break them into several smaller stories, it also encourages some teams to be more optimistic and choose smaller numbers. It can encourage teams to invent new numbers in the scale, reducing the value we get from the sequence.

No estimates

As we have mentioned earlier, it can be easy to get carried away with estimates and try to make them more and more precise. There is also an opposite trend, sometimes characterised as '#noestimates',[110] which is to avoid them altogether.

This is not as daft as it sounds. On average, all stories are the same size, so as long as we have enough information to decide whether we can do this story in this iteration that may be all the estimation we need. The iteration planning is effectively the same but collapses the estimation into two buckets – this story can be done in this iteration, or it cannot and must be split.

---

110 The #noestimates Twitter hashtag was first used by Woody Zuill in 2012 when describing a project he worked on at Industrial Logic, where they refused to give estimates and just focused on delivering the most important stories one at a time. https://www.infoq.com/interviews/zuill-mob-programming/.

The originators of no estimates advocate working on a single story at a time (Woody Zuill is also a pioneer of mob programming described later in this chapter) but, even when a team works on several stories at a time, the relative size of the stories isn't always that helpful to document.

If we apply the simplicity principle and try to maximise the work that we don't do, then we should examine **why** we think we need estimates. If there isn't a good answer, then we shouldn't need to do them.

In our experience, by far the most valuable part of any estimation approach is the conversations between the team and the stakeholders. The actual estimate isn't often that much use once the story is prioritised into the iteration.

PRIORITISATION

Agile teams usually use a Product Backlog to show the priority of their work, with items at the top a higher priority than those further down. There are several practices used to help identify where items should go and provide relative priority for items within an iteration.

Force ranked backlog

This is the simplest and arguably the best way to prioritise. Each item has a unique number with the item at top of the backlog being priority one, the next priority two and so on. The unique number forces each item to have a unique priority.

Now, next, later

As we described earlier, and show in Table 10.4, this is a simple way to group items into three groups. Keeping the 'Next' group small (a form of limiting WiP) is good practice and a nice way to help manage stakeholder expectations.

Fixed capacity

When priorities change, stakeholders often want to move a newly prioritised piece of work further up the backlog. In a traditional project this causes scope creep and can cause projects to overrun cost and/or schedule. This can be prevented by insisting that any new work must be matched by removing work from scope that is the same size or greater.

MoSCoW

The MoSCoW method for prioritisation was developed by Dai Clegg in 1994 as part of his RAD approach.[111] It became a core part of the Agile framework Dynamic System

---

[111]   Clegg, D. and Barker, R. (1994) *CASE Method Fast-Track: A RAD Approach*, Addison-Wesley, Boston, MA.

Development Method (DSDM), which is now known as AgilePM.[112] It is an iterative prioritisation method that allocates each item to one of four states each time it is applied: Must have, Should have, Could have or Want to have, but won't have this time (see Table 8.2).

Table 8.2 MoSCoW states

Must have	These are the Minimum Usable SubseT (MUST) of requirements without which there would be no point in delivering the solution. However, if only these requirements were delivered, then the solution is viable and can provide value to the customer.
	If any of these cannot be met, then the delivery is not viable and should be cancelled.
Should have	These requirements are important, but not vital initially. They may be painful if left out or require some work arounds, but the delivery is still viable.
Could have	These requirements are wanted or desirable, but less important. There is less impact if they are left out.
Want to have, but won't have this time	These requirements are optional and have been considered, but will not be included in the current scope of the prioritisation.

MoSCoW works well when it is applied iteratively, and can be a hierarchical method, applied at a whole project level and again at each release or product increment and again at each iteration. Each time the method is invoked is a brand new decision for each item. The states are not a progression. At the lower levels, items prioritised as 'won't have this time' could be prioritised at any level next time, even 'must have'.

MoSCoW can be very powerful at iteration planning, particularly when limits are applied. A common rule of thumb we use is for 'must have' items to be no more than 60 per cent of the iteration. Any more than this and it is highly likely that at least one will not be met and therefore the iteration goal fails. To achieve this, use the goal splitting techniques in this chapter and in Chapter 10, and be very critical about what 'must' happen for the goal to be met.

Good-Better-Best

Jeff Patton describes a really powerful prioritisation and story splitting approach in his book *User Story Mapping*.[113] He calls it the Good-Better-Best game. We start with a story – this is the overall goal we are working towards. We then break it down to create smaller stories in three groups.

---

112   Chapter 10 Moscow prioritisation. Agile Business Consortium. https://www.agilebusiness.org/page/ProjectFramework_10_MoSCoWPrioritisation.

113   Patton, J. (2014) *User Story Mapping: Discover the Whole Story, Build the Right Product.* O'Reilly Media, Sebastopol, CA.

First, one or more stories that would just barely satisfy the goal. Users probably wouldn't love it, but they could get by; it is **good enough for now**.

Next, we discuss what stories would make it **better**. These will improve the user experience, add new features, improve performance and so on.

Finally, we find stories that make this the **best** we think we can make it. Be bold here, they aren't requirements, they are just ideas; but sometimes it is the wild and crazy ideas that spark other great ideas.

At the end of the game, we have replaced our one big story with at least three, but sometimes many more, smaller stories that can now be independently prioritised.

This game is good to play as part of backlog refinement or as an ideas generation stimulant when we are doing high-level product development. It also works really well when we have too much work in an iteration or have too many 'must haves' following a MoSCoW prioritisation. We can take all the Must have stories and split them into Good-Better-Best, then apply MoSCoW again to see if we can meet our goal with less work than before.

Weighted shortest job first

Weighted shortest job first (WSJF) is a prioritisation technique first proposed by Don Reinertsen in his book *Principles of Product Development Flow*,[114] and evolved as part of SAFe.[115] It helps teams to prioritise for maximum economic benefit by using cost of delay and job duration to calculate a number (see Figure 8.5). Prioritising by this number (largest first) will deliver the maximum economic benefit.

Figure 8.5 Weighted shortest job first

$$\text{WSJF} = \frac{\text{Cost of Delay}}{\text{Job Duration}}$$

Reinertsen places great emphasis on cost of delay, saying: 'If you only quantify one thing, quantify the Cost of Delay.' The cost of delay is the economic impact of not doing a job; this could be lost revenue, increased costs elsewhere or costs associated with increased risk. Doing jobs with a high cost of delay early will therefore reduce your overall costs. If these jobs can be done quicker, then those costs will be saved earlier. The WSJF encourages quick, high value jobs to be done first.

Reinertsen's model requires that you know the cost of delay and the duration of the job. This implies a level of certainty we don't expect with Agile deliveries, particularly large or complex ones. SAFe solves this by using relative estimation and the modified

---

114 Reinertsen, D. G. (2009) *Principles of Product Development Flow: Second Generation Lean Product Development.* Celeritas Publishing, Redondo Beach, CA.

115 https://www.scaledagileframework.com/wsjf/.

Fibonacci scale described earlier to calculate numbers that allow the WSJF of work items to be compared and prioritised. They break cost of delay into three components that add together:

- **Value to the user or business** – Including penalties or other negative outcomes if it is delayed.
- **Time criticality** – Does the value decay over time or have a cut-off date?
- **Risk reduction or opportunity** – Will this delivery make other deliveries less risky or quicker? Will it provide any other opportunities?

For each work item being prioritised, the team considers each of the three elements independently. They identify which work item should have the lowest score: this is a score of 1. Then each of the other work items is compared to that and a score from the Fibonacci sequence assigned; this is repeated for all three elements. The scores are added together to produce the cost of delay for each work item. If the job duration is also not easy to estimate precisely, the same relative sizing exercise can be applied.

As with most estimation, it's best not to try to get too accurate. A good enough score will still give better prioritisation results than pure guesswork.

SOFTWARE DEVELOPMENT

The Agile Manifesto was devised by people from the software world, so it should be no surprise that there are lots of Agile practices that have come from software development.

Pair programming

Pair programming is a practice popularised as part of XP,[116] and, as discussed in Chapter 7, involves two developers working together with one keyboard and one computer. One person is the driver and they do all the typing. The other is the 'Observer' or 'Navigator' and they review all the code. Together they discuss what they are doing and collaborate to get the best solution. It is described nicely by Birgitta Böckeler and Nina Siessegger on Martin Fowler's blog.[117]

Although it seems counter-intuitive, it is a more efficient and effective way to do work than to divide the work between all the people and have them work independently. This is because a relatively small amount of time spent coding is actually typing. A lot is thinking through the problem, refactoring what you have already done and considering higher level design elements. All these activities are accelerated and improved with two brains instead of one. An added benefit is that design and code review is happening while the work is being done, meaning review or approval stages are not required – as soon as the code is ready it can be released.

---

[116] Beck, K. (2004) *Extreme Programming Explained: Embrace Change* (2nd edn). Addison-Wesley, Boston, MA.

[117] Böckeler, B. and Siessegger, N. (2020) On pair programming. MartinFowler.com. https://martinfowler.com/articles/on-pair-programming.html. Martin Fowler was one of those who created the Agile Manifesto.

The traits described above are true for many other types of knowledge work and other elements of product or solution delivery, so pairing can work just as well for many other types of task. The software company Menlo pairs every single job, including project managers, business analysts and sales.

Mob programming

Mob programming is similar to pair programming except the whole team is involved, still with one keyboard. It was introduced in *Extreme Programming Perspectives* in 2002,[118] and has been championed recently by Woody Zuill.[119]

Again, it can feel counter-intuitive, but the experience of Zuill and others is the opposite. The resulting code is better quality with fewer bugs, and over time the team delivers more work than when they work in parallel. One reason for this is that is takes Little's Law and limiting WiP to the extreme – the team is working on just one task at a time. They don't context switch, and instead focus on completing that task before starting another.

Test driven development

Another XP and Kent Beck idea, test driven development (TDD),[120] is the practice of writing the test before writing the code. Then you write just enough production ready code to pass the test, and no more. Then write another test and iterate the code until that passes. This process iterates until there is sufficient test coverage to satisfy the customer, then that version of the product is released.

It is often combined with behaviour driven development (see Chapter 10), which writes the tests from a business, not a technical, perspective. For example, a TDD approach for the loyalty card sign-up is shown in Table 8.3.

The team take each test in turn and create one or more test artefacts (code, test data, instructions, etc.). They then execute the test, and it will fail. Then the team implement the functionality and run the test again, iterating the code until it passes. They then move on to the next test and repeat the process. Each step is a working version of the solution, although not always a version we would want to release.

This practice reinforces the simplicity principle by ensuring that the solution delivered is the minimum necessary to pass the tests. It also ensures 100 per cent test coverage, thus improving quality. Since each iteration is small, bugs are easier to find and integration into the main codebase is simpler.

118   Marchesi, M., Succi, G., Wells, D. and Williams, L. (2002) *Extreme Programming Perspectives*. Addison-Wesley, Boston, MA.

119   Zuill, W. and Meadows, K. (2021) *Mob Programming: A Whole Team Approach*. Leanpub. https://leanpub.com/mobprogramming.

120   Beck, K. (2002) *Test Driven Development: By Example*. Addison-Wesley, Boston, MA.

Table 8.3 Test driven development example

Test	Description	Implementation
1	A new customer signs up with correct details and succeeds	A version of the product that only works when a new customer signs up with correct details
2	A new customer tries to sign up with incorrect details and fails	A version of the product with some specific error checking of the sign-up details (that would be specified in the test)
3	An existing customer tries to sign up and is reminded they already have an account	A version of the product that includes a workflow for existing customers' email address being used to sign up
4	A new customer signs up but doesn't validate their email address	A version of the product that includes a workflow dealing with missing email validation

Refactoring and emergent design

As each new test is written, the existing design is analysed to check whether it is still the best approach to the problem. If so, then it is extended to meet the new tests. If not, then it is refactored into a new design or architecture that both satisfies the existing tests and the new ones.

This element satisfies the principle of emergent designs. As we add features and complexity to our product, our design and architecture evolves. Importantly, this evolution only happens when the new features are added – we do not anticipate future requirements in our design.

We can see this in action with the loyalty card product. Early versions are simple, with limited data and no complex analysis necessary. Even though we know we will need complex analysis and lots of data capacity in the future, we don't need it **now**. Figure 8.6 shows how a data architecture can change through frequent refactoring.

Figure 8.6 Refactoring the architecture during development

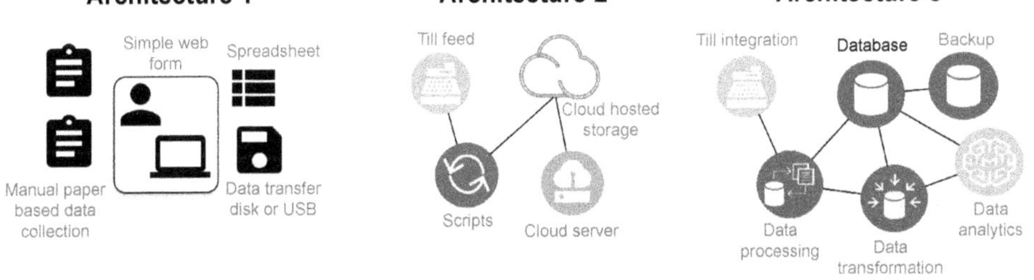

145

To begin with, we can choose a simple implementation – perhaps a spreadsheet with manual data entry – that is quick, easy and passes the early tests. It only needs to solve the simple problem, so we choose a simple solution. Later on, we can replace this with some cloud computing elements and some automation of data loading. Eventually, we add more complex data processing, analysis and storage. Even when Agile teams are not using TDD, this practice of refactoring is still helpful as it encourages deferring decisions until they need to be made, and not over-complicating early versions.

It can seem wasteful – if we know the spreadsheet won't be in our final solution, surely it is a waste of time to deploy it in the first place? We should just deploy the database at the start. The problem with this approach is that the database is inevitably more complicated to deploy and configure than we think, and there is more to go wrong with it. It will take more time to deliver, delaying when our customers get value, and may need to be paid for. It will be really tempting to add in things we don't need now but may need later. This leads to more up-front analysis and design and a higher risk that we implement things early that we will subsequently decide we didn't need after all. This is why deploying software that we fully expect to throw away later isn't as wasteful as it may appear.

Continuous integration/continuous deployment (CI/CD)

The two practices of continuous integration and continuous deployment are commonly tied together as CI/CD because they are such satisfactory bedfellows.

With CI, we aim to avoid having multiple versions of our solution maintained separately. Often, when a developer (or a pair) start working on a new feature or story, they take a copy of the code (called a branch) that they can work on knowing that other people can't change it. Meanwhile, others have been doing the same, meaning that each developer or pair has their own version of the product with their changes in it, but only their changes. Once they are complete, they merge their changes onto the main branch (sometimes called the 'trunk').

If the trunk hasn't changed, this will be a trivial process, since the only changes are those made by the developer. However, if another developer merged their changes onto the trunk before you try to, there are now unknown changes that could conflict with your changes, as shown in Figure 8.7. Tests that passed on your version of the branch may fail once the other changes are present. This makes the second developer's task more complicated and higher risk. The longer you have had your branch, and the more other branches there are, the more change has happened that you don't know about and the more likely you are to have problems when you merge.

With CI, we aim to merge our branch onto the trunk as frequently as possible, perhaps many times a day. In this way, each merge is dealing with less change, often just our own changes, and problems will be easier to find as we have written less new code since we created our branch. This helps to reinforce the principles of always having working software (since to be on the trunk it must work) and to keep our batch size small.

Figure 8.7 Branching and merging

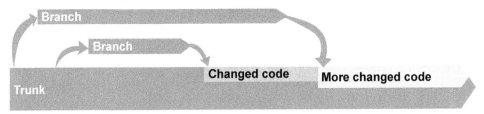

With CD, every time code is integrated it is also deployed, meaning that the version of the product that is live is always the most up-to-date version possible. This means that the testing must be robust enough to trust these frequent new versions.

Both practices are greatly enabled with automation.

MEASURING SUCCESS

The Agile Manifesto makes frequent reference to two important elements of delivery: the customer and the team. Therefore, focusing on these two things is a good place to start when measuring performance:

- Is the customer happy?
- Are the team happy?

This could be as simple as conducting a survey. We aim for all customers and all the team to be very happy with the work being done.

In practice, that isn't usually enough for most teams (or their managers), so more detailed metrics are often required. The Agile Manifesto principles (see Chapter 5) state that Agile teams deliver value frequently and that the best way to measure progress is through working software, so that's another good place to start.

Successful Agile teams provide value to their customers through products that they can use early and are updated frequently. Customers may have their first version of the solution within a few days or weeks. New or improved capabilities and features will be added frequently, at least each iteration, but perhaps every day or more frequently.

Software teams using automated build processes and practising CD can deploy new versions of their product many times a day. Where there are lots of teams, this can aggregate to an astonishing number of deployments – Amazon Web Services, Netflix and Facebook deploy code thousands of times each day.[121]

---

121   In 2016, Facebook committed code over 500 times each day: Feitelson, D. G., Frachtenberg, E. and Beck, K. L. (n.d.) Development and deployment at Facebook. https://research.fb.com/wp-content/uploads/2016/11/development-and-deployment-at-facebook.pdf.

Accelerate four key metrics

Deployment frequency is just one important metric. In 2011, Alanna Brown and Dr Nicole Forsgren began surveying teams who practised an emerging way of working called DevOps and asking them questions about what they were doing and how well it was working for them. They published their findings as the 'State of DevOps'.[122] Due to Nicole's academic background and her scientific rigour, they used their initial analysis to shape questions for the next survey. This allowed them to test their assumptions and conclusions in a scientific way.

Over the subsequent years they, and their collaborators, gathered a huge amount of data on how teams were working and, crucially, whether those teams were successful or not. One important assumption they tested was that, despite DevOps being software-centric, their recommendations would not only improve software companies, but almost any large company. This is because, like it or not, software systems are so critical to virtually every organisation that every company is a software company. Even if their headline business is banking, manufacturing, shipping, media or almost anything else, most organisations depend on software, often bespoke software that is created by or for them. Therefore, optimising DevOps and software performance will have an effect on the whole organisation's performance. For this reason, the conclusions they reached on creating successful organisations have widespread relevance, beyond just the technology sector.

WHAT IS DEVOPS?

There isn't a universally agreed definition of DevOps other than it is a contraction of the words development and operations. It emerged in response to the inefficient traditional approach where development teams and their functions tended to be separate from the operations and IT infrastructure teams. The development team would hand over their finished software to the operations team, who would be responsible for deploying and running it.

Our favourite definition is that DevOps is the combination of cultural philosophies, practices and tools that bring together development and operations in the same team in order to deliver software at a faster pace. In practice, this means that teams applying a DevOps approach make heavy use of automation, configuration management, tooling, cloud services and security practices to ensure that their software is always able to be deployed in a safe, secure and compliant way, and take responsibility for deploying and supporting it themselves. This makes DevOps a natural fit for Agile teams, and vice versa.

In 2018 Nicole Forsgren, together with Jez Humble and Gene Kim, drew the results of all the state of DevOps research together in their book, *Accelerate*.[123] *Accelerate*

---

122 The State of DevOps research is now carried out by DevOps Research & Assessment (DORA). https://www.devops-research.com/research.html.

123 Forsgren, N., Humble, J. and Kim, G. (2018) *Accelerate. The Science of Lean Software and DevOps: Building and Scaling High Performing Technology Organizations*. Trade Select, Portland, OR.

describes the 24 concrete, specific capabilities that, when optimised, will result in higher performing organisations. These capabilities interrelate and those relationships, and their effect on organisational performance are backed up by the research and scientific analysis from the surveys. In other words, they aren't just proposing good ideas, they can prove that they are good ideas. The capabilities span technical, process, measurement and cultural areas.

Their research also indicated that there are four key metrics that organisations should seek to optimise to improve their overall software delivery performance and therefore their overall organisational performance. Performance against these metrics can be used to classify teams or organisations as low, medium, high and now Elite[124] performers. The four key metrics are described in Table 8.4.

Table 8.4 The Accelerate four key metrics

Deployment frequency	How often do you deploy your primary application or service to production or release it to end users?
	From on-demand (multiple times a day) for Elite, to less than every six months for low.
Lead time for changes	How long does it take for changes to be implemented, i.e. from code committed to code successfully running in production?
	From less than one hour for Elite, to more than six months for low.
Time to restore service	How long does it generally take to restore service when a service incident or defect that impacts users occurs? (Note that this is to restore service, not necessarily fix the root cause of the problem.)
	From less than one hour for Elite, to more than six months for low.
Change failure rate	What percentage of changes to production or released to users result in degraded service (e.g. bugs or outages) that subsequently require remediation?
	From 0–15% for Elite and 16–30% for all the others.

It is important to optimise for all four metrics as they can impact one another. For example, increasing deployment frequency alone may introduce more defects that affect time to restore and change failure rate. Each metric has a strong customer focus – either helping customers to get value faster or ensuring that the current capabilities continue to provide value – and directly support the Agile values and principles.

The Accelerate research shows how the 24 factors affect these metrics, and provides strong guidance for how teams can improve their performance. Many are also recommendations that we make in this chapter and elsewhere in this book to create high-performing Agile teams.

---

124 The Elite organisation metrics have been added by DORA since the book was first published.

Customer lead time

The Accelerate lead time measure is the lead time from a feature being complete to it being available for use. While useful, this isn't really what a customer would consider to be lead time; they would define it as the time between asking for a feature and being able to use it. While this can be a useful metric, it doesn't take account of the team's throughput. A better metric is the lead time between committing to a story or feature and it being available.

We can calculate a simple or rolling average (for example, over the past three months the lead time of a feature from commitment to delivery is four weeks), but to be most useful the work items must be of a similar size. The four weeks example is still true, but much less helpful when half the stories take one week and the rest take seven weeks.

Having stories roughly the same size helps us to manage stakeholder expectations better. It also allows us to optimise for small batch size according to Little's Law and be better at splitting big goals into smaller goals.

Continuous improvement

A second expectation on Agile teams from the Agile Manifesto is that of continual improvement, both of the product – through iterative and emergent architecture and design – and of the team themselves.

The simplest way to measure this is by measuring the improvement actions or tasks that the team commit to in each planning session. For a while, the Scrum framework even made an improvement goal mandatory – making it as important as the iteration goal.[125]

Identifying improvement actions are an explicit purpose of a retrospective, but are useless unless the improvements are implemented. The important thing to measure is commitment to and achievement of improvement actions – not just the identification of them. That's why we still encourage teams to commit to including improvement goals or actions in every iteration.

It is important that the team's stakeholders, including their customers and leadership, also view continuous improvement as a priority. When this isn't the case, we often see teams fail to meet improvement goals and de-prioritise actions from retrospectives.

Team health and happiness

A happy and well-motivated team will do better work than one that is not. Therefore measuring and tracking attributes of team health can be an excellent indicator of their potential performance. There are many ways to do this, from a simple single question survey to more complex suites of questions.

---

125 Scrum is updated every two years or so. The mandatory improvement goal was removed from the 2020 version as part of the move to simplify the framework.

Music streaming company Spotify developed and published a series of indicators they regarded as important to their teams. They call it a Squad Health Check.[126] There are 11 indicator cards and each one has a description of what it should be like, and a description of what it shouldn't. For example: **Learning:** 'We're learning lots of interesting stuff all the time, or 'We never have time to learn anything.' The indicators are: Support, Teamwork, Pawns or Players, Mission, Health of Codebase, Suitable Process, Delivering Value, Learning, Speed, Easy to Release and Fun. Sometimes, additional cards are added that are specific to a particular team, and teams should iterate and improve the questions to suit their circumstances. For each indicator, each team member looks at the card and considers how they feel at that point in time. They then vote as per the layout in Table 8.5.

Table 8.5 Spotify health check scoring

Green	We might not be perfect, but I am happy with this indicator at the moment, and I don't see any major need for improvement.
Yellow	There are some important problems that we could do with improving, but it's not a disaster.
Red	This really sucks and needs to be improved as soon as possible.

The team discuss what they think and, by comparing their answers today with previous iterations, they can spot trends. For example, they may notice that their satisfaction with the health of the codebase is declining as the product gets bigger, or they have less fun when annual performance reports are being written. The teams also evolve the indicators, choosing new ones when they need to and retiring any that stop being useful.

If there are several teams, then trends across teams can also be analysed. For instance, if most teams think there are serious problems with learning, then perhaps that's a systemic problem that requires a more strategic response.

There are other sources of team health that you may also consider, such as the Scrum health check,[127] Patrick Lencioni's five dysfunctions of a team,[128] the Project Aristotle[129] dynamics of effective teams, Amy Edmundson's psychological safety[130] questions and, of course, you can come up with your own questions.

---

126 https://engineering.atspotify.com/2014/09/16/squad-health-check-model/.

127 Scrum checklist. Crisp. https://www.crisp.se/gratis-material-och-guider/scrum-checklist.

128 The concept. TableGroup. https://www.tablegroup.com/product/dysfunctions/; Lencioni, P. (2002) *The Five Dysfunctions of a Team*. Jossey-Bass, San Francisco, CA.

129 Guide: Understand team effectiveness. Re:Work. https://rework.withgoogle.com/print/guides/5721312655835136/.

130 Unlock the full potential of your team. The Fearless Organization. https://fearlessorganization.com; Edmundson, A. (2018) *The Fearless Organization: Creating Psychological Safety in the Workplace for Learning, Innovation, and Growth*. John Wiley & Sons, Hoboken, NJ.

Our advice is to start simple. It is more important to get data you can trust and understand than to try to collect huge volumes. The more effort it is for the team to provide these data, the less likely they are to continue providing them, or to be thoughtful, open and honest with their answers.

Leading and lagging measures

A leading measure is one that you can use to help judge whether you will meet a particular goal. A lagging measure is one that tells you that you have met a particular goal. For example, team health is a good leading indicator since teams will begin to mark themselves down in particular indicators before their work really starts to suffer; this allows us to correct the problem and avoid performance being badly affected.

Leading indicators often measure outcomes such as the four key metrics described earlier or progress through states in Kanban or those defined in the OMG standard, Essence.[131] Assessing a product or feature against the states[132] can be a good leading indicator of progress or problems. For example, recognising that stakeholders have changed could be an indication that strategic direction may change, or seeing features reach 'Operational' indicates that customers are getting iterative value.

Lagging indicators are often those that measure outputs, and are less valuable. Measuring how many stories remain on the backlog doesn't tell us how likely we are to deliver them, nor whether they are likely to cause us problems.

Similarly, measuring stories completed or Story Points completed can only be leading indicators if our work is sufficiently homogeneous that the work of the past is so similar to the work in the future that we can assume it will be delivered in the same way and in the same time. In practice we rarely see this to be true – teams change, the nature of the work changes, the expectations of the customers change. All these changes make lagging indicators like data about work completed less helpful to predict anything about the work in the future.

Velocity

Team velocity is a measure of the average amount of work completed by the team. Often a rolling average of the past three iterations, it can be a helpful indicator of the rough capacity of the team and is, by definition, a lagging indicator. However, we must be very cautious of using it for anything else, particularly anything contractual. This is because there are too many variables to allow us to trust it and, because of those variables, it is too easy to game the result. Some of the challenges are shown in Table 8.6.

Despite these challenges, velocity can sometimes be valuable as long as its accuracy is also understood. Abstracting up to story level can be useful as, over the length of a delivery, on average each story is the same size. Therefore, counting the number of

---

131   https://www.omg.org/hot-topics/essence.htm.

132   Alpha state cards (PDF version). Ivar Jacobson International, Essence in Practice. https://www.ivarjacobson.com/cards.

stories a team delivers on average during each iteration can give a rough indication of how many stories they may deliver in the future. This lets us estimate how many stories may be delivered in a given time, or how long it may take to deliver a given number of stories.

Table 8.6 Challenges using velocity as meaningful measure

The team doing the work must remain stable	Their available time, skill level, work rate, ability to solve problems, coding accuracy, etc. must all remain roughly the same.
The type of work must remain the same	The type, complexity, implementation technology, estimation unit, etc. must all be comparable across all the work items.
The acceptance criteria must remain the same	The tests, criteria, thresholds, etc. all remain the same or, if they change, then they take the same time and effort to apply.
The work items must be of similar size	The more disparate the size of items, the harder it is to compare them, particularly if we are using a modified Fibonacci estimation scale. This implies future work needs to be broken down to a similar size to the work items we have historic data on, which usually means a lot of up-front analysis is necessary.
The estimates must be trustworthy	This is particularly the case if we want to use Story Point velocity as a contractual metric; we must trust the numbers. However, since estimation is a human activity and needs to involve the team, the estimates are easy to influence or game to get the desired result.

SCRUM

The State of Agile Report is the longest continuous annual series of reviews of Agile techniques and practices. The most popular Agile method used by their respondents has consistently been Scrum or hybrids of Scrum. In 2021 the 15th version reported that 66 per cent of teams use Scrum and a further 15 per cent use hybrids of Scrum.[133] Therefore it's worth mentioning Scrum here, although a comprehensive (and up-to-date) description is found on the website scrumguides.org.[134] The Scrum framework is freely available and licensed under the Attribution Share-Alike licence of Creative Commons.[135]

---

133 15th annual state of Agile report. Digital.ai. https://digital.ai/resource-center/analyst-reports/state-of-agile-report.

134 https://scrumguides.org/index.html.

135 https://creativecommons.org/licenses/by-sa/4.0/legalcode.

Figure 8.8 The Scrum framework

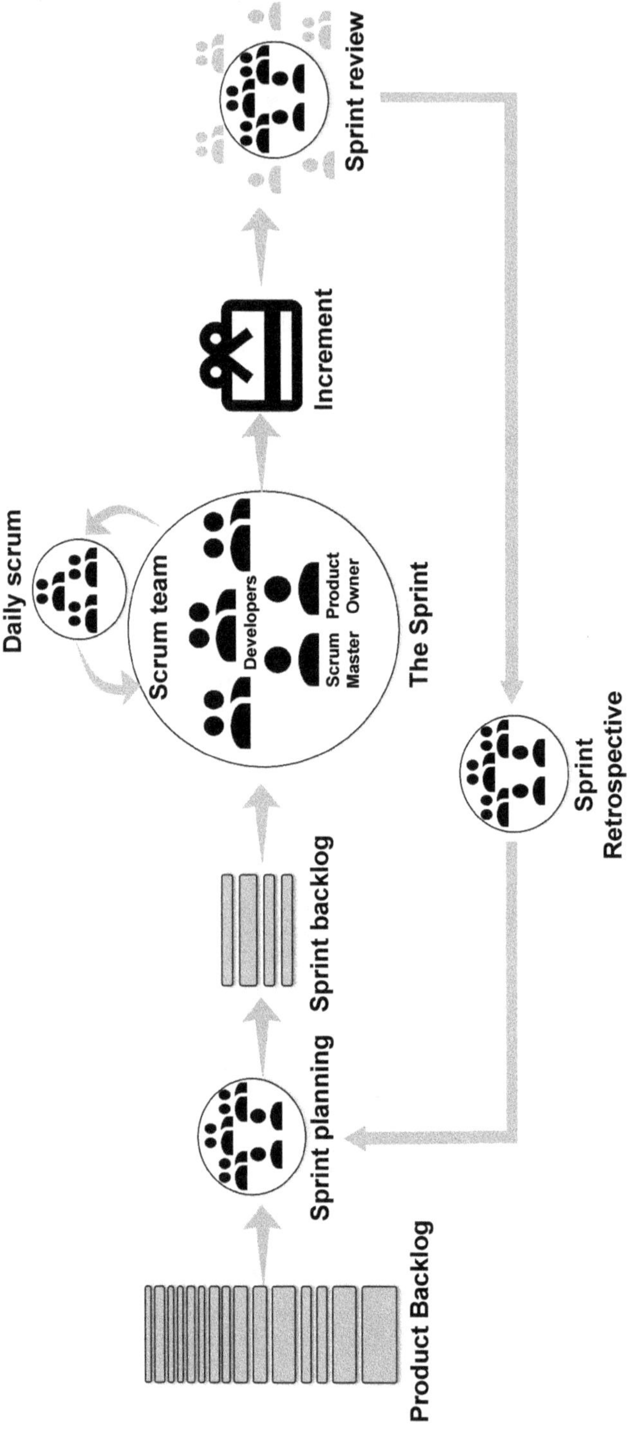

Scrum is a lightweight framework that helps people, teams and organisations to generate value through adaptive solutions for complex problems. It embodies many of the Agile values and principles described in this book and, when followed properly, allows teams to be Agile. Despite being relatively simple to understand – the latest (November 2020) version of the Scrum Guide is only 13 pages long – it is deceptively difficult to master, and although Scrum co-founder Jeff Sutherland's 2014 book promises fantastic benefits,[136] many teams who start using Scrum struggle to get the value promised.

Scrum consists of some theory, values and a framework of three accountabilities, five events and three artefacts. As a framework, it describes what teams need to do, but not how to do it (see Figure 8.8). The theory is based on empiricism and includes the three pillars of transparency, inspection and adaptation described in Chapter 6. The Scrum values are commitment, focus, openness, respect and courage. They give direction to the Scrum team with regard to their work, actions and behaviour.

As we described in Chapter 7, the Scrum team accountabilities are Product Owner, Scrum Master and Developer (see Table 8.7). They are a small, cross-functional team with all the skills and authority needed to create a valuable increment, and they are all focused on the same product.

Table 8.7 Scrum accountabilities

Developer	Developers are the people in the team committed to creating any aspect of a usable increment in each iteration.
Product Owner	The Product Owner is accountable for maximising the value of the product resulting from the work of the team.
Scrum Master	The Scrum Master is accountable for establishing Scrum as defined in the Scrum Guide. They do this by helping everyone to understand Scrum theory and practice, both within the Scrum team and into the wider organisation.

The Scrum team take part in five events to create three artefacts. The events are time-boxed and all except the Daily Scrum are proportional to the Sprint length – so the review of a two-week Sprint will be half the duration of that of a four-week Sprint. The five events are shown in Table 8.8. The three artefacts iterate and evolve through the life cycle of the delivery, and are shown in Table 8.9.

---

136 Sutherland, J. (2014) *Scrum: The Art of Doing Twice the Work in Half the Time.* Crown Business, New York.

Table 8.8 The Scrum events

Sprint	The Sprint is the core of Scrum. It is a fixed length of less than one month, during which time the team work together to deliver the agreed Sprint goal and a new version of the product increment.
Sprint Planning	The Sprint starts with the whole team collaborating to agree the most important items on the Product Backlog and how they contribute to the Product Goal. They agree the goal for this Sprint and what work must be completed to meet it.
Daily Scrum	In the Daily Scrum the developers inspect progress towards the Sprint Goal and adapt the Sprint Backlog as necessary, adjusting the upcoming planned work.
Sprint Review	The Sprint Review allows the team and wider stakeholders to inspect the outcome of the Sprint and discuss progress towards the Product Goal, including future adaptations.
Sprint Retrospective	The Sprint Retrospective allows the team to identify and plan ways to increase quality and effectiveness. The Scrum team inspects how the last Sprint went with regard to individuals, interactions, processes, tools and their definition of done. They agree changes to address as soon as possible.

Table 8.9 The Scrum artefacts

Product Backlog	The Product Backlog is an emergent, ordered list of what is needed to improve the product. It is the single source of work undertaken by the Scrum team and includes the current Product Goal.
Sprint Backlog	The Sprint Backlog is composed of the Sprint Goal (why), the set of Product Backlog items selected for the Sprint (what) and an actionable plan for delivering the increment (how).
Increment	An increment is a concrete stepping stone towards the Product Goal. It is the 'working software' we measure progress by. In order to provide value, the increment must be usable.

THE KANBAN METHOD

A *kanban* system is a Japanese manufacturing system, originating from Toyota, where the supply of components is regulated through the use of an instruction card sent along the production line – that production card is called a *kanban*. When a process uses some resource, it sends a *kanban* to the supplier to signal that the resource needs to be replenished. This implements a pull system, where inventory is pulled in when required rather than being pushed onto the line when it is created. A *kanban* system reduces inventory and transportation wastes and improves production flow.

In 2010 David Anderson published *Kanban*,[137] where he described how the principles of the *kanban* system could be applied successfully to knowledge work and software systems, not just manufacturing. He called this the 'Kanban Method'[138] (also often abbreviated to 'Kanban'). Since then, the Kanban Method has become a popular way to visualise and manage work in Agile teams, often alongside other methods such as Scrum. Like Scrum, however, Kanban is also easy to misunderstand and abuse. Some teams struggle to see beyond the Kanban board and don't get the potential value they could. We often see teams who struggle with the discipline of Scrum decide to move to Kanban thinking it is simpler and easier.

In fact, the Kanban Method is about a lot more than just having a board with columns and pieces of card – even *Essential Kanban Condensed* runs to more than 70 (small) pages covering the foundational principles of Kanban, flow systems, its general practices, the roles and guidance on forecasting and metrics.[139] At its heart, Kanban is a method that simply shows us how our work works. By visualising our work on a Kanban board we make it transparent. We can see where problems lie, making it easier to solve them and improve our delivery. By applying limits to our WiP[140] we focus on flow and create a pull system that ensures we continually complete and deliver work. This helps teams with sustainable pace and measuring progress by the delivery principles of Agile.

Like Scrum, Kanban has a set of values: transparency, balance, collaboration, customer focus, flow, leadership, understanding, agreement and respect. These values complement and reinforce the Agile Manifesto values and principles, although the Kanban Method does not have to be applied in an Agile context.

Kanban agendas

To help reinforce these values, Kanban recognises three agendas, as shown in Table 8.10.

Table 8.10 Kanban agendas

Sustainability	This is about finding a sustainable pace and improving focus.
Service orientation	This is about focusing on customer satisfaction and performance.
Survivability	This is about staying competitive and being adaptive.

Remaining focused on these three agendas helps to build teams that are resilient to change and able to adapt to keep them current and able to survive. Their customer focus helps to ensure their services remain fit for purpose and are valued.

---

137 Anderson, D. (2010) *Kanban: Successful Evolutionary Change for your Technology Business*. Blue Hole Press, Sequim, WA.

138 When referring to or abbreviating the Kanban Method, we capitalise Kanban. When referring to the Japanese word for the card or the *kanban* system, we do not capitalise it.

139 Anderson, D. and Carmichael, A. (2016) *Essential Kanban Condensed*. Blue Hole Press, Sequim, WA.

140 As discussed earlier in this chapter, the term 'WiP' originated in manufacturing where it stands for 'work in process' (i.e. work that is still within the manufacturing process). Many teams prefer the expression 'work in progress' as it sounds better. In his books on the Kanban Method, David Anderson uses 'Work in Progress'.

Kanban principles

The foundational principles of Kanban are split into two groups, as shown in Table 8.11.

Table 8.11 Kanban principles

Change management	As we mention throughout this book, people are not naturally inclined to think and behave in an Agile way. They resist change, and this must be addressed to make progress. Kanban proposes three principles to help instil this change: • Start with what you do now. • Agree to pursue improvement through evolutionary change. • Encourage acts of leadership at every level.
Service delivery	Teams tend not to exist in isolation, and neither do their products. At an organisational level, value to the customer is generally delivered through an ecosystem of interdependent services. Kanban defines three principles to apply not just to one service but to the whole network: • Understand and focus on your customers' needs and expectations. • Manage the work, and let people self-organise around it. • Evolve policies to improve customer and business outcomes.

Again, these principles align well with those in the Agile Manifesto. They help us to focus on the important things and to guide teams in their decision making.

The Kanban board

The most significant and visual element of Kanban is the board that teams use to visualise the flow of their work and to help them improve the value they provide to their customers. In Figure 8.2 we show an example Agile board. Although many teams would describe this as a Kanban board, it omits some important aspects. To be a Kanban board, several conditions must be met:

- There must be signals to limit the WiP, usually in boxes at the top of the relevant columns.
- There must be clear 'Commitment' and 'Delivery' points that denote the start and end of the WiP but also provide explicit agreements between the customer and the team on the work and its acceptance criteria.

An example Kanban board that meets these criteria is shown in Figure 8.9. The Kanban board also allows us to define some import metrics that we can use to measure performance, as shown in Table 8.12.

Figure 8.9 Example Kanban board

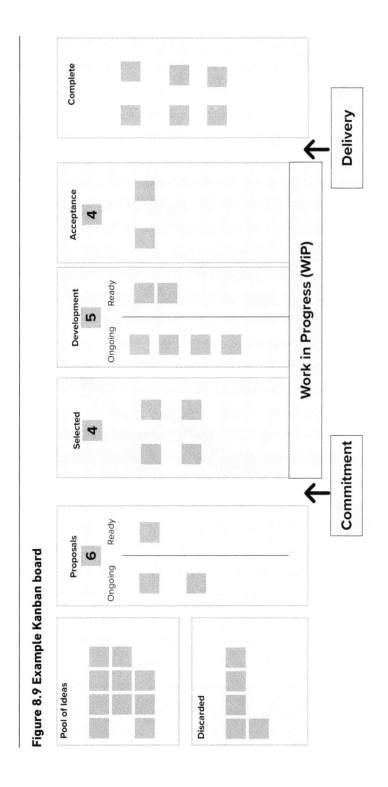

Table 8.12 Kanban metrics

Lead time	This is the time that a work item is in process between being committed to and being accepted as complete. It may be different from the customer lead time, which will be from customer request to receipt.
Delivery rate	This is the rate at which items are delivered: the throughput.

As we described earlier in this chapter, Little's Law tells us that limiting WiP will reduce our lead time and increase delivery rate. This is why the WiP limits are so important. These metrics can be portrayed graphically over time in a cumulative flow diagram (see Figure 8.10) and used to provide some prediction of future delivery rate based on historical data.

Figure 8.10 Example cumulative flow diagram

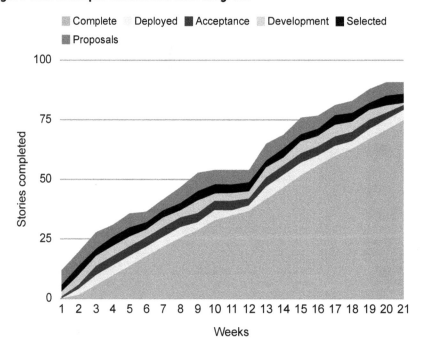

Kanban practices

The Kanban Method describes a number of practices that help teams to see the work, and policies that dictate how the work is processed and how they can improve their process. The general practices are given in Table 8.13.

Table 8.13 Kanban practices

Visualise	Visualising not just through a visual board, but also visualising and making obvious the policies that affect the work and common criteria such as definitions of done or ready.
Limit work in progress	Limiting WiP forces a pull process since space must be created from the end of the process in order to start new work at the beginning. It also forces people to work where they are needed rather than where they may prefer to.
Manage flow	The movement of work through the system can be managed in various ways, including prioritising work with a high cost of delay, ordering work by classes of service and use of service level agreements.
Make policies explicit	Policies that affect process should be visible and explicit. This is partly to expose when they should be changed, but also to ensure that they are clear to everyone.
Implement feedback loops	Although Kanban does not use fixed length iterations like other methods, it does require frequent feedback loops with cadences to ensure they happen regularly. It is explicit with the range of things to seek feedback on and includes areas such as strategy, risk management and operational coordination that are often overlooked by Agile teams.
Improve collaboratively, evolve experimentally	The best way to identify improvements is when we involve the whole team, and empirically making and testing improvements helps to ensure that they are having the impact we expect.

As we can see from this brief description of the Kanban Method, there is significantly more to Kanban than putting sticky notes on a board and forgetting about iterations. Kanban is underpinned by science, psychology and a shared understanding; applying it successfully requires discipline and rigour, but when this happens it provides a solid baseline for strong Agile delivery.

Because Kanban is so aligned with the Agile values and principles, it is a natural accompaniment to other processes such as Scrum or many of the scaled approaches. Particularly when teams adhere to the principles and practices, Kanban can help teams to apply other approaches more purely and successfully.

SUMMARY

Agile's simplicity is also its complexity. Four values, that on first glance seem like common sense, can be surprisingly hard to adhere to without structure and guidance from methods, techniques, patterns and practices. Fortunately, there is plenty of support available.

Through this chapter we have introduced a vast array of practices – some from larger methods, such as SAFe, AgilePM or XP, and others that have emerged on the sidelines or in related fields. These are just a taster of some of our favourites. They are briefly described here so that you can explore them in more detail if you feel the need.

There are two areas – leadership and product management – that we consider so significant to doing Agile well that we have devoted Chapters 9 and 10 to them. There, we will scratch the surface a little deeper but still leave room for further study. Many of these practices have entire books written about them, so our aim here is merely to introduce them to you, not teach them to you. However, they are all worth learning.

A method or framework is rarely a perfect match, and you should be cautious of assuming that one size fits all. However, tinkering with a method without fully understanding it can do more harm than good (see *Shu Ha Ri* in Chapter 11). When coupled with the foundations of Agile covered in the previous chapters, applying these practices will stand you in good stead whichever framework you choose to use or not use. These practices are some of the fundamental building blocks of Agile that are important to demonstrating an Agile mindset and being able to continually deliver value in a VUCA world.

9 AGILE LEADERSHIP

It isn't enough for just teams to understand Agile; their leaders, managers and organisation must also become Agile

We already know that working in an Agile way requires teams to think and behave in different ways, but this is true for managers and leaders too. In fact, some of the changes they must make are even more profound and uncomfortable than those of their teams. Yet, this is not always acknowledged and not always discussed. It is easy to read a book on Agile or attend a training course as a manager and leave assuming that all the changes will be in how other people act. This failure to acknowledge the significance of good Agile leadership in the success of any Agile endeavour is important – it is a key reason why many Agile teams struggle or fail.

So, why is this the case? Why don't leaders see that adopting Agile also requires a shift in their mindset? There are, of course, many reasons, but an important one is that the kind of cultural shift required of leaders is hard and it is uncomfortable. It requires rejecting decades of practices, beliefs and behaviours that don't seem to be obviously broken. These same behaviours are often the things that are sought out when promoting and appointing leaders, therefore perpetuating the cycle.

Yet when we look at where those established management practices came from, we can see that they originate in an environment that is very different from the VUCA world we find ourselves in today. The work is different, the challenges are different, the people are different. When things change, we ought to respond to those changes – and that includes how we lead and manage.

This chapter explores some of these factors. It will help to explain the different styles of leadership and how we can change to better enable Agile behaviours in our teams, and why these changes make our teams more effective. We will briefly introduce several leadership ideas and theories, but for more thorough coverage we recommend the references.

This chapter will cover:

- Why we lead and manage the way that we do.
- What is different in Agile leadership.
- How leadership influences the ways Agile teams behave.

EVOLUTION OF LEADERSHIP

Most organisations are led and managed in similar ways, irrespective of their sector, purpose or history. There is a top level that sets direction and strategy for the rest of the organisation to implement. This top level wants to ensure that their instructions are adhered to, so they implement a management and oversight structure to provide that assurance. This management structure usually involves setting out what needs to be done at the next layer down and monitoring that this happens. There are usually several layers of control necessary to be able to break down the tasks to the level at which the work is assigned to a person. We can trace this approach back to the late 19th century and the work of Frederick Winslow Taylor.

Taylorism

While managing the factory floor of a steelworks in the US, Taylor noticed that, when left to their own devices, the workers would take different approaches to the same task. The difference in productivity was less to do with the hard work (or laziness) of the workers and more to do with the lack of a system that described the most efficient approach for each task. He believed there was 'one best way' to perform each task and set about identifying and describing this. He broke the tasks down to their simplest steps and directed the workers to follow them to the letter. He selected and trained the workers for the tasks and followed a principle whereby the managers performed the thinking and the workers focused on performing the task.

His impact was profound. By splitting the work into detailed, specified tasks, focusing workers on a small set of tasks each and rigorously monitoring them, he proved repeatedly that this would improve productivity. In 1911 he published his findings in his book, *The Principles of Scientific Management*,[141] which has gone on to influence virtually every large organisation in the world with its premise that management is a discipline, that managers are separate from workers and that managers think and workers do.

Meanwhile, in Europe, Henri Fayol was also concluding that strong management practices were key to predictability and efficiency. Learning from his experiences in mining, in his 1916 book, *Administration Industrielle et Générale*,[142] he defined five functions of management – planning, organising, commanding, controlling and coordinating – underpinned by 14 principles of management. This encouraged organisations to seek to specialise and control their workforce to become more productive.

Where Taylor drew his conclusions in a steelworks environment, Henri Fayol reached similar conclusions in mining and Henry Ford famously adopted the production line for motor car manufacture. It appeared that this top-down, management-centric approach worked in multiple sectors, so it isn't surprising that it caught on.

---

141   Taylor, F. W. (1911) *The Principles of Scientific Management*. Dover Publications, Mineola, NY.

142   Fayol, H. (1949) *General and Industrial Management* (English trans. Constance Storrs). Pitman, London.

Theory X and Theory Y

What these approaches have in common is that they focus on the perspective of the managers and the business. They assume that workers are there to be controlled and are not a sentient part of the system; the managers do the thinking because the workers aren't capable of it. This leads to several other assumptions made of workers that Douglas McGregor identified in his 1960 work, *The Human Side of Enterprise*,[143] and described as Theory X.

Theory X managers believe that:

- The average person prefers to be directed, to avoid responsibility, is relatively unambitious and wants security above all else.
- The average person dislikes work and will avoid it if they can.
- Therefore, most people must be forced with the threat of punishment to work towards organisational objectives.

This theory fits well with the recommendations of Taylor and Fayol and may well be true for the work environments they created: workers performing repetitive, low skill tasks dictated to them by managers and held to strict criteria.

However, McGregor believed that there was an alternative theory that was far more suited to the kinds of work that were emerging in the later 20th century; work that is less certain, where workers need to apply some thought to their work. We call this 'knowledge work', a term coined by Peter Drucker in 1959 and described in his 1967 book, *The Effective Executive*.[144] McGregor describes this alternative as Theory Y.

Theory Y managers believe that:

- Work can be as natural and as enjoyable as play.
- People don't require external control or threat of punishment to apply self-control and self-direction to achieve organisational objectives.
- Commitment to the objective is in itself part of the reward, not just achieving the goal.
- People usually accept and often seek responsibility.
- Most people have the capacity to use a high degree of imagination, ingenuity and creativity to solve problems.

This is a wholly different approach to leading and managing than Theory X. In fact, it is such a paradigm shift that many managers cannot even contemplate it being true. When we look at how many organisations are currently structured – their HR policies and processes, how they task or allocate work, their oversight and governance mechanisms, the organisation of their teams and team management – we can see a clear skew

---

143 McGregor, D. (1960) *The Human Side of Enterprise*. McGraw-Hill, New York.

144 Drucker, P. (1967) *The Effective Executive* (reprinted 2007). Routledge, Abingdon, UK.

towards Theory X assumptions. This is despite them being based on observations more than 100 years old, and from industries that are completely different from today's knowledge-worker dominated environment – and that's before we even think about how well suited they are to the VUCA environment we described earlier.

WHAT IS AGILE LEADERSHIP?

Until this point, we have used the word **manager** a lot. This is intentional. The dominant focus of leadership in the past has been to **manage** the work, implying that the jobs that need doing are well known and the role of management structures and managers is to check that they are being done and being done properly. This is reinforced by titles such as managing director, general manager, management committees, project manager and many more. When we call somebody a manager, we are priming them to expect to manage and priming those around them to be managed.

That is not what is required in Agile organisations. In fact, the complete opposite is true. The people best placed to make decisions on what needs to be done are the people doing the work, not those above or around them. Therefore, good Agile teams don't have or need managers. However, they do require **leadership**, and good leadership is a prerequisite for being able to pivot away from a culture built on the manager-centric ethos of Taylor and Fayol.

The good news is that good Agile leadership is not a million miles away from the leadership being advocated by management experts today. As we will see later in this chapter, psychologists, military historians, naval captains and other progressive leaders are describing approaches that fit perfectly with Agile leadership, although none of them reference the Agile Manifesto nor profess to be Agile experts.

We can also find good examples of Agile leadership from history. In Chapter 8 we quoted German Field Marshal von Molkte, who served in the Prussian army in the 1800s. His view on what constitutes an order is a perfect example of Agile leadership. He said: '... an order should contain all, but also only, what subordinates cannot determine for themselves'.[145] In other words, give the team enough, just enough, information to achieve the desired outcome, letting them work out for themselves everything they possibly can.

Agile leadership begins with the team. Valuing the left-hand side of the Manifesto means trusting individuals, relying on collaboration more than paperwork and processes, and assuming that any decision might need to be revisited if things change. This means that a classic top-down cascade of ideas and tasks cannot work. Instead, we move as much decision making as we can into the team and defer decisions until as late as possible.

Working out which decisions can be moved into the team, and how late decisions can be deferred, is the role of the leadership. There will still be some decisions the team can't or shouldn't make, and some decisions that need to be made earlier than we may prefer. The challenge is balance – doing just enough, just in time.

---

145 Bungay, S. (2011) *The Art of Action: How Leaders Close the Gaps Between Plans, Actions and Results.* Nicholas Brealey Publishing, Boston, MA, p. 62.

MINDSET SHIFTS FOR LEADERS

Creating the right environment to optimise Agile leadership requires leaders to adopt a different mindset from what many are used to. The traditional approaches, still wedded to Taylorism and Theory X assumptions, don't allow Agile teams to thrive, and in many cases will conspire to do harm and prevent success.

> Some leadership shifts are simple. In David Marquet's book, *Leadership Is Language*,[146] he explains why **what** you say can have tremendous impact on your teams. For example, he suggests saying 'What am I missing?' rather than 'Does that make sense?' or 'On a scale of 1 to 5, how useful would it be for me to come on site?' rather than 'Tell me if you need me to come over.' This changes the question into a request for information that requires the other person to think before answering, involving them more in the decision and making it more likely to elicit useful and honest answers.

In this section two models are explained that help to describe the kinds of mindset shift necessary to become an Agile leader.

Become a corporate rebel

In January 2016, Joost Minnaar and Pim de Morree quit their jobs and set out around the world to seek out inspirational leaders and interview them. Over the next few years, they spoke to people in large and small organisations, in the public and private sectors delivering services, manufacturing, healthcare, entertainment, in fact almost any type of business you would care to imagine. They document their experiences in their book, *Corporate Rebels*, and on their website.[147]

What makes the inspirational people they meet special is that they are doing things differently from their peers. In many cases, radically differently: some allow their staff to set their own salary, others have no expenses policies, others have extreme approaches to innovation and experimentation. But they also have things in common. Through their research, Joost and Pim identified eight trends[148] that separated these bold, innovative and pioneering workplaces from the norm. These eight trends also describe what it means to be an Agile leader. They are described in a similar way to the Agile Manifesto, as a journey from one mindset to another:

- From profit **to** purpose and values.
- From hierarchical pyramids **to** a network of teams.

---

146   Marquet, D. (2020), *Leadership is Language: The Hidden Power of What You Say and What You Don't*. Portfolio Penguin, New York.

147   Minnaar, J. and de Morree, P. (2020) *Corporate Rebels: Make Work More Fun*. Corporate Rebels, The Netherlands. https://corporate-rebels.com.

148   https://corporate-rebels.com/trends/.

- From directive leadership **to** supportive leadership.
- From predict and plan **to** experiment and adapt.
- From rules and control **to** freedom and trust.
- From centralised authority **to** distributed authority.
- From secrecy **to** radical transparency.
- From job descriptions **to** talents and mastery.

Much like the Agile Manifesto, history, experience, dogma and discomfort will keep many leaders towards the status quo. It can be uncomfortable and lonely to be moving towards the right of this set of values, but, as the Corporate Rebels have found, those who make the shift are rewarded.

Three key mindset shifts

In his book, *The 6 Enablers of Business Agility*,[149] Karim Harbott explains that adopting the latest Agile tools and practices won't be enough to make your organisation Agile; there are six key enabling factors that you must focus on to become a high-performing Agile organisation: leadership, culture, structure, people, governance and ways of working, and for leaders there are three key mindset shifts required. Making these changes is critical in enabling the environment we describe in the rest of this chapter. The three mindset shifts are shown in Table 9.1.

Table 9.1 Three key mindset shifts for Agile leaders

Mindset shift 1	Focus less on the work and more on the culture.
Mindset shift 2	Decentralise as much of the decision making as possible.
Mindset shift 3	Encourage and support the growth and development of those around you.

While these mindset shifts may not appear all that profound, we frequently see leaders (and managers) in so-called 'Agile' organisations do the opposite. We see a focus on outputs, decisions referred upwards and personal development left to the individual to manage in whatever spare time they can find.

SIX LEADERSHIP OUTCOMES

Agile leadership can be broken into broad leadership outcomes. These are distinct things that Agile leaders should seek to achieve. They are shown in Figure 9.1 and we will explore each of them in the following sections.

---

149   Harbott, K. (2021) *The 6 Enablers of Business Agility: How to Thrive in an Uncertain World.* Berret-Koehler Publishers Inc, Oakland, CA.

Figure 9.1 Six leadership outcomes for high-performing teams

Servant leadership	Psychological safety	Intrinsic motivation
Trusted, empowered people	Self-organising teams	Strategic alignment

These six outcomes are not independent of one another. They are different perspectives and lenses on the same thing: how to create high-performing teams. Focusing on any of them should bring some improvement but, since they reinforce one another, focusing on them all will bring the best results.

Servant leadership

The term 'servant leadership' was first coined by Robert Greenleaf in his 1970 essay 'The Servant as Leader',[150] and was inspired by reading Hermann Hesse's *The Journey to the East*.[151] In the story, Leo is the servant to a group of travellers, yet when he disappears the group falls into disarray and they have to abandon the journey – it is only sometime later that the narrator discovers that Leo was actually the head of a noble order, he was its guiding spirit and a great leader. The group had been completely unaware of Leo's status, had assumed he was a mere servant and they only made the progress they did because of Leo's influence and wisdom. Greenleaf used his coined term to describe a better way of leading than traditional command and control. In his essay, he says:

> The servant-leader is servant first – as Leo was portrayed. It begins with the natural feeling that one wants to serve, to serve first. Then conscious choice brings one to aspire to lead. That person is sharply different from one who is leader first, perhaps because of the need to assuage an unusual power drive or to acquire material possessions. For such it will be a later choice to serve – after leadership is established.

A servant leader is a **low ego** leader. They are not seeking their own success and recognition, they are seeking success and recognition for their team first. This is how an Agile leader should behave.

They should seek to serve first, to help their teams become the best they can be, to allow them to take decisions, make mistakes and learn, for the team to feel ownership of the problem and connection to the purpose. They should identify and remove blockers to the team's progress. They should celebrate success as the team's success, encouraging

---

150 Greenleaf, R. K. (1970) *The Servant as Leader* (reprinted 2008). Robert E. Greenleaf Center for Servant Leadership, South Orange, NJ.

151 Hesse, H. (1932) *The Journey to the East* (reprinted 2021). General Press, New Delhi.

and championing them. They encourage the team to reflect on their progress, to identify ways they can grow and to use each task or activity as an opportunity to learn and improve.

> Servant leadership shares many attributes with good coaching. Developing and using coaching skills – asking powerful questions, actively listening, focusing on future goals – will help to develop good servant leadership behaviours.

When the team needs guidance or direction, the Agile leader gives them just enough guidance to allow them to proceed once more and just enough information to allow them to start making their own decisions again. They involve the team in decisions and strategy, helping them to understand the bigger picture and their place within it.

An Agile leader's first instinct is to step back; to trust that the team knows what they are doing and will make the best decisions. This is an uncomfortable and unfamiliar place for many leaders. It can trigger feelings of inadequacy and a reduction in status – after all, if the team is doing all the work, what role does the leader have now? It is tempting to want to step in, particularly if you know the answer or can think of a better way, but the best way to improve and develop is from within. Teams make more progress when they identify their own improvements.

Psychological safety

In 2012, when Google set out to identify what makes an ideal team, they expected that their research (codenamed Project Aristotle[152]) would confirm that putting the best and brightest people together would be important, as would ensuring that the team members were from similar backgrounds and got on well with one another; however, that wasn't what they found.[153] Who was on the team didn't seem to matter. Instead, what was more important was **how** the team worked together. They identified five aspects that were common in high-performing teams. The last four were dependability, structure and clarity, meaning, and impact, but the most significant and important aspect was that the team exhibited psychological safety. They described psychological safety as:

> [A]n individual's perception of the consequences of taking an interpersonal risk or a belief that a team is safe for risk taking in the face of being seen as ignorant, incompetent, negative, or disruptive.

In a team with high psychological safety, teammates feel safe to take risks around their team members. They feel confident that no one on the team will embarrass or punish anyone else for admitting a mistake, asking a question, or offering a new idea.

---

152 https://rework.withgoogle.com/print/guides/5721312655835136/.

153 Duhigg, C. (2016) What Google learned from its quest to build the perfect team. *The New York Times* magazine, 28 February. https://www.nytimes.com/2016/02/28/magazine/what-google-learned-from-its-quest-to-build-the-perfect-team.html.

The phrase 'psychological safety' was coined by Amy Edmondson in 1999 and described in her 2018 book, *The Fearless Organization*.[154] Creating the conditions for psychological safety requires trust, openness, curiosity about our colleagues and a non-judgemental culture. It also requires an absence of fear.

Fear holds us back from being innovative and creative and even from contributing to discussions and collaborating with our colleagues. There can be many sources of fear – for instance, some people fear public speaking or running workshops – and even for those who take public speaking in their stride, expecting a hostile audience or being in a new venue can turn a safe environment into a fearful one.

Creating an inclusive environment is also critical. When people can be themselves at work, they have more capacity to devote to do their best work. This doesn't just mean that we should not tolerate discrimination, however slight, it also means that people should be comfortable being themselves at work and not be fearful of how their colleagues would react to their sexuality, background, education or anything else. When we hide things from our colleagues because we are worried about the consequences, it consumes mental capacity that we can't devote to other things.

A consequence of a cognitively diverse team is that different opinions, experience and ideas cause challenge. Psychologically safe teams disagree and challenge one another, but they do this in a kind, helpful and constructive way. They provide 'tactful challenge'.[155] Having psychological safety doesn't mean everything needs to be 'nice'. A culture of nice is not a good thing as it leads to people trying to avoid conflict, sugar-coating issues and hiding mistakes. Being nice isn't the same as being kind. Instead, we want teams focused on the same goal and constructively using challenge to result in innovation, creativity and ultimately better solutions.

The SCARF model

David Rock created the SCARF model[156] to describe five domains of human social experience (see Table 9.2) that can trigger the brain's fight or flight response in much the same way we evolved to detect danger from tigers in prehistoric times. Perceiving an increase or decrease in these domains triggers our brain's limbic system to respond, depleting energy from the rest of the brain. The problem is that these five domains are easy to find in the workplace and can easily become threats.

Anything that decreases these domains can compromise psychological safety, while things that increases them can help to create psychological safety.

Agile leaders encourage and facilitate psychological safety in their teams. They create space for team members to get to know each other at a deeper level, and understand the similarities and differences that combine to make each team unique, even if the overt skills and job titles are the same. They become comfortable with exposing weaknesses

154 Edmundson, A. (2018) *The Fearless Organization: Creating Psychological Safety in the Workplace for Learning, Innovation, and Growth*. John Wiley & Sons, New York.

155 Reed, A. (2021) Change initiatives blog post, 15 June. CMC Partnership Consultancy Ltd. https://consultcmc.com/the-art-of-the-tactful-challenge/.

156 Rock, D. (2008) SCARF: A brain-based model for collaborating with and influencing others. *NeuroLeadership J.*, 1, 1–9.

and learning from failures and experiments. They encourage tactful, kind challenge and maximise opportunities for feedback. Overall, they treat people as people, leading with compassion and consideration.

Table 9.2 The SCARF model

Status	our sense of relative importance to others
Certainty	our ability to predict and be certain of the future
Autonomy	our sense of control over events
Relatedness	our sense of safety with others – friends not foes
Fairness	our perception of fair exchanges between people

Intrinsic motivation

One of the secrets of a high-performing team is that its members are motivated to do good work. The role of leaders is to create the optimal conditions for motivated people. The source of motivation can come from internal or external stimuli – creating intrinsic or extrinsic motivation.

Intrinsic motivation is where we do something because we want to. Our internal satisfaction is enough of a driver. Extrinsic motivation is where we do something to gain a reward or avoid a punishment – this is what most classic management approaches assume will create higher performing people, so we see policies such as bonuses, targets, stack-ranking performance assessments, on-target earnings, commissions, employee of the month and so on.

In a study of motivation, Daniel Pink discovered that for the types of knowledge work we do today, not only is intrinsic motivation a better way to create high-performing individuals and teams, but extrinsic motivation (such as bonuses for completing a task quicker) can actually lead to **poorer** performance. This finding was so profound and paradigm shifting that he called his book *Drive: The Surprising Truth About What Motivates Us*.[157]

Pink goes on to uncover what exactly intrinsic motivation means and describes three key elements that are necessary for highly motivated people and teams – once the basic hygiene factors, such as having enough pay to live on and a nice-enough working environment, are good enough to not be demotivators. Those three elements are: autonomy, mastery and purpose, as shown in Table 9.3.

Creating environments that maximise these three factors can make leaders feel uncomfortable. Increasing autonomy usually means allowing the team to make decisions that used to be made by others, such as managers or senior practitioners. Creating conditions for mastery and continuous improvement means expecting people to push themselves, work outside their comfort zone and to do new work they haven't

---

[157] Pink, D. H. (2011) *Drive: The Surprising Truth About What Motivates Us*. Canongate Books Ltd, Edinburgh.

done before. This can feel riskier than tasking the team with work you are certain they can do. Sharing the overall purpose can feel like an unnecessary distraction for the team, particularly when their tasks are clear. However, for knowledge work in a VUCA world, this discomfort in leaders is essential for teams to succeed.

Table 9.3 Factors that drive intrinsic motivation

Autonomy	The ability to have control over your life and work; to have choices and take decisions on what to do, when to do it and with whom. Autonomy and freedom motivate us to think creatively and to experiment.
Mastery	The desire to improve; to be challenged and to get better at your chosen craft.
Purpose	Working towards a meaningful and purposeful goal. The knowledge of how your work fits in to a bigger picture.

Agile leaders have to overcome this discomfort, to seek ways to provide teams with autonomy and adopt a position where the default response to any decision is for the team to make it. One way to easily increase autonomy is to increase the level of tasking. Let teams solve bigger problems with more opportunity to consider options and make decisions. This creates more opportunities for mastery by making it easier for the team to vary their level of challenge. This also requires the team to be willing and competent to make decisions themselves, which isn't the case for all teams.

The third element of intrinsic motivation – purpose – ought to be easier for Agile leaders to provide, yet it is often overlooked or the team is assumed to know it already. To test this, why not ask the team what the purpose of the product is and see how similar the answers are? When we have done this, the range of answers is staggering and there is usually at least one person who says they aren't really all that sure.

JFK AND THE JANITOR

There is a well-known story that exemplifies the effect of connecting a person to the purpose of their work.

The story goes that when JFK first visited NASA in 1961, he encountered a janitor carrying a broom. He approached him and said: 'Hi, I'm Jack Kennedy. What are you doing?'

The janitor replied: 'Well, Mr President, I'm helping put a man on the moon.'

Bringing the purpose and impact of the work to life for the team is an important role for an Agile leader. This is why the customer collaboration value is so important – when we collaborate with our customers, we understand what our work means to them. The easiest way to do this is for the work of the team to have a clear and direct connection to the purpose. For some organisations that is easy; but it isn't always clear, especially when your team isn't directly connected to the end customer or the organisation's core purpose. However, there are still things that Agile leaders can do to provide that connection. Consider things such as objectives and key results (OKRs), customer journeys or asking senior leaders to come and explain to the team how they value the work they are doing.

> The National Cyber Security Centre (NCSC) is the part of the UK Government responsible for cybersecurity advice and support. Their stated purpose is 'Helping to make the UK the safest place to live and work online.' It is easy to see how a team in the NCSC can directly connect their work to that high-level purpose.

Trusted, empowered people

The first value in the Agile Manifesto is about valuing individuals and interactions over processes and tools and requires trust and the assumption of noble intent. Many organisations ask managers to fear the worst of their people. They administer processes designed to prevent bad behaviour with approvals, monitoring and oversight. Consider expenses policies: in most companies, these run to many pages, with limits, exclusions, approvals and sanctions.

> Netflix explicitly states that they value 'people over process'[158] and prove it with an expenses policy for travel, entertainment, gifts and other expenses that is five words long: 'Act in Netflix's best interest.'

In 1999, David Marquet was faced with a problem. He was expected to be in charge, and to instruct his team what to do, but he hadn't been around long enough to know everything and didn't have time to learn. What's worse is that his team were widely regarded as the most poorly performing team. He took an unusual step and did the opposite of the expectations. He vowed never to give another order and turned to his team to decide what to do.

What's even more surprising is that Captain David Marquet was the commander of the USS *Santa Fe* at the time – a US Navy nuclear submarine. For a captain to ask his crew what to do instead of telling them was unheard of. Captain Marquet was creating a system he called Intent Based Leadership, and he describes it in his book *Turn The Ship Around*.[159] His crew came to him saying things such as 'I intend to take the ship down 400m' and he replied 'Very well.' His crew knew their mission and were empowered to make decisions about how best to deliver it. They knew the controls of the ship better than the captain and they made better, faster decisions when they were allowed to. On

---

158   https://jobs.netflix.com/culture.

159   Marquet, D. (2015) *Turn the Ship Around! A True Story of Turning Followers into Leaders*. Penguin, New York.

the *Santa Fe*, there wasn't just one brain deciding what to do, there were 134. The ship's performance improved, and within a couple of years their performance rating was the highest level ever assessed.

David Marquet had come to a similar conclusion as W. Edwards Deming did with his 95/5 rule – 95 per cent of the variation in a system is caused by the system itself, only 5 per cent is caused by the people.[160] By changing how the crew were led, the worst performing crew in the fleet became the best.

Sadly, it isn't as simple as just handing over control to the team. Not every team needs the same level of empowerment and autonomy; sometimes, too little direction and control can lead to teams freezing – unable to make progress because they don't have the confidence or the knowledge to do so.

ONE SIZE DOESN'T FIT ALL

I was leading an organisation with around 100 software engineers in Agile teams, and had fostered a culture of high autonomy and empowered teams. Not all of the teams seemed happy, and neither were all of our customers.

I conducted a survey asking the teams a number of questions, including one about autonomy. I asked if they had enough, too much or too little autonomy. The results surprised me. Only around 50 per cent said they liked the amount of autonomy they had. Of the rest, about half wanted more and half wanted less.

Trying to take all teams to the same level of empowerment had not worked. Some needed to take smaller steps; they needed more direction and less freedom, at least for the moment.

Ladder of leadership
Marquet describes this problem with his ladder of leadership.[161] This is a staged approach with seven rungs to the ladder – intent-based leadership is rung 5. Teams cannot jump up too many rungs at once, so a team or person on rung 1 or 2 may take some time and several intermediate hops before being able to reach intent-based leadership.

- At level 1 people ask to be told what to do.
- At level 2 they can explain what they see that might affect what the right decision is.
- At level 3 they say what they think should be done.
- At level 4 there is more confidence and they say what they would like to do.

---

160   The Deming statement is from his Introduction in Scholtes, P. R. (1988) *The Team Handbook: How to Use Teams to Improve Quality*. Joiner Associates, Madison, WI.

161   https://intentbasedleadership.com/.

- At level 5 they explain what they intend to do.
- At level 6 they describe the decision or action they have done.
- At level 7 the timeframe has increased and they say what they have been doing.

Agile leaders start with the assumption that people are trying to do good work and that, in most cases, poor performance is likely to be the fault of the system rather than the person. They assume trust and find ways to show that trust by delegating decision making downwards and asking teams to solve problems rather than perform tasks. They find ways to remove or mitigate processes and behaviours that remove decision making from the team.

Their role is to ensure that the work being done by the team is valuable to their stakeholders and that the team is competent and willing to complete it. Crucially, as we have already said, they must ensure the team knows the purpose of their work and are clear on the intent they are working towards.

Self-organising teams

Principle 11 of the Agile manifesto states that the best architectures, requirements and designs emerge from self-organising teams. It is rare for the most valuable work to always require the exact same mix of skills, so Agile teams adapt their composition, focus and skills to fit the work. In practice this means the specific tasks people carry out will vary and might not always be their preferred role. However, it can be tempting to pick lower priority work that you enjoy rather than more valuable but less enjoyable work. This delays value getting to the customer and risks starting work that never becomes a priority.

The best way to create a self-organising team is to hire a team that can adapt, change and learn. Hiring for fixed roles and specific skillsets might seem sensible when you understand their first project, but it doesn't help when the skills need to change. Instead, 'T-shaped professionals' have one or more main skills but are also able to do other roles, perhaps at a lower skill level. This means they are much more flexible, and it is much more likely that across the whole team, they will have all the skills necessary to deliver the highest value work.

The second critical attribute for self-organising teams is to be able to learn new skills. Particularly in fast changing technical roles, skills don't stay current for long and there are always new technologies, frameworks, systems and approaches to learn. Practices such as pair programming, buddying, mentoring and internal TED-style talks can help team members to learn from one another, but leaders must also invest time for more formal or directed learning. Once again, hiring people with a passion for learning and staying up to date is a good start.

People with a passion to learn and experiment can't always find the opportunities to do so in their team. So why not find another way?

Since 2005, software company Atlassian have been hosting quarterly events for their employees where they have 24 hours to work on anything they want. They self-organise into teams, get creative and spend the day (and night) working together on something they can deliver. Originally called 'FedEx days' (because they had to deliver in 24 hours), they are now called 'ShipIt days'[162] and are a core part of their culture. They foster creativity and innovation and are a safe place to try new technologies.

Agile leaders expect change and expect their teams to respond to that change. They hire and form teams based as much on aptitude and potential future skills as for current ability. They create opportunities for people to grow and build team environments where moving around to create a better skills mix or a development opportunity is welcomed. Their teams are optimised for the work being done today and aren't afraid to rebalance, reset and evolve to match the shape needed for tomorrow's work.

This doesn't always mean teams must be stable. While long-lived teams can be high performing, it is also possible to create high-performing teams that are short-lived or change frequently – in fact, dynamic reteaming is a core attribute of the Agile approach FAST (see Chapter 11). In our experience, the stability of team membership is far less significant in creating a high-performing team than the other factors we describe in this chapter. The benefits of being able to flex a team to optimise it for the changing needs of its members and the business far outweigh the risk that they take a little time to get themselves up to speed.

Creating strategic alignment

We know from Dan Pink's work that high levels of autonomy are a powerful contributor to intrinsic motivation in knowledge workers (see Intrinsic motivation in this chapter). For startups and small, independent teams this can be straightforward to create, but it presents a problem in larger organisations, particularly those with more traditional structures and management approaches.

If the team is deciding what they do, how do you know they are doing the right thing? If you are lucky, the team might be connected to the high-level vision and be well enough informed that all their actions will be completely aligned with it. However, that isn't always the case, so it is the role of a good leader to provide that alignment.

This combination of alignment and autonomy is not as contradictory as you may think. Alignment is not the opposite of autonomy; instead, it is better to think of them as two axes that we can move along in either direction. This concept was introduced in Stephen Bungay's *The Art of Action*,[163] where he used his military historian background to explain leadership theory. In a military context, the generals simply cannot micromanage the war fighters on the ground. Instead, they set clear direction for the soldiers (the what

---

162 https://www.atlassian.com/company/shipit.

163 Bungay, S. (2011) *The Art of Action: How Leaders Close the Gaps Between Plans, Actions and Results.* Nicholas Brealey Publishing, Boston, MA.

and the why) and trust their training and competence with high levels of autonomy in how they achieve the objective.

The music streaming company Spotify is famous for their approach to Agile, with their unique language and innovative style to applying an Agile methodology to their development. In 2014, one of their coaches, Henrik Kniberg, used quirky diagrams in presentations to explain their method.[164] Part of their approach is a version of Bungay's alignment and autonomy graph. The original described alignment (the intent; the what and the why) and autonomy (the how) as two axes and shows that when both are high, we achieve the best results. Kniberg's Spotify model is described in his YouTube video,[165] making it more relatable. Our version, based on the loyalty card case study, is shown in Figure 9.2.

Figure 9.2 Balancing alignment and autonomy

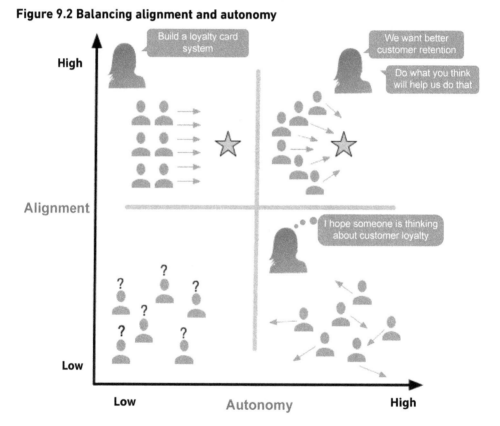

Balancing alignment and autonomy
The role of the leader is to provide sufficient alignment and strategic direction for the team, while also providing sufficient autonomy for them to make their own decisions

164 https://engineering.atspotify.com/2014/03/27/spotify-engineering-culture-part-1/.

165 Kniberg, H. (2015) Alignment autonomy clip. YouTube. https://www.youtube.com/watch?v=_qlh2sYXcQc.

and set their own direction. Too much alignment without autonomy requires the leader to have lots of detailed information and leads to feelings of micromanagement in the team. Too little alignment with high autonomy and the team can do what they want, but don't really understand why they are doing the work. They risk building the wrong thing. Too little alignment and too little autonomy and the team doesn't feel empowered to work out what to do and isn't given instruction. This leads to confusion, inaction or irrelevant work being done.

Get both elements right, however, and the team is clear on its purpose (one of Dan Pink's drivers of motivation) and clear on what they can do to achieve it. There is just enough control for the leader to be confident that the team is working on the most valuable work, and just enough direction that the team has control and autonomy over what they are doing and how they are doing it.

But it isn't as simple as that. Alignment isn't just with the high-level strategic goal, or the highest priority user needs. It also applies to technical decisions, style, branding, security, compliance, people processes and many other aspects. Each of these dimensions may require different levels of alignment and autonomy. The leader's role is to get the balance right for all of them.

Three levels of autonomy
Table 9.4 breaks autonomy down into three distinct levels.

Table 9.4 Three levels of autonomy

Level 1	pure autonomy
Level 2	constrained autonomy
Level 3	no autonomy

The first level of autonomy, **pure autonomy**, is where the team has complete control over what they do. Examples of this may be how they implement an algorithm, what font they choose for their report or what their definitions of done are. For some teams, this could extend to all their work, but for other teams this isn't true.

At the other end of the scale is **no autonomy**, where the team has no choice. For example, there may be a corporate design system that defines what colours and fonts to use on the website; a particular logging or auditing standard may be required for security reasons; or perhaps certain products or technologies must be used. Large organisations usually have fixed people processes, such as leave policy, sickness absence reporting, and so on; most teams will have some elements in this category.

In between pure autonomy and no autonomy lies **constrained autonomy**. This is where the team is still responsible for their decisions, but they must consult with a wider set of stakeholders to be confident that they are making the right decisions. They aren't asking for permission or conceding the decision elsewhere, but there are factors outside their immediate team that may affect their decision and it is imperative that they know this. For example, their system may include a payment component; while they could implement this themselves, it's possible that other teams may have already implemented something they can reuse, or have experience the team could benefit from. Or perhaps other teams may reuse something that this team is creating for the first time, so perhaps that may make the team implement it differently.

The role of an Agile leader is to create an environment where these connections and conversations happen. One where the team has the humility to ask for help and has a network of people who can provide that help.

It is important that the team still makes the decision. Managers (especially those with a Theory X background) tend to want to control more. This can move decisions away from the team. Perhaps the manager doesn't trust that the team will do the necessary consultation, or will make the decision for the team, turning it into a constraint, not a choice.

Another risk is that constraints aren't challenged, meaning opportunities to improve, update or replace them are lost. In the payment system example, perhaps there have been advances in technology that means our team should build a new solution rather than reuse an existing one. This should be the team's choice, but one that is made in consultation with other teams and other stakeholders.

CREATING HIGH-PERFORMING TEAMS

The six key outcomes we have just described are all independently valuable, but deliver best results when implemented together. However, like much in Agile, they don't come for free and just hoping they will happen won't be enough. The Agile leader must actively create the environment for these six outcomes to establish, flourish and be sustained.

This is usually easier with small teams and becomes harder as the number of people and teams grow. As we seek to lead more people, the tendency to move towards Theory X management – adding processes, tools and even additional managers – can be strong. It is easy to justify each small, individual change, but, when they begin to add together, the impact on the culture and environment can be catastrophic.

A public sector organisation was struggling to respond to the pace of change their customers expected. They had established teams that were using Agile practices but were still in a more Waterfall mindset. To solve this, they opened a new office, hired for culture fit and an Agile mindset, and started applying Agile approaches from the outset.

This worked well, and grew to well over 100 developers. They kept a relatively flat hierarchy and adopted many of the qualities we describe in this book: they were transparent, balanced autonomy with alignment, focused on development and continuous improvement and had highly engaged and motivated people.

Three years later, however, they looked and felt very different. There were still roughly the same number of people, but now had more management, oversight and non-delivery focused roles, mainly resourced from jobs that used to be developers. Teams that had felt part of a wider, bigger development were now focused on developing just one component. Divestment went up, engagement and motivation went down, and they are now almost indistinguishable from their parent organisation's teams.

Each small change, such as establishing a test lead, adding a more senior manager (to show how important the area was) or creating roles for outreach and innovation, made sense in isolation – and each of these changes was a well-intentioned attempt to make the organisation better – but each change also diluted one or more of the six leadership outcomes. They changed the opportunities for teams to have impact on the wider organisation and changed the emotional contract each person had with the organisation. Each change moved the organisation more towards the right of the Agile Manifesto and further from the ideals of the Corporate Rebels.

Creating and maintaining high-performing teams is a tricky balancing act for an Agile leader. Not only must you seek to maximise the six outcomes we have described, but, once there, you must also stop them being eroded. It is a bit like plate spinning in that it requires initial effort to get going but without a little involvement now and then to maintain momentum, the plates come crashing to the ground.

DON'T ASK WHY, ASK WHY NOT?

Agile teams are self-organising and have the skills, resources, authority and ability to deliver products of value to the end customer.

As teams and organisations grow, it can be common to see elements of that delivery taken out of the team and moved elsewhere – to another team or perhaps a newly created manager role. Rather than seek to provide justification as to why that is a good thing, concentrate on identifying the reasons why it might not be a good idea. What are the negative consequences to the change? Very often, the negatives quickly outweigh the positive reasons.

Teams contain individuals

To achieve high-performing teams also requires balancing the needs of the team with the needs of the individuals in the team. Great teams manage to align those two needs, but it can take some effort and it is easy to undo.

We have all probably experienced that state where we get so engrossed in our work that time seems to stand still, we forget about eating and drinking and, when we eventually look up, hours have passed. This is when we do some of our best work, and why multi-tasking and being constantly interrupted is so damaging.

Psychologist Mihaly Csikszentmihalyi describes this state as 'flow'[166] – when skill and challenge are balanced. This presents leaders with a challenge themselves:

> Surely, we want team members to be doing tasks we know they are good at, and we know they will successfully complete. But that work may not help them get into flow.

> If they need new, challenging work to get into flow, how do I know they can do it? Doesn't that add too much risk?

Of course, it's not always that bad. Sometimes, part of the challenge can be work that is new, interesting or high purpose, even when it is something you have done lots of times before and are certain to do well. However, in time, carrying out homogenous work will increase your skill level to the point where you cease to find it challenging. You risk slipping into boredom and apathy, when, ironically, the quality of your work will often suffer.

High-performing teams adjust the work so that each team member is challenged, interested and productive. They need sufficient autonomy and complex and interesting enough work to be able to do this. This is easier when they start with larger, more complex work that they can break down in different ways to achieve the right mix of complexity.

Sometimes, the best thing may be to adjust the team membership. Some people believe that only stable, long-lived teams can be high performing. This isn't true. Some very poorly performing teams are stable and long-lived, and some high-performing teams have constant movement of membership. What is important is that the change in team membership comes from the team; when they initiate the change, they will welcome and assimilate the new people quickly. Frequently welcoming new people also makes teams used to sharing their approaches and information and reduces silos of knowledge and single points of failure.

These approaches allow professional and personal development to be advanced along with product delivery, but it does require the encouragement and trust of leaders. Agile leaders understand the importance of high-performing teams and the actions that create, maintain and damage them.

THE IMPORTANCE OF CULTURE

The story of the software team that changed with new management initiatives in the previous section is an example of how the culture of an organisation can quickly change even though most of the people don't; David Marquet's story of the *Santa Fe* is another. But one of the most powerful stories of culture change being a product of the system, not the people, comes from motor manufacturing. It is an appropriate setting, given how the production line innovation of Henry Ford shaped much of today's thinking of management, and the Toyota Way brought us Lean process improvement

---

166 Csikszentmihalyi, M. (2011) *Flow: The Psychology of Optimal Experience*. Harper Collins, New York.

and influenced many of the Agile practices we have discussed. It is a story involving Toyota and their partnership with General Motors (GM) in the United States – New United Motor Manufacturing Inc (NUMMI).

In 1982 GM closed their manufacturing plant in Fremont, California. It was one of their poorest performing factories. There were over 6000 grievances on the books, drugs and alcohol were rife, absenteeism was over 20 per cent and it was regarded as the worst plant in the company. Two years later, NUMMI – a joint venture between GM and Toyota – reopened the plant and within one year absenteeism dropped to 2 per cent and the plant was rated as GM's best. The most surprising thing was that this was done with the same people who worked at the previous plant – including the 'troublemakers' – and with the same unions and union leaders. They even had a 'no lay-offs' policy.

What Toyota had managed to do was completely change the culture of the plant without needing to change the people. As John Shook described in *MIT Sloan Management Review*,[167] they didn't seek to change how people felt or thought – instead, they focused on changing how people **behaved**. It was influencing what people did that made the most significant impact on how they felt and thought. The different behaviours led to the different culture.

Some of these behaviour changes were simple: managers and staff were more equal; there were no separate canteens or reserved parking spaces; there was a flat pay structure. Some changes were more extreme: if there was a problem, any worker could pull the 'Andon Cord', which would stop the line, causing everyone to come over to help solve the problem. When things go wrong, the Toyota Way is not to attribute blame – instead, problems are treated as an opportunity to make improvements.

Establishing and maintaining a new culture is difficult. The GM managers were frequently tempted to revert to old ways, to cut corners to keep the production line moving or to compromise on quality, but by staying true to the system – keeping their faith, recognising their mistakes and working with the workforce, not against them – the plant continued to thrive until it eventually shut in 2010. It is now owned by Tesla.

The culture of a team is critical to its success. While culture can come from the people, it is defined by how those people behave, not by who those people are. Agile leaders focus on the behaviours they want to see and assume that the people can adapt to those new behaviours. Conversely, no matter what you ask of your people, when their behaviours and actions do not change, neither will the culture. You cannot transform by continuing to do the same things as you used to do, even if you pretend you are by using new names or giving yourself a new job title.

LEADERSHIP IN AGILE TEAMS

We have spoken in this chapter about the importance of leadership for Agile teams, but where do we find it? The simple answer is that it should be everywhere. Agile teams are not hierarchical. Self-organising teams specifically don't need a hierarchy, which means

---

167   Shook, J. (2010) How to change a culture: Lessons from NUMMI. *MIT Sloan Man. Rev.*, Winter. https://www.lean.org/ Search/Documents/35.pdf.

that anyone can take on a leadership role, but there are some roles that lend themselves more towards some elements of leadership than others, even with simple frameworks.

The Product Owner role is a natural role to provide leadership on alignment, strategy and purpose. The role is to ensure that the team is delivering the work of highest value, so requires them to know what that is.

The Scrum Guide explicitly states that the Scrum Master is a servant leader. So, the Scrum Master role is well placed to provide leadership on team practices, encouraging the team to self-organise, collaborate, learn from one another and so on. They can also initiate events that can grow psychological safety or create alignment, such as Agile chartering/Liftoff[168] or the daily check-in protocol.[169]

There are also opportunities to lead for everyone in an Agile team, particularly in fostering psychological safety, and creating intrinsic motivation, self-organisation and trust. However, as we saw in the case study earlier, it is leaders (and managers) outside the team that can have the greatest impact – both positive and negative. Anyone that the team interacts with can be in a leadership role, including people who may not think they need to know anything about Agile. However, as we have shown in this chapter, Agile leadership is a critical enabler to the advantages of Agile and it is imperative that leaders – wherever they are – know this and are actively seeking ways to demonstrate Agile leadership.

Leadership roles in scaled approaches

We should mention other roles that exist in the various scaled Agile approaches, but do so with some hesitation. As we explore in Chapter 11, there are specific leadership roles defined in some Agile methods. It should be logical to assume that these roles would promote good Agile leadership; however, while that may be the intention of the method creators, in practice it isn't always what we see. Instead, we often see these roles interpreted in ways that do not promote good Agile behaviours nor demonstrate good Agile leadership. We see a lot of Theory X management behaviours, a lot of decisions taken away from the teams, a lot of approvals, gates and delays, and a lot of people behaving in the same ways they did when they were in traditional, heavyweight programme delivery jobs.

Whatever role you are in, whatever job title you have and whatever other people are doing, we implore you to stick to the principles and values of Agile. This chapter and this book will help you to do that.

AGILE COACHING

One of the most effective ways to optimise your Agile leadership is to engage an Agile coach to help you. A good Agile coach will help to challenge, support and encourage you to become a better Agile leader.

---

168   Larsen, D. and Nies, A. (2016) *Liftoff: Start and Sustain Successful Agile Teams* (2nd edn). Pragmatic Bookshelf, Dallas, TX.

169   https://thecoreprotocols.org/protocols/checkin.html.

Agile coaching is something you should expect to see at all levels within your organisation – working with individuals, teams and leaders. It isn't a one-way role. Good Agile coaches have coaches themselves. We do, and so do our coaches. The principle of continuous learning means that we always have room to grow, develop and improve. Coaching can help us with that growth no matter how skilled we already are.

What exactly is an Agile coach?

Many people are familiar with executive or leadership coaches. An Agile coach is similar and can provide many of the same benefits; however, what sets an Agile coach apart is that they come with a bias towards Agile. This sounds obvious, but it means that an Agile coach will generally have more tools at their disposal to help their coachee. In addition to the skills of an executive coach, they are also experienced in a wide range of Agile practices and approaches.

In an Agile coaching conversation, an Agile coach can move between three stances – coaching, mentoring and consultancy/teaching – as shown in the Agile coaching model in Figure 9.3.[170]

Figure 9.3 Agile coaching model

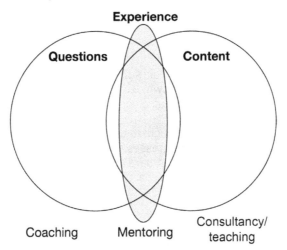

Sometimes an Agile coach uses powerful questions with their clients, but success depends on the client being able to reach the answer themselves. Sometimes, an Agile coach is teaching or consulting on a specific topic, where success depends on that specific topic being the right one for the client. By bringing broad Agile expertise and knowledge to the engagement, an Agile coach can help to bridge this gap with mentoring – combining powerful questions and active listening with information, experience, stories and advice that is tailored to the context of the situation. This helps the coach to

---

170 Coaching model developed from an idea from John McFadyen.

accelerate the client's growth towards an Agile mindset by adapting to their needs and having a broad toolkit of models, practices and ideas to draw upon.

Ideally, coaches will be mostly on the questions side, but sometimes the right thing is to provide content and answer questions, not ask them. Just as we adjust our leadership styles based on the maturity and preferences of the teams, we also adjust our coaching style.

Coaching teams

One-to-one coaching with an Agile coach is a powerful way to develop and advance Agile skill and competence. Agile coaches can also have a powerful impact on teams. As we discuss throughout this book, Agile is challenging to do well and it is easy for teams to lose focus. An Agile coach can help to identify this happening and coach the teams in how to bring themselves back on track.

Agile coaches can be full-time members of the team, or they can coach multiple teams. Each approach can work well. Coaches within the team can help to optimise practices and facilitate team events. Coaches outside the team can bring a detachment that could provide insights that the team miss as they are too close to the problem.

For more guidance on Agile coaching, see Lyssa Adkins' fabulous book *Coaching Agile Teams*.[171]

Measuring value

By definition, any coach aims to help their subject, whether individual or team, reach their own conclusions and make their own decisions; the coach doesn't tell them what to do. This can make measuring the value of coaching incredibly difficult.

The primary impact of Agile coaching ought to be more value for the customer, because the team optimises the work as it progresses so that a higher proportion of the work done is useful to the customer. This is hard to attribute to the coaching, since the decisions are made by the team, not the coach.

In 2005, internet giant Yahoo was adopting Scrum and Agile throughout the organisation. Gabrielle Benefield was one of the consultants helping them and describes the rollout in her paper, 'Rolling out Agile in a Large Enterprise'.[172] To begin with they got good feedback, with 64 per cent of teams reporting that using Scrum was making them deliver more business value; but as they scaled, they began to experience the kinds of challenges we describe in this book. Just encouraging teams to adopt Scrum didn't seem to be enough for lasting improvement.

---

171 Adkins, L. (2010) *Coaching Agile Teams: A Companion for Scrum Masters, Agile Coaches and Project Managers in Transition*. Addison-Wesley, Boston, MA.

172 Benefield, G. (2008) Rolling out Agile in a large enterprise. http://static1.1.sqspcdn.com/static/f/447037/6486321/1270929190703/YahooAgileRollout.pdf.

In response, they introduced a coaching model to help teams navigate these new ways of working and make the best of them. However, measuring the effectiveness of the coaching was harder to do. In the end, they settled on asking teams if they felt they were more productive. This is a subjective and non-ideal measure, but it did give them some powerful results. They found teams consistently reported productivity improvements at an average of 39 per cent. This self-reporting also led to an increase in coaching sessions as teams and their customers sought to maintain these levels of productivity.

The work mentioned above at Yahoo led to some statistics on the power of Agile coaching that are still realistic today:

- One Agile coach can coach around 10 teams a year.
- If each team is around 10 people, each coach has a reach of around 1:100.
- With a (conservative) 30 per cent improvement in productivity, each Agile coach creates the equivalent of an **additional 30 team members** per year.

That is an attractive return on investment.

A word on quality

As with many skills in Agile and IT, there is no quality threshold to call oneself an Agile coach. This means that people can (and do) market themselves as an Agile coach when they have little skill or experience in the craft. Sadly, poor coaches can do more harm than good by embedding poor practices, failing to identify systemic problems and focusing on the wrong things.

In an article by enterprise coach John McFadyen,[173] he compares Agile coaches to sports coaches. Some are entry level, capable of doing a good job teaching teams the basics. Like a Sunday league coach, they mostly teach rather than coach, but do so with skill and passion.

The next level is intermediate; the public, minor leagues. Here we have player-coaches, those who are in a coaching role, but also on the team themselves, often the best player on the team. They know everyone's role inside out, and can play well in most positions. They become a coach because they love helping others and are using the mix of practitioner and coach to hone their coaching craft.

At the final level, we have professional coaches. Their skill as a player isn't enough to make them a good coach; they need new skills and the time and opportunity to hone them. They progressively improve and validate their skills and can help others be better practitioners than perhaps they could be themselves. This is the level of coach we need for larger transformations or complex Agile challenges.

---

173 McFadyen, J. (2020) Agile coaching capability. Agile Centre. https://www.agilecentre.com/resources/article/agile-coaching-capability/.

Good Agile coaches recognise this transition and have invested in their coaching skill and craft. This may be though Agile certifications, such as those from Scrum Alliance or ICAgile, or could be from pure coaching training, but they will certainly be able to describe their journey, which is unlikely to be smooth. They will be able to tell stories of the problems they have faced, the mistakes they have learned from the people and books that have inspired them and where their journey is going now. If they can't convince you of this, perhaps they aren't the right person to help you on your path to being a great Agile leader.

SUMMARY

Most Agile teams do not exist in isolation, and they will not thrive if the leadership, management and governance around them is not also Agile. Yet, Agile leadership is not well described and often overlooked in Agile transformations in favour of applying Agile practices in delivery teams.

The default style for many managers and leaders is based on the industrial styles of management that were developed in the early 20th century. While these work well for predictable, repetitive work such as production lines, they are not well suited to the knowledge work that most organisations depend upon today. Instead, Agile leaders should seek to achieve for their teams the six leadership outcomes in Table 9.5.

Table 9.5 Six leadership outcomes for Agile leaders

Servant leadership	Leaders act with low ego. Their first objective is to serve their teams, not direct them.
Psychological safety	Teams trust that they can speak out, challenge and be themselves at work without fearing the consequences.
Intrinsic motivation	People motivate themselves when they have autonomy, can build mastery and have clear purpose.
Empowered, trusted teams	The people closest to the information will make better, data-driven decisions when they are trusted to do so.
Self-organising teams	Teams that have all the skills, experience and authority to deliver value for the end user. When those people are 'T-shaped' they can self-organise to ensure the most valuable work is always being done.
Strategic alignment	Autonomy must be balanced with alignment. Agile leaders connect teams with the strategic purpose of their work at the right level to empower and not micromanage them.

Each of these six outcomes will help teams work in an Agile way, but they are not simple or easy to achieve. They will feel alien, counter-intuitive and even wrong to many people used to traditional management. However, persevering will result in more empowered, engaged and motivated teams that make better decisions and deliver more value for their customers.

When trying to achieve and sustain these six outcomes, Agile coaches can be an invaluable support. Good Agile coaches support and empower teams and help leaders to identify challenges and blockers to their Agile journey.

10 MANAGING THE PRODUCT

The product is the single most important artefact in Agile; understanding how to create and manage it is vital

There is no point in leading the perfect teams and developing the product impeccably if it won't provide value to the customer. The Agile Manifesto is clear that the customer and the business are critical elements of an Agile delivery, so it follows that managing the product and ensuring it will deliver value to the customer is extremely important.

Some requirements practices were introduced in Chapter 8, but this chapter goes into more depth to help you focus on managing the product, including identifying customers and stakeholders, understanding their needs and validating that those needs have been met.

Throughout this book we have emphasised the value and benefits Agile methods can bring. However, few Agile approaches discuss in much detail how to identify user needs and requirements in the first place, a well-formed backlog is just assumed to exist. Yet, without a clear view on the user need, we will struggle to maintain a focus on value.

In fact, it is often the case then even the customer isn't clear on what they need. It is common for customers to describe the product or solution they think they need, but this solution focus can often mask their real needs. We must find ways to better understand those needs while still adhering to the Agile values and principles and avoiding big up-front requirements capture.

This chapter will uncover and share techniques to help you:

- understand customer needs;
- capture product ideas in roadmaps;
- break those ideas down into manageable work items;
- organise them in product and iteration backlogs.

UNDERSTANDING AND MANAGING STAKEHOLDERS

'Those who build the product must speak to those who will use it', Mike Cohn.[174]

---

174 Cohn, M. (2004) *User Stories Applied: For Agile Software Development.* Addison-Wesley, Boston, MA.

The statement above seems obvious, yet all too often we see products not meeting customer expectations and disappointment experienced by both the customer and the delivery team. There may be many reasons for this, but essentially it comes down to not properly understanding the customer or wider stakeholder needs or expectations.

First, it is useful to define what we mean by stakeholder. We define a stakeholder as **anyone who has a vested interest in, or is affected by, the product**.

A stakeholder, therefore, is wider than just the user and customer and can include many people with knowledge or interest in the product, such as:

- the person paying for the product, who may not be an end user;
- subject matter experts;
- managers of end users;
- external partners and suppliers;
- technology specialists and architects;
- security experts;
- legal advisors or lawyers;
- user experience designers;
- sales and marketing.

Each of these stakeholders needs to be understood, as well as the more obvious customer or user, as they may have an impact on whether our product is successful. If we only focus on the customer or end user, we could deliver a product that meets user expectations but may fail in other ways, such as not integrating with other systems, being too expensive to produce, failing legal or security compliance or addressing the wrong market segment.

For the rest of this chapter, we will focus on understanding and building a relationship with the customer who will benefit most from the product. However, all these techniques can, and should, be applied more widely to other stakeholders.

Challenges in understanding customer needs

We know that understanding your customer is critical to the success of the product, yet this is not always as easy as it should be. Some of the challenges we can face are discussed in Table 10.1.

There are several techniques that we can use to understand our customers and their needs. Some of our favourites are shown in Figure 10.1 and described in the following sections.

Context diagrams

Before delving into user stories or identifying user needs for a product, it is a good idea to first understand and agree the initial context of the product. This is a starting point for defining the scope, which is important for managing user expectations.

Table 10.1 Challenges in understanding customer needs

Customer expressing a solution, not their need	Many customers find it easier to state the solution they want rather than expressing what they actually need. While their solution may provide them with the value they desire, there may also be better, cheaper or faster ways to address the underlying need. As car manufacturer Henry Ford's (probably apocryphal) quote goes: 'If I had asked people what they wanted, they would have said "Faster horses".'
	This doesn't mean every solution needs to be a radical innovation, but understanding the customer's underlying needs affords the delivery team much more flexibility to design a solution that best meets that need.
	A question we often ask when a customer proposes the solution is: 'What is the problem for which this is the right solution?' This can often uncover the real user need.
Managing customer expectations	In the early stage of product development, it can be easy to agree a vision for the product with the end users that may not be achievable with the time or money available.
	Be mindful of the Agile values and don't commit to an end goal at the start. Instead, treat the goal as desirable but be prepared to change and evolve it as new ideas and information emerge during development.
	Visions and roadmaps iterate and evolve just like other product artefacts. We must avoid them becoming contracts or commitments just because they have senior stakeholder support when they are first agreed.
No customer availability	When working in an iterative and incremental way it is imperative to have access to the customer to collaborate and ask them questions.
	In reality, customers tend to be busy doing their day job and can struggle to find the time to be available as much as the development team would want.
	One way to mitigate this is to help them focus their time on the highest value activities such as iteration planning, backlog refinement and iteration reviews. Agreeing small amounts of time regularly (say, 15 minutes each day) can be more valuable than longer meetings less frequently. This means the team can always have urgent questions answered relatively quickly.
	Another useful strategy is to have several other subject matter experts whom the main customer trusts to answer on their behalf.
The wrong customer	Sometimes the person working with the development team in the Product Owner role may not have the skills, knowledge or authority necessary.
	It is important to recognise if you are in this situation and try to resolve it, particularly when they don't have the right authority. The Product Owner must be empowered to make decisions about the product.
	Where the person is lacking skill or experience, the development team, along with specialists such as business analysts or UX designers, can support them.

Figure 10.1 Techniques to help understand our customers

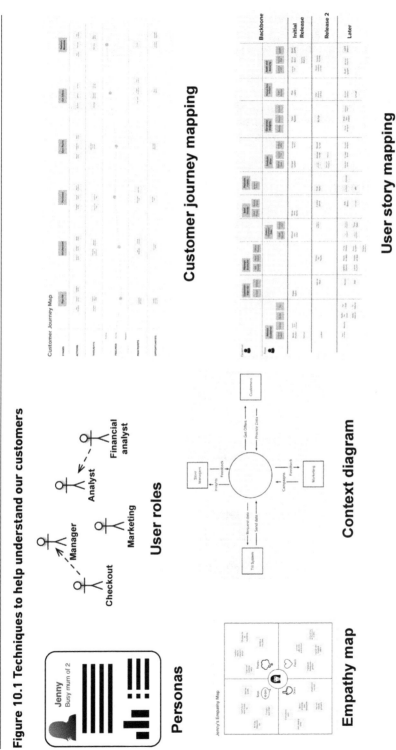

There will always be more potential work than you will have time or resource to accomplish, and customers are adept at identifying more once you begin. Thus, defining and agreeing an initial scope boundary is key to meeting product goals.

A context diagram shows the interactions between a product, or system, and the things outside that product/system; these interactions can be people, other systems or other organisations. It provides a solid foundation for exploring these interactions with the context of the product, and is a great starting point to explore user roles. An example of a context diagram, for our loyalty card programme, is in Figure 10.2.

Figure 10.2 Context diagram

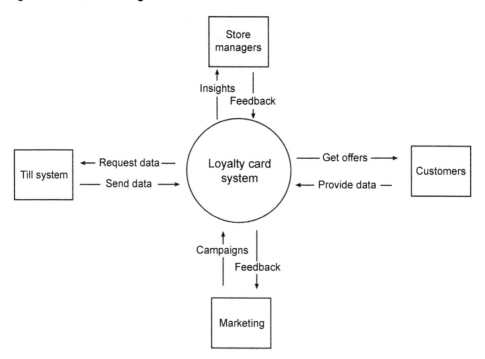

Context diagrams are one way to understand and define a product context. They are also described as 'boundaries and interactions' in Diana Larsen and Ainsley Nies's book, *Liftoff*.[175] Examining boundaries and interactions is important throughout Agile chartering – in purpose and alignment but especially in context, where understanding the external relationships and dependencies is critical to success. Exploring the context can identify (or confirm) where the team relies on others for an element of the solution. For example, teams often forget about internal stakeholders such as sales, marketing, legal or security whose involvement is essential to the product delivering value.

---

175 Larsen, D. and Nies, A. (2016) *Liftoff: Start and Sustain Successful Agile Teams* (2nd edn). Pragmatic Bookshelf, Dallas, TX.

Empathy mapping

The empathy map[176] was designed by David Gray as part of a toolkit called Gamestorming.[177] It helps teams to obtain shared understanding and empathy for others, which particularly helps to improve customer experience. It also works well in conjunction with personas (described next). The empathy map contains seven key areas, as shown in Table 10.2.

Table 10.2 The seven key elements of empathy mapping

The goal	**Who** are we empathising with?
	What do they need to do?
Their expertise	What do they **see**?
	What do they **say**?
	What do they **do**?
	What do they **hear**?
What goes on inside their head?	What do they **think** and feel?

Considering each of these elements helps us to 'walk a mile in the customers' shoes' and can lead to more insightful analysis of requirements and better alignment of priorities with customer needs. Building empathy with your customer will also improve your relationship with them.

Personas and user roles

Once the product context is understood we can set about better understanding the customers of the product. Personas and user roles are two such techniques for this; however, we often see them being misused or amalgamated into one, so they are worth considering together.

Personas and user roles are complementary, yet distinctly different, techniques that both help us to understand our customer better. They can be used separately, but are most powerful together. The main distinctions are discussed in Table 10.3.

Figure 10.3 shows the relationship between role and persona and shows the differences. Creating personas will help to add value to our understanding of a role by helping us to consider the emotional and behavioural aspects that different types of user bring.

---

[176] Gray, D. (2017) Updated empathy map canvas. The XPlane Collection, 15 June. https://medium.com/the-xplane-collection/updated-empathy-map-canvas-46df22df3c8a.

[177] Gray, D., Brown, S. and Macanufo, J. (2010) *Gamestorming: A Playbook for Innovators, Rulebreakers, and Changemakers.* O'Reilly Media, Sebastopol, CA. See also: https://gamestorming.com.

Table 10.3 Personas and user roles

User role	Describes the tasks or activities performed within a given system by an individual in a specified role.
	Roles, such as use case actors or user roles, represent a single user group (e.g. loyalty programme customer) and focus on how that user/group interacts with the system, the steps they take and the tasks they perform.
Persona	Describes fictional, yet realistic, characteristics of a typical or target user. They are an archetype not an actual living person and used to understand the motivation and drivers from a customer perspective.
	They are used in marketing or in UX design as part of user research to empathise with a user group/role and understand their personal needs, concerns and goals.

A common mistake is to extend personas to cover both the role and the persona. This is unnecessary, confuses the distinct value brought by the two perspectives and results in duplication where multiple personas all share the same role.

Figure 10.3 Relationship between role and persona

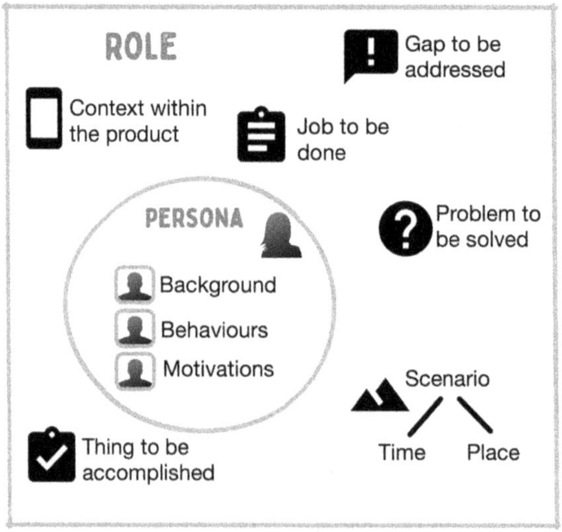

Personas can represent a range of users, not always a single user role, and a single user role can be taken by many personas. For example, within our loyalty programme we have a user role that is Loyalty Card Customers. They perform tasks such as view loyalty points, earn loyalty points, spend loyalty points. Some personas associated with the Loyalty Card Customer role include:

- elderly customer with no IT;
- tech-savvy customer;
- cost-conscious customer.

While they will all want to earn loyalty card points and view their current loyalty points, they may also have different needs determined by the persona. For instance, a teenage customer who is technology savvy may only want to engage through a mobile app, while an elderly customer without a smartphone may only want to interact by post or telephone.

Knowing the relative percentages of personas is important: if 15 per cent of customers don't have or don't want to use IT, we still need to consider their needs in our product development, but we may want to focus on the other 85 per cent first. Conversely, if the 15 per cent are higher spenders or more frequent shoppers, we may want to focus on them first.

Similarly, our cost-conscious customer persona could also work for the store and therefore sometimes be in the Cashier User role and interact with the system in a different way. Examples of a role description and a persona are shown in Figures 10.4 and 10.5.

Figure 10.4 Role description example

Role Description	Loyalty Card Customer

The Loyalty Card Customer is a customer of AG Stores who is eligible to obtain a loyalty card. The loyalty programme results in more frequent and higher value spending and a more positive impression of AG Stores.

Actions they may take include:
- Apply for a loyalty card
- View and manage their account
- Cancel account
- Collect points
- Redeem points for rewards
- Receive information and marketing

One simple way to avoid confusing roles and personas is to ensure that each role has multiple personas associated with it. Having a 1:1 relationship is an anti-pattern that should be avoided, as shown in Figure 10.6.

If you are struggling to find more than one persona for a role, you may find it more useful to just have one role and use empathy mapping (discussed earlier in this chapter) against that role. Creating just one persona is probably creating more work than is necessary and doesn't really add much value.

Figure 10.5 Persona example

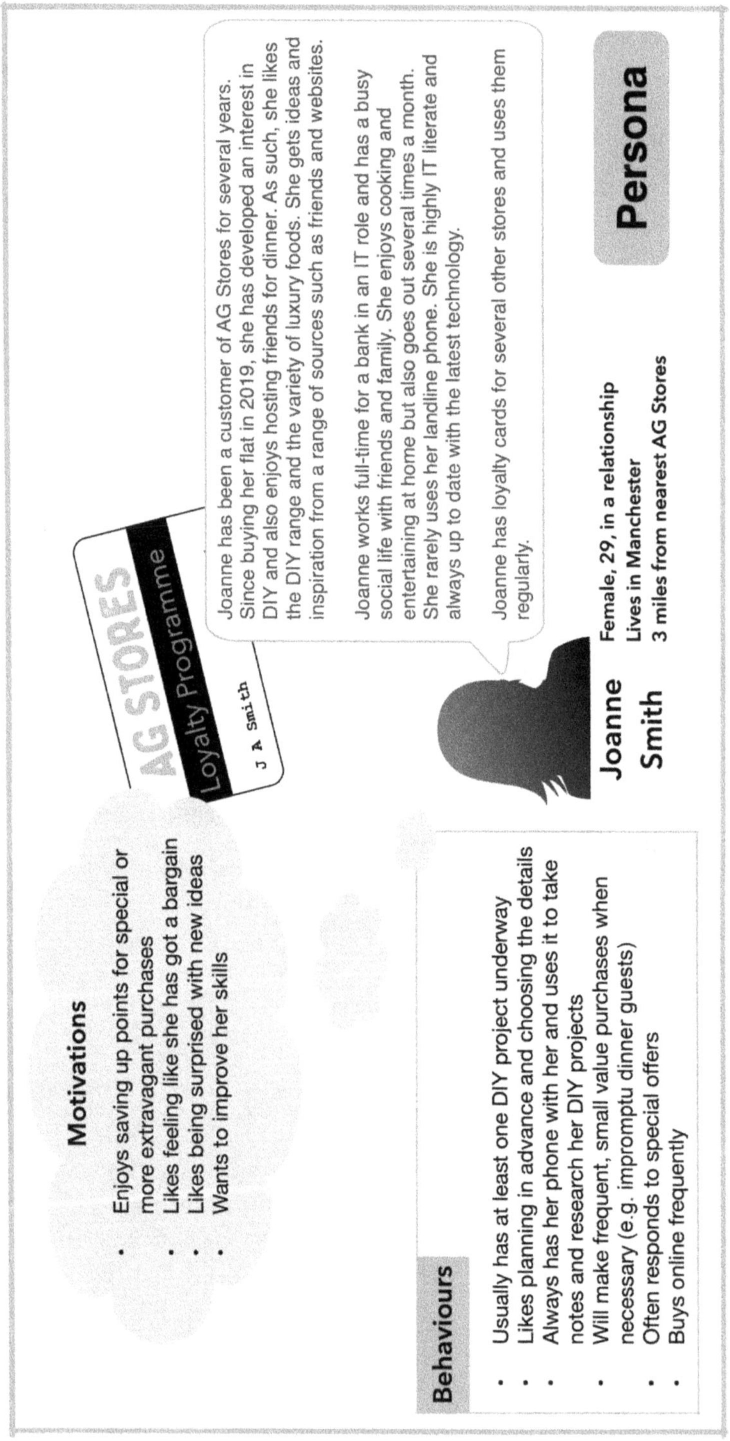

Persona

Joanne Smith

Female, 29, in a relationship
Lives in Manchester
3 miles from nearest AG Stores

AG STORES
Loyalty Programme
J A smith

Joanne has been a customer of AG Stores for several years. Since buying her flat in 2019, she has developed an interest in DIY and also enjoys hosting friends for dinner. As such, she likes the DIY range and the variety of luxury foods. She gets ideas and inspiration from a range of sources such as friends and websites.

Joanne works full-time for a bank in an IT role and has a busy social life with friends and family. She enjoys cooking and entertaining at home but also goes out several times a month. She rarely uses her landline phone. She is highly IT literate and always up to date with the latest technology.

Joanne has loyalty cards for several other stores and uses them regularly.

Motivations

- Enjoys saving up points for special or more extravagant purchases
- Likes feeling like she has got a bargain
- Likes being surprised with new ideas
- Wants to improve her skills

Behaviours

- Usually has at least one DIY project underway
- Likes planning in advance and choosing the details
- Always has her phone with her and uses it to take notes and research her DIY projects
- Will make frequent, small value purchases when necessary (e.g. impromptu dinner guests)
- Often responds to special offers
- Buys online frequently

Figure 10.6 The 1:1 role:persona anti-pattern

2..n

1

Role Description   **Loyalty Card Customer**

The Loyalty Card Customer is a customer of AG Stores who is
eligible to obtain a loyalty card. The loyalty programme results
in more frequent and higher value spending and a more
positive impression of AG Stores.

Actions they may take include:

- Apply for a loyalty card
- View and manage their account
- Cancel account
- Collect points
- Redeem points for rewards
- Receive information and marketing

1

1

Role Description   **Loyalty Card Customer**

The Loyalty Card Customer is a customer of AG Stores who is
eligible to obtain a loyalty card. The loyalty programme results
in more frequent and higher value spending and a more
positive impression of AG Stores.

Actions they may take include:

- Apply for a loyalty card
- View and manage their account
- Cancel account
- Collect points
- Redeem points for rewards
- Receive information and marketing

Customer journey mapping

Mapping the customer's journey through your system will help you to understand their needs and identify possible pain points or new opportunities. A customer journey map is developed from the perspective of the customer and explores the path they take to achieve a goal or objective, such as 'Register for loyalty card'. It includes emotions and feelings as well as functional steps, so can also help to feed into an empathy map.

The first step is to break the journey into small and simple steps such as 'Find Registration Page' or 'Confirm Email Address'. Then, capture the experience of the customer while navigating these steps. This is usually done by observing the customer and asking them how they feel at each interaction, but you can also ask them to provide feedback through a questionnaire or interview. This technique will give the best results with real customers using the product for the first time. The information is captured in a map (see Figure 10.7) along with other observations, such as opportunities to improve that you have identified or additional feature ideas.

You will probably need to repeat this with different scenarios to get a complete picture. For instance, in our example we may want to have different journeys for people using a mobile device or a desktop computer, or people who use password managers and those who don't. Some things to consider when creating a customer journey map include:

- Be clear of the goal to be achieved by the customer journey.
- Ensure you have defined personas with clear goals listed.
- Identify the steps and interactions you expect the customer to take to achieve their goal.
- Take the customer journey yourself.
- Observe the customer as they carry out the steps to achieve their goal, listing their emotions and experience at each step/interaction (e.g. happy, sad, need more info, not sure what to do).
- Let them make mistakes, and don't correct them. Seeing where they went wrong can be very useful.
- Make improvement/changes as necessary and repeat the process until the customer journey is optimised.

Story mapping

Customer journey mapping is a great way to understand the external view the customer takes, but sometimes we need a little more structure to explore a problem in more depth. One of our favourite ways to do this is to apply Jeff Patton's user story mapping approach.[178] User story mapping allows us to visualise product delivery in a way that promotes early delivery of value yet still retains the ability see the whole system and make changes easily.

---

178   Patton, J. (2014) *User Story Mapping: Discover the Whole Story, Build the Right Product.* O'Reilly Media, Sebastopol, CA.

Figure 10.7 Customer journey for loyalty programme registration via website

Customer Journey – Loyalty Programme Registration via Website

STAGES	Find Registration Page	Enter Details	Choose Password	Confirm Email	Account Created
ACTIONS	Navigate to Website / Search / Click Banner / Navigate Menu	Complete Form Correctly / Confirm	Choose Password / Follow password rules / Confirm password	Receive email / Click to confirm / Redirected to logged in account	Browse account / See point balance / See offers and bonuses / No points yet
THOUGHTS	Website could be easier / How long will it take? / What information will they want?	Could it auto complete? / Personal Information	Complicated rules / Can I think of a good password? / Does it integrate with my password manager?	That was easy!	Simple layout / When can I use my new account next? / No points yet
FEELINGS (Positive / Neutral / Negative)					
PAIN POINTS	Loading time	Data Protection / Lots of typing	Choosing a good password / Remembering the rules	Check the spam folder	No physical card
OPPORTUNITIES	Direct navigation from adverts	Auto-complete integration / Spell-check	Password suggestion ideas / Integrate with password managers / Non-password 2FA solution	Reward for creating account?	Request additional data? / Feedback form? / Surveys?

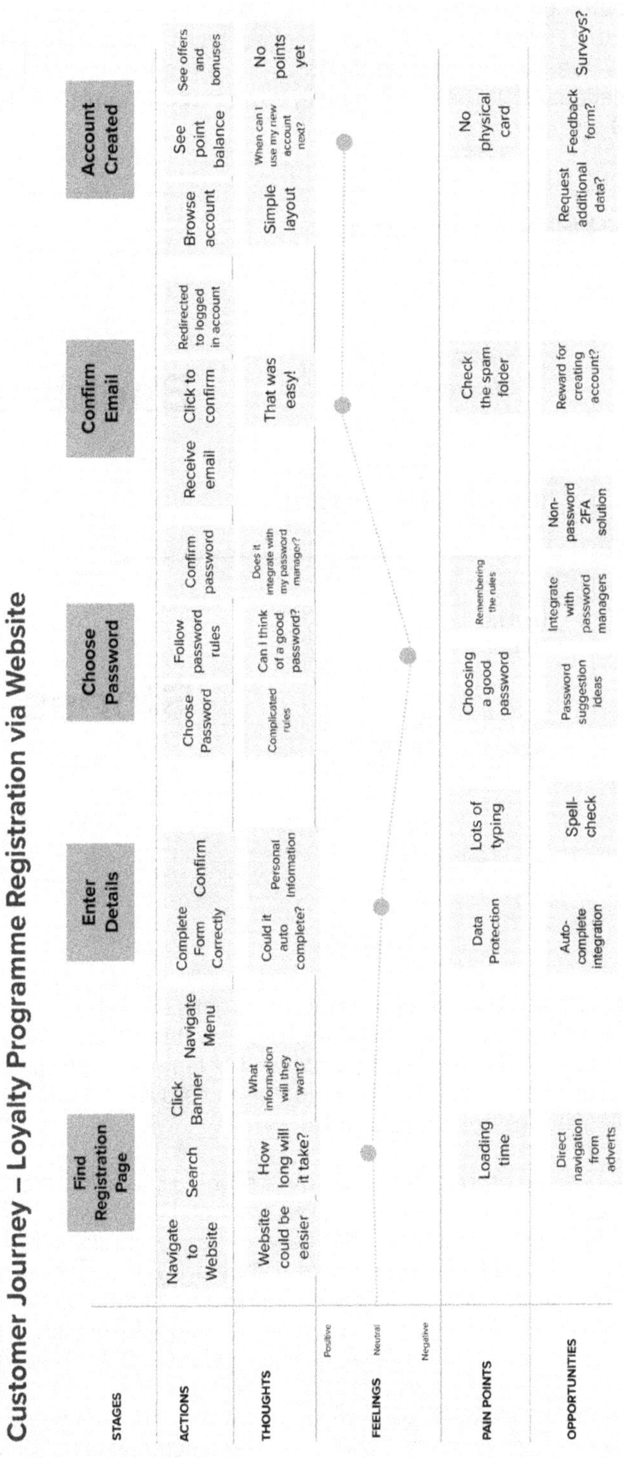

A user story map is created on a wall, and organises the work into two dimensions. Across the top is the value stream: the types of changes, tasks or actions that need to occur to deliver the value that we are aiming for. This is the **backbone**. Then we brainstorm all the detailed tasks, stories, that we can implement. Figure 10.8 shows a snapshot of this process.

Figure 10.8 Creating the backbone and stories

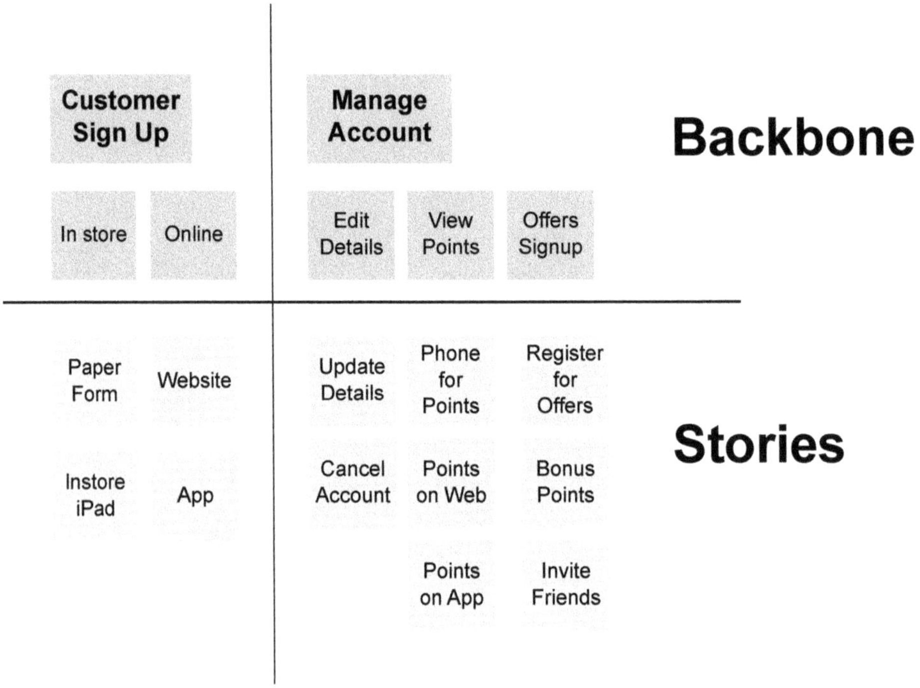

The creation of the backbone and stories is a powerful way to get a shared understanding across the team and customers of how the product will create value. When it represents the customer's journey, it helps to build empathy between the team and the customers. It focuses the work on things that will impact the customer and provide them with value. At this point the underlying stories are not prioritised.

The next step is to organise the stories vertically by arranging them into horizontal rows, each representing one iteration or release of the product. Each row contains the specific things under each backbone element that need to happen to deliver value to the customer. Backbone elements are moved down if they are not essential to that particular iteration. Not every part of the backbone needs to be incremented at each iteration, for example the 'Generate Insights from Trends' column for our loyalty card system doesn't have any effort until after several iterations. Figure 10.9 shows this.

All the items are represented by sticky notes and can be moved up or down the board easily. This promotes powerful conversations with customers about what is important

Figure 10.9 Story map example

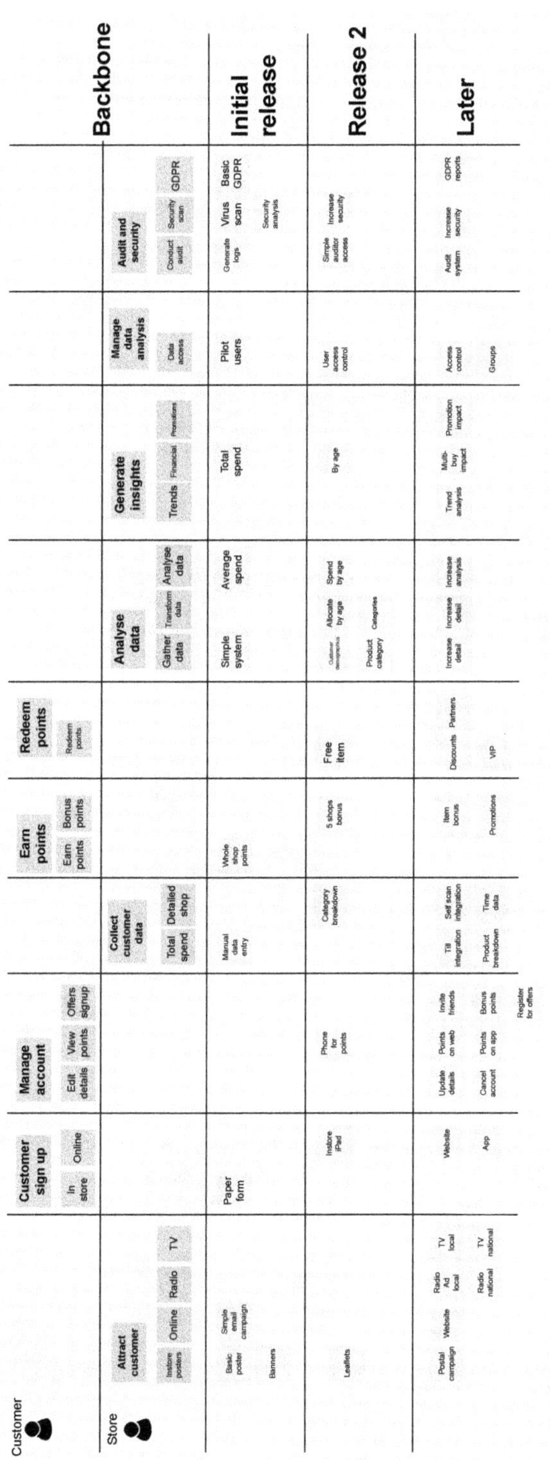

Customer

	Attract customer	Customer sign up	Manage account		Earn points	Redeem points
Backbone	Instore posters · Online · Radio Ad · TV	In store · Online	Edit details · View points · Offers signup		Earn points · Bonus points	Redeem points
Initial release	Basic poster · Simple email campaign · Banners	Paper form				
Release 2	Leaflets	Instore iPad	Phone for points		5 shops bonus	Free item
Later	Postal campaign · Website · Radio Ad local · TV local · Radio national · TV national	Website · App	Update details · Cancel account · Points on web · Points on app · Invite friends · Bonus points · Register for offers		Item bonus · Promotions	Discounts · Partners · VIP

Store

	Collect customer data	Analyse data	Generate insights	Manage data analysis	Audit and security
	Total spend · Detailed shop	Gather data · Transform data · Analyse data	Trends · Financial · Promotion	Data access	Conduct audit · Security scan · GDPR
Initial release	Manual data entry	Simple system · Average spend	Total spend	Pilot users	Generate logs · Virus scan · Basic GDPR · Security analysis
Release 2	Category breakdown	Customer demographics · Product category · Allocate by age · Categorise · Spend by age	By age	User access control	Simple auditor access · Increase security
Later	Till integration · Product breakdown · Self scan integration · Time data	Increase detail · Increase detail · Increase analysis	Trend analysis · Multi-buy impact · Promotion impact	Access control · Groups	Audit system · Increase security · GDPR reports

in early releases and helps us to identify the minimum set of features necessary for the customer to get some value –the MVP we discussed in Chapter 7.

One nice aspect is that it allows us to visualise all the possible product features on one map. This means that stakeholders can find their ideas on the map and see where they are in relative priority to other features. This makes the likely order of delivery clearer and it's easier to see why a particular story is where it is.

Being able to see their stories on the map gives comfort to stakeholders that their stories haven't been forgotten. Because we get them involved in deciding their position, there are fewer problems with stakeholders trying to bump their stories into an earlier release.

Because the backbone represents the intrinsic value chain of the product, it changes less frequently, meaning we can be more certain of it. Conversely, the things that are likely to change – the priority of specific features and stories – are easy to change since we just move them up or down the map.

An initial user story map can be created in a workshop over a couple of hours and evolved as everyone's understanding of the problem grows. Even though they can be detailed and quite large – in Jeff's book, he gives some examples that represent years of work for quite a large team – they can still be created in a day or two, even for large and complex products. We have also used them very effectively for small products.

Other useful mapping techniques include Gojko Adzik's impact mapping[179] and Simon Wardley's Wardley mapping.[180]

Customer discovery and Lean Startup

Agile teams are highly customer-centric, so techniques that place the customer at the centre are a natural fit. 'Customer discovery' is a term used by entrepreneur Steve Blank,[181] and is exemplified by his mantra 'get out of the building' – customer discovery involves finding out what your customers need by asking them, and you can't do that by sitting in your office.

You might find out what they want by better understanding their needs or pain points, or you might find out whether a product or idea of yours would be attractive to them. In either case, you start with a hypothesis, conduct some experiments or tests and evaluate the results.

---

179   Adzik, G. (2012) *Impact Mapping: Making a Big Impact with Software Products and Projects*. Provoking Thoughts, Woking, UK. https://www.impactmapping.org.

180   https://learnwardleymapping.com.

181   https://steveblank.com/tools-and-blogs-for-entrepreneurs/.

Ideally, this process is quick and cheap, so it is important to find the smallest possible experiment that will give you some useful information. By using real customers, we get data that we can trust far more than our own guesses. That's why it is important to get out of the building. This type of information is validated learning.

Steve Blank worked with and mentored Eric Ries, who founded the Lean Startup movement with his book of 2011.[182] Lean Startup combines ideas from Agile, Lean, customer discovery and elsewhere into an approach for making startups more successful.

One principle is that entrepreneurs are everywhere, so it doesn't just apply to new companies but to any new idea or endeavour even within large organisations. The Lean Startup way is to identify assumptions and quickly and cheaply test them, preferably with real customers, to get validated learning. Then apply a build-measure-learn iterative cycle to evolve your product, deciding in each cycle whether to persevere, pivot or fail.

The Strategyzer[183] series of books and models from Alex Osterwalder are a great source of ideas for customer discovery and identifying or developing your product. The Business Model Canvas, Value Proposition Canvas and Customer Gains and Pains can help with aligning the team with a common purpose and help to identify your high-level product goals and vision.

ROADMAPS IN AGILE DELIVERY

An Agile iteration is usually short; one to three weeks is common. This allows frequent delivery and presents a timeframe within which drastic change is unlikely, but it makes longer-term planning hard. Most real-world products will take several months, or even years, to complete.

Despite wanting to keep our options open and respond to change, we often need to have a longer-term plan or view on the development of our product. This may be required to secure funding, align with other initiatives or to inform things like marketing plans or hardware procurement. More often, however, it is required on the whim of a senior stakeholder who thinks having a longer-term plan written down will make it more likely to be true. The challenge for Agile teams is to provide enough clarity on longer-term delivery without resorting to detailed planning that is likely to be wrong.

While storing this detail in one place, such as a backlog (see Managing the Backlog later in this chapter), may seem logical, it can become unwieldy over time and prone to

---

182   Ries, E. (2011) *The Lean Startup: How Today's Entrepreneurs Use Continuous Innovation to Create Radically Successful Businesses.* Crown Publishing Group, New York.

183   https://www.strategyzer.com/books.

becoming too detailed. Instead, we create a separate artefact often called a 'roadmap'. The roadmap makes it easy to distinguish between short-term and long-term needs and makes the work more manageable.

We can create a trustworthy roadmap by abstracting the detail to a level we can be sure is unlikely to change. The items are bigger, but we don't need to go into detail. This could be in the form of a product vision or a roadmap of large features, for instance we may have a roadmap item to implement personalised offers to the customer. We don't need to decide which kinds of offers they will be, what customer data are used for the personalisation or how they are distributed, all that detail can be left until later.

A roadmap isn't a plan, it's just our current ideas of what we think we may do. To help stop people thinking of it as a plan, it's a good idea not to have any dates on it. Instead, structure the roadmap in three sections: Now, Next, Later, as shown in Table 10.4.

Table 10.4 Now, next, later

Now	The things we are currently working on.
Next	The things we will probably prioritise to do next.
Later	The things we think we will want to do later.

In this way, stakeholders can understand the overall scope of the product, retain the ability to change priority, and add or remove features without worrying about replanning. The Later section can be prioritised to indicate the rough order of delivery, and we can estimate the relative sizes to help understand the overall size of the delivery. However, you don't have to do that; a simple list of things for the future is good enough.

Another approach we can take is to set bigger goals than can be delivered in a single iteration. These could be on a longer cadence (perhaps a couple of months) or be a variable length depending on the goal itself. These goals could represent the set of capabilities that allow a formal release or the minimum set of features for a particular set of users. We would still have goals in each iteration, but they would contribute towards the higher-level goal (see Figure 10.10).

We want our roadmap to have just enough detail to be useful and not be so intricate or detailed that we are reluctant to change it. The 'Endowment Effect' (see Chapter 4) and the 'Sunk Costs Fallacy'[184] make us less likely to want to change something we have invested time and effort into. Making these artefacts simple to change and easy to replace will help to avoid that.

---

184   'The general tendency for people to make decisions to continue a behaviour or endeavour based on previously invested resources (time, money or effort) rather than future value': Arkes, H. R. and Blumer, C. (1985) The psychology of sunk costs. *Organ. Behav. Hum. Dec.*, 35, 124–140.

Figure 10.10 Now, next, later roadmap

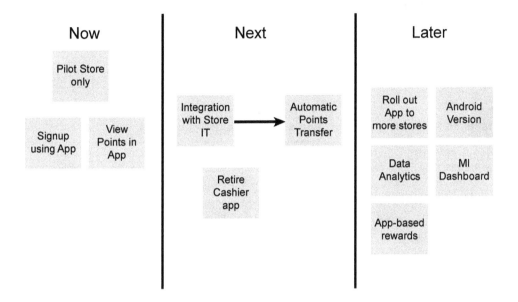

AGILE REQUIREMENTS

The word 'requirement' has been around for decades and is commonly used in many traditional and Agile teams. It is used to describe a feature or need from a stakeholder that may form part of a solution or system. Some requirements represent the usability or functional needs of the solution, whereas others will impose constraints on the solution, such as an architectural constraint, or non-functional requirements, such as a performance target.

In more traditional approaches formal requirements are elicited and documented up front, in advance of development work. They are often validated through formal review or sign-off processes to ensure they are correct before development begins. As discussed in Chapter 4, this creates a form of contract, sometimes even a legally binding contract. This approach is shown Figure 10.11.

The problem with traditional requirement approaches

There are many problems associated with conducting requirements work in this way. Some of these are included in Table 10.5.

Figure 10.11 Up-front requirements

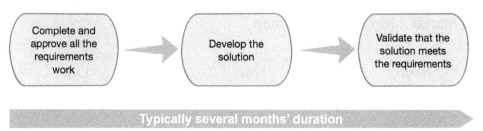

Table 10.5 Problems with traditional requirements approaches

Requirements will change	Requirements will change over time. That is guaranteed. Even the most thorough analysis by the most experienced people will not reliably predict the needs of customers months or years into the future.
	This means that requirements elicited and/or fully documented in advance of being developed are likely to change. The more detailed the requirement, the higher the likelihood it will change.
	Best case scenario, the team spots the change and responds, resulting in the early requirements work being thrown away. This is rare, however. More commonly, the change isn't identified until after the requirement is implemented and the user either rejects it, complains about it or just never uses it.
	Because the work is front loaded, so too is the customer engagement, leading to a long hiatus between the customer's last interaction with the team and seeing the final product. This gap in engagement leads to mistrust from the users, especially if what is delivered is not what they want anymore.
Up-front detail inhibits later collaboration	To attempt to create accurate requirements up front, analysts will usually document in great detail. This is partly a trap to force the customer to sign up to a very detailed specification that will be costly to change, but it is also an attempt to prove that the analysis was very thorough and can be trusted.
	Sadly, this detail usually also consumes a lot of customer and stakeholder time, which makes them reluctant to spend further time with the team once they begin development. This compounds the problem. Not only are the delivery team losing the chance to collaborate with the customer and forced to trust the document implicitly, but this lack of collaboration means they won't pick up any clues that the customer needs may be changing.

(Continued)

Table 10.5 (Continued)

	Even if they want to be able to 'Respond To Change', they won't have the information from the customer that would let them.
Change management becomes change prevention	The majority of change management processes put in place mechanisms to minimise change, rather than manage and embrace change. Sometimes these are explicit – acceptance gates lock in specifications that are delivered whether they are needed or not – but sometimes they are more opaque. Change can only be approved at infrequent meetings of busy, important people who are frequently absent and often defer a decision until the next meeting.
	This can incentivise a creative and innovative sub-culture where the metrics that trigger the change management process are manipulated and massaged to avoid the change process being invoked. We sometimes call these 'watermelon projects' – they are green on the outside, but look inside and you will find they are red.
	However, when change is prevented or avoided then the only possible outcome is that the product will deliver functionality that is out of date or nobody wants to use. Whether the project is contractually correct to deliver will be no comfort to the users, who will not have their needs met.
Avoiding scope creep	Many project managers following structured project management methodologies are measured and rewarded on delivering the project scope on time and within budget.
	This is a problem because of the so-called 'iron triangle' first described by Dr Martin Barnes in his work on construction projects.[185] The three points of the triangle are quality (scope), cost and time – and one cannot change without the others also changing. Since change to agreed requirements usually means adding new requirements, this increase in scope will lead to increased cost and time.
	While project tolerances can cope with a certain amount of change, too much change will blow the budget and the project will be deemed a failure. This results in project managers trying to avoid changes to the scope. We frequently hear arguments such as 'this was only signed off 6 months ago', or 'this is what you agreed to'. These are contract negotiation conversations, not responding to change or customer collaboration.

An Agile requirement approach

So, what is the alternative? In Agile delivery the requirements should evolve over time. Requirements artefacts are lightweight and produced at the point they are needed and not in advance. There is high emphasis on collaboration – those that build the solution

---

185 Barnes, M. (1988) Construction project management. *Project Man.*, 6 (2), 69–79.

must speak to those who will use it if they are to fully understand what they are trying to achieve. Lastly, the requirements do not get 'signed off' in an Agile approach. As more value is placed in working software than comprehensive documentation, it is the working software that is signed off.

As explained in Chapter 6, Agile teams deliver value incrementally and iteratively, delivering increments of value early and frequently. They set goals that are valuable to the customer and deliver them quickly. Since small goals can be completed quicker than large goals, Agile teams focus on small units of value. This approach is shown in Figure 10.12, and the advantages of an Agile approach include those listed in Table 10.6.

Figure 10.12 An Agile requirements approach

Table 10.6 Benefits of an Agile requirements approach

Requirements elicited just enough, just in time	Rather than big, lengthy requirement documents captured 6–12 months ahead of when they are needed, Agile requirements are captured in just enough detail, just in time for being developed and implemented. They may not even be in a document; they could be written on an index card or sticky note.
	Only once a requirement has been prioritised for development within an iteration is it elaborated in detail by the developer and the customer. This ensures the detail is up to date and necessary. As more value is placed on 'working software', the validation occurs once the requirement has been approved by the customer and they can use it.
	If details need to be documented, this is ideally done within the product – often in the code. This reduces the need for long requirement documents and emphasises the left side of the Agile Manifesto.
Requirements evolve over time	It is impossible to get all the requirements correct at the start of product development, so we don't try to. Instead, Agile requirements start as a broad set of ideas and concepts that may, or may not, be fulfilled. As we go through the development, these big ideas are refined and fleshed out. Once development starts on one, that's when the final details are agreed.

(Continued)

Table 10.6 (Continued)

	As the team learns about the problem and the customer, these big ideas change, evolve and disappear and new ones emerge. The set of requirements reflects what we know at this particular point in time. The team still has a rough outline of the overall solution, but the only place they need detail is in the work they've begun and are likely to do next.
Start delivery early	Since Agile teams do not need to have fully detailed requirements in advance of starting development, they can begin development sooner. The focus on delivering 'working software' means that the customer gets something of value much earlier than with traditional development.
	This early delivery drives further change. Once a customer starts using a product, they get a far clearer idea of what they need and what they don't. This allows the backlog to be prioritised to maximise value far more accurately than without real-world customer use of the product.
Change is continuous	Because Agile teams operate on short iterations, the opportunities to change direction are frequent. This allows the team to match the pace of change and change their iteration length if necessary.

Adopting an Agile requirements approach can be challenging, since the alternative is so prevalent in organisations and project management culture. Requirements skills are typically restricted to specific roles such as requirements engineers, business analysts or systems engineers, yet the people most affected by the quality of requirements are the users and developers of the solution.

The most successful teams bring together technical and analysis skills coupled with business knowledge. The developers can bring solution-centric ideas and innovations. After all, the end users may not be experienced software developers and therefore cannot know the art of the possible. Equally, the user view is important, perhaps to temper a deeply technical solution that may be far more complicated than the user actually needs.

This section necessarily is talking a lot about 'requirements'. However, even the word 'requirement' can be problematic since it is related to the verb 'require'. This leads people to believe that a 'requirement' on a backlog is 'required'. As we have said repeatedly, this is wrong. Backlog items are options that may be prioritised in the future, but may not be. They are certainly not 'required'. For this reason, it can be helpful to avoid using the word 'requirement' when trying to adopt an Agile mindset. We talk about backlog items, stories, epics, roadmap items, goals, features, capabilities, constraints, definition of done and so on. We try not to talk about requirements.

REQUIREMENT TECHNIQUES

It is important that we choose techniques that enable the user needs to be elicited just enough and just in time. Just enough so that there are enough work items in the backlog for the team to elaborate for development in the next iteration; just in time to ensure that we are not eliciting and detailing requirements that may not be important, therefore creating requirement inventory and risking the detail becoming out of date.

There are many methods that assist with articulating and navigating requirements within an Agile context. Some of the more popular techniques are shown in Figure 10.13 and described in this section. For a more thorough discussion, see the BCS book, Agile and Business Analysis.[186]

Figure 10.13 Requirements techniques

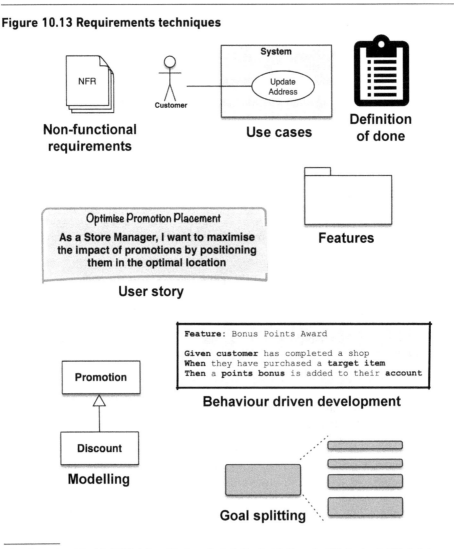

---

186   Girvan, L. and Paul, D. (2017) *Agile and Business Analysis: Practical Guidance for IT Professionals*. BCS, Swindon.

User stories

A user story is a short description of value and often follows the following format, pioneered by Connextra in 2001,[187] though it doesn't have to:

> As a <role> I can <capability> so that <receive benefit>

For example:

> **As a** Loyalty Customer **I can** view my points balance on my phone **so that** I can decide whether to redeem my points in store.

This format helps teams to focus on who the benefit is for and why they want it. It lends itself to short, specific requirements, helping teams to keep their batch size small. Traditionally, a user story is written on an index card, which also helps to limit size by limiting the amount of space there is.

The small, simple nature of a user story also requires the team to talk to the customer before they can implement it. Alistair Cockburn first coined the phrase 'A user story is a promise of a conversation',[188] which is an excellent way to help us focus on the customer collaboration side of the Agile Manifesto rather than the contract negotiation side. User stories must also have acceptance criteria that describe how the team will know that the story is complete.

The small scope of a user story means that there may be many stories in a product compared to other approaches for documenting requirements, such as use cases (discussed later in this chapter). Where a use case would describe a higher-level requirement with multiple steps and paths, a user story could represent a single scenario or path. For example, in the use case 'Manage Points' there would be many additional tasks that a user may want to do, not just view their points balance. Each of these could be an independent user story, prioritised and estimated independently. User stories are also limited to the user's needs – they don't imply any solution.

For more information on user stories, see Mike Cohn's book *User Stories Applied*.[189]

Epics and splitting them into smaller stories

User stories are intended to be small enough to be completed within one iteration. When they are too big, they are called an epic.[190] Other terms used for large 'stories' include feature, capability, goal.

---

187 https://agilecoach.typepad.com/agile-coaching/2006/12/as-a-coach-i-want-a-story-template-so-that-people-ask-questions.html.

188 Alistair Cockburn coined this phrase during a visit to the Chrysler C3 project team in Detroit in 1998. It is referenced in an article on his website that is now unavailable but linked in his tweet: https://twitter.com/totheralistair/status/897894659544031232.

189 Cohn, M. (2004) *User Stories Applied: For Agile Software Development*. Addison-Wesley, Boston, MA.

190 The word 'epic' is also used with other meanings, including in some Agile methods. We find this meaning most useful and use it in this book.

When we first come up with things that our product can do, it is common for many of these ideas to be quite big, even if they can be written in the user story style. For example, one of the later stories in the loyalty card example might be:

> As a store manager, I can use the data to help me decide how to manage in-store promotions so that our promotions can be more effective.

That story probably won't be able to be done in one iteration, so it's not a story, it's an epic.

When an epic is prioritised to the top of the Product Backlog, we will need to split it into multiple, smaller stories and then reprioritise them before we can choose what can be done in the next iteration. There are several ways to do this, some that result in the epic being replaced entirely by lots of smaller stories, and others where small, achievable stories are sliced off the epic but the rest remains as an epic, to have further stories sliced from it later. Some useful techniques on splitting stories, epics or goals are shown in Table 10.7.

Table 10.7 Techniques for splitting large items

Type of story	Story or epic	Ways to split
Task or step	As a loyalty card holder I want to view my loyalty card points so that I know how many points I have.	• Telephone call centre, for enquires by telephone. • Monthly email. • Via the mobile app. • Via the website. • Printed monthly statement in the post.
Business rules	As a loyalty card holder I want to redeem my points.	• In one transaction. • Multiple transactions. • Part payment.
Data sets	As a marketing manager I want to review loyalty card management information (MI) so I can report return on investment.	• Points earned through sales for past week. • Points redeemed this month/quarter/year. • Number of new loyalty card customers. • Percentage of loyalty card customers that haven't made a purchase.

(Continued)

Table 10.7 (Continued)

Type of story	Story or epic	Ways to split
Data/content entry	As a marketing manager I want to make loyalty customers aware of promotional offers.	• All offers displayed in all apps. • Targeted email campaign. • Tailored ads in app based on past customer behaviour.
CRUD	As a call centre handler I want to manage customer details.	• Create a new account. • View (read) customer details. • Update customer details. • Delete customer account.
UI	As a user of a particular interface I want to know my points balance before I visit the store.	• Mobile or web. • Android or iOS. • Web browser type. • Call centre access. • Access from corporate network.

Table 10.7 shows how relatively small stories can be split into even smaller stories. We also need to split things that are even bigger than epics. Often, there are huge chunks of functionality that we capture but don't want to break down until later. For example, the loyalty card system has identified a business need for data analysis including using artificial intelligence to generate insights into customer spending.

That's huge and can be broken down in different ways. In that example, a good tactic is to treat it like an iceberg. Identify a small goal that is part of it and slice it off – for example, Offer Penetration: how many app users view the offers in their AG Stores app when they get a notification that a new offer is available? This new story is 'calved' from the Data Analysis iceberg. The rest of the iceberg stays where it is without any further decomposition necessary until data analysis becomes a priority again.

Some other tactics for dealing with very large roadmap or backlog items include:

- **Scenario flow** (basic flow, alternative flow, exceptions) – Often there are many ways that a user can achieve a result. There are also often several ways their attempt can fail. This can result in there being many different possible permutations. Each of these can be split out and implemented separately.[191] Use cases (described later) provide a nice structure where identifying these flows is straightforward.

- **User type/persona** – Different users or personas can give us a different view of the system from a user perspective, so can be used to help us take a generic story and spit it into multiple stories for each perspective. For example, different persons may access a product or service in different ways.

---

191 See Behaviour driven development (later in this chapter) and Test driven development (Chapter 8) for examples where this would be useful.

- **Good-Better-Best** – Jeff Patton introduced this concept in his book *User Story Mapping*.[192] For each story/epic consider what needs to be in place to make it just good enough, what more can be added to make it better and what is the best it can be. This would create at least three stories and help to focus on the most important things first and prevent over-engineering solutions.

Examples are given in Table 10.8.

Table 10.8 Good-Better-Best example

As a loyalty card customer, I want to know how many loyalty card points I have.

Good	Customer phones helpline and is told their balance.
Better	Customer logs into website, where points are updated every week.
Best	Customer app displays current points balance on front page, which is always up to date. Same information is available on website and through phone support.

Each of the above examples of Good-Better-Best are stories in their own right and all achieve the goal of providing customers with an update on their loyalty card points. However, how this can be achieved varies and enables us to consider different initial options for the MVP.

This technique is particularly useful if you are trying to deliver more than one story in an iteration. Split them down into Good-Better-Best and use MoSCoW to prioritise them. Ensure that 'Must' stories are no more than 60 per cent of your available capacity.

In any elaboration or further analysis of requirements it is important to bear the simplicity principle in mind: maximise the work not done. Only split out what you need to in order to deliver the maximum value to the customer. Nothing more.

The three Cs

Ron Jeffries introduced the term the '3Cs' in Essential XP.[193] This describes the three critical elements of a user story: card, conversation and confirmation (see Table 10.9).

Use cases and Use-Case 2.0

Use cases were developed by Ivar Jacobson and presented at the OOPSLA conference in 1987.[194] They became a very popular way to describe and model requirements of both large and small systems. They are integral to the Unified Modelling Language (UML) and a core component of the Rational Unified Process (RUP). They evolved into Use-Case

---

192 Patton, J. (2014) *User Story Mapping: Discover the Whole Story, Build the Right Product*. O'Reilly Media, Sebastopol, CA.

193 https://ronjeffries.com/xprog/articles/expcardconversationconfirmation/.

194 The Object Oriented Programming Systems, Languages and Applications conference. The conference would see the first public presentation of Scrum eight years later.

2.0[195] to better support Agile delivery and are still a popular and powerful requirements tool today.

Table 10.9 The three Cs

Card	The user story is written on an index card. This is a token for the story, to represent it and remind the team of it. It will not be able to contain all the information about the story, but just enough.
	The team write on the card to update it, things such as estimates of size or value, priority, customer contact, etc. The card is moved around the Agile board as it is worked on.
Conversation	The actual requirement is the result of conversations and exchanges of knowledge between the development team and the customers. This is how assumptions are tested, details are refined and ideas discussed.
Confirmation	It is important to agree criteria for accepting that the story is complete. Ideally this is a working version of the solution that the customer can use to solve a real problem. There may also be criteria regarding security, audit, performance and other non-functional aspects. Traditionally, the confirmation would be summarised on the back of the card.

Use cases are a lightweight, iterative way to describe what a system is going to do and, by intentional omission, what it is not going to do. They tend to describe larger, more comprehensive pieces of functionality than user stories, but the two approaches often successfully complement one another.

There are six key principles that underpin Use-Case 2.0, as shown in Table 10.10.

Table 10.10 The six principles of use cases

1	**Keep it simple by telling stories**	Telling stories is a powerful way to communicate and share knowledge. Use cases use a narrative structure to tell stories about how to achieve the goal and how to handle problems along the way. The level of detail in the stories increases as the use case iterates.
2	**Understand the big picture**	A use case diagram can convey the whole system scope, including the people interacting with the system, in a clear, simple way. This provides context that helps with the detail.

(Continued)

---

195   https://www.ivarjacobson.com/sites/default/files/field_iji_file/article/use-case_2_0_jan11.pdf.

Table 10.10 (Continued)

3	**Focus on value**	Concentrate on how the system will be used to achieve a specific goal for a particular user. Start with the simplest way to deliver the value, then add detail by specifying all the alternative ways value could be achieved.
4	**Build the system in slices**	A use case slice is a small piece of end-to-end value through the use case. Often, these map to the stories that describe the different paths to the value. Implement each slice before starting the next one.
5	**Deliver the system in increments**	Each increment is a demonstrable or usable version of the system that adds one or more slices of capability. Expect to make many increments of the system.
6	**Adapt to meet the team's needs**	Elaborate each use case as little as you can, but as much as you need to. Minimising detail will make it easier to adapt and change.

Use cases are iterative and progress through a series of states, as shown in Figure 10.14.

Figure 10.14 States in Use-Case 2.0

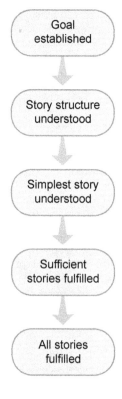

Teams often use a template for use cases with sections for narrative descriptions of the use case in increasing detail. For instance, there are often sections for brief description, main path, pre-conditions, post-conditions, alternate flows, exceptions and so on. Each of these is an opportunity to describe the use case in more detail, each section building on the others. Ideally, this detail is added in business-friendly language such as a story, but use cases can also form part of detailed UML models where multiplicity, inheritance and other technical details can be documented.

Despite their potential for complexity, use cases can be extremely valuable in their simplest state – with just the overall goal described. This is often enough to prioritise the system development, create an initial backlog and begin identifying the highest priority use case slices or user stories. Low priority use cases may not need further elaboration until much later in development, perhaps never if their priority changes and they are not required.

At this high level, a use case diagram (see Figure 10.15) can be a very useful way to express the scope of the system and keep stakeholders informed. These are quick to create and provide a system- or subsystem-wide scope that can help communication and planning. More complex modelling of use cases can elicit more detail but remember the simplicity principle.

Figure 10.15 Use case diagram

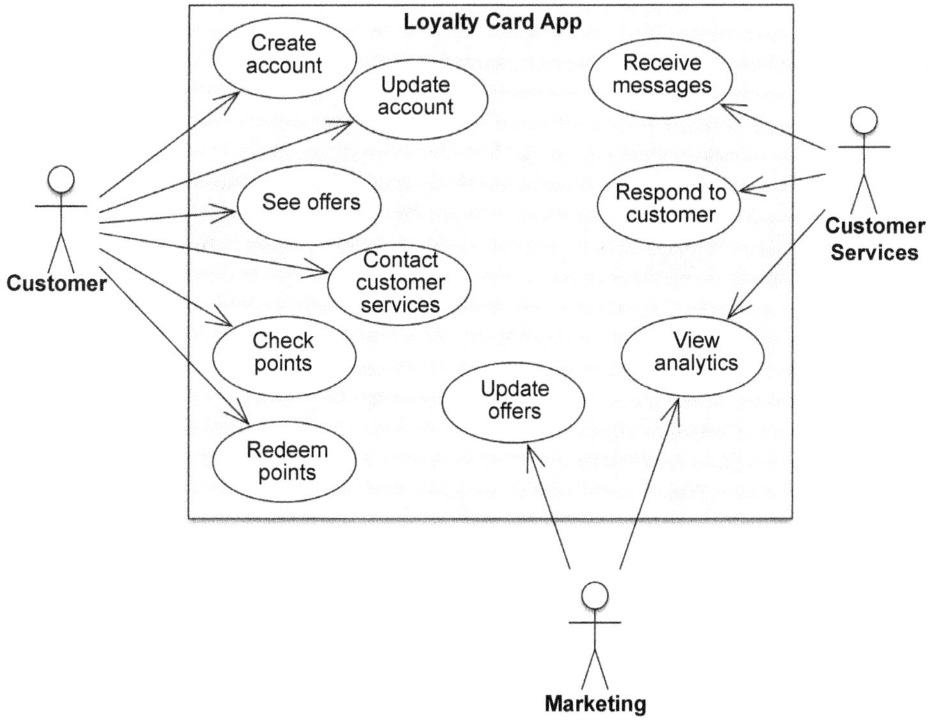

Non-functional requirements

It is easy to overlook non-functional requirements when so much effort is expended on understanding and managing the customer needs and expectations. However, non-functionals, or 'NFRs', are just as critical to the product success as functionality and can cost more in the long term if not considered. The difference between functional and non-functional requirements is defined in Figure 10.16.

Figure 10.16 Functional and non-functional requirements

What the
product/system
needs to do

**Functional
requirements**

How well the
product/system
does it

**Non-functional
requirements**

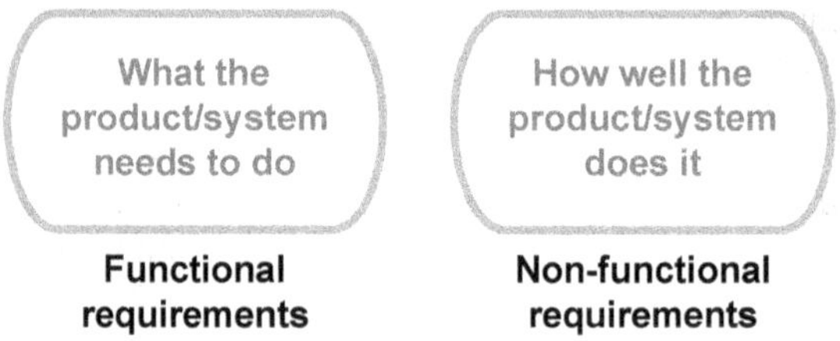

In many ways non-functional requirements define the quality characteristics of the solution. They define things such as performance, reliability, security and the service level agreements that document how the solution will be maintained and supported through its lifetime. We categorise them in two ways, as in Table 10.11.

Table 10.11 Types of non-functional requirement

Global non-functionals	Global non-functionals persist across numerous iterations and will never be completed; things such as security architecture, technology interface compatibility or legal requirements. While we may not need to have them met in the first very few iterations, they will need to be in place for any live deliveries including the MVP. Therefore, it is important they are captured and understood at the start otherwise they can slow down or hold up progress later.
Associated non-functionals	Associated non-functionals tend to be operational in that they make the functionality better. They are often associated with one or more functional requirements, for example every story that is implemented in a mobile app may have the same associated non-functional requirements. Stories implemented in cloud-hosted micro-services may have different associated non-functionals.
	These types of non-functionals can evolve with functional requirements and can be considered as part of the acceptance criteria for a functional requirement.

Both types of non-functional requirements need to be documented and managed. One strategy that we recommend is as follows:

- **Global non-functional** requirements are formal requirements and should be managed in a formal, version-controlled system. In some cases (such as pharmaceuticals, finance or defence industries), they may be subject to audit and compliance, which may require a formal, external process to be followed. They should be considered and documented early in the product life cycle as they can describe quality criteria that can influence architecture decisions.

- **Associated non-functionals** relate to functionality within the system, so are directly related to groups of stories. Rather than copy them into every relevant story's acceptance criteria, it makes more sense to write them once – perhaps in a behaviour driven development (BDD) language such as Gherkin (discussed later) – and refer to them in each relevant story. It can be convenient to use the same document as the global non-functionals.

For both types of non-functional requirement it is important not to forget about them, which can happen when details are hidden away in documents. To overcome this, add them as sticky notes on your backlog or Agile board. This helps to make them more visible, as stories and other backlog items are considered each iteration. They can then be included in the acceptance criteria for the story – the non-functional requirements themselves are never 'completed' and do not go through the same workflow as functional requirements do.

Behaviour driven development and acceptance criteria

BDD was introduced in the 2000s by Dan North.[196] It emerged in response to TDD (see Chapter 7) as a way to help prevent misunderstanding between development and testing in Agile teams by creating a language for testing business value and behaviour at the acceptance level. BDD aims to provide a shared understanding between the different perspectives of the developers, end users and testers by ensuring that only software that meets the business need is built.

The language used for BDD is called Gherkin. It is based on the user story format of 'As a ... I want ... so that ...', but uses the construct given-when-then, which is defined in Table 10.12. Figure 10.17 is an example of a BDD scenario for our loyalty programme.

Table 10.12 Behaviour driven development

Given	a context
When	an action occurs
Then	an outcome is achieved

---

196 http://dannorth.net/introducing-bdd/.

Figure 10.17 BDD example

Given A customer purchases a product in store and presents their
valid loyalty card

When The purchase is completed and the loyalty card is registered
as part of the purchase

Then The loyalty account will be credited with 1 loyalty card point
per pound spent

The scenario can contain more detail, which can help when using automated testing systems. Figure 10.18 shows a more detailed version of this scenario with actual values.

Figure 10.18 Detailed BDD example

Given A customer purchases a product for £20 in store and presents
their valid loyalty card

When A purchase is made at the till and the loyalty card number
543672 is registered as part of the purchase

Then The loyalty card 543672 is credited with 20 loyalty card
points

The relationship between BDD and user stories does not stop at the similarity in format used. In fact, every user story can have multiple BDD scenarios to test the behaviour and value of the story. In this way, they can become the acceptance criteria and tests for the story. For example:

As a Customer I want to register for a loyalty card via the website so I can earn and redeem loyalty card points.

The BDD scenarios that may be used to test this story include the examples shown in Figures 10.19 and 10.20.

It is easy to see how BDD can be used to write tests or meet the acceptance criteria as part of the user story confirmation. However, it should be noted that BDD tests should only be written once a story is in an iteration. They are developed by the Agile team in conjunction with the end user or subject matter expert. Writing BDD scenarios for stories that are not yet prioritised into an iteration can be an incredible waste of time. It

Figure 10.19 BDD example – correct details

```
Given the customer selects 'Register' to register for the programme

And they enter  customerDetails(<first name>, <surname>, <DOB>,
<Address> <email address>) correctly

And they confirm their customer details are correct

When they click on 'submit'

Then they should be presented with a success message saying
'Success: you are now registered as a Loyalty Card customer. Your
customer details will be sent in a separate email.'

And An automated email should be sent to <email address> containing
their customer details and customer number
```

Figure 10.20 BDD example – incorrect details

```
Given the customer selects 'Register' to register for the programme

And they enter one or more of customerDetails(<first name>,
<surname>, <DOB>, <Address> <email address>) incorrectly

And they confirm their customer details are correct

When they click on 'submit'

Then they should be presented with the message 'you have not
entered the customer detail (#customerdetail) correctly, please
amend and re-submit'
```

also usually means that the development team has not been involved in writing them, increasing the risk that they will be wrong or misunderstood.

BDD also makes it easy to implement TDD (see Chapter 7). The first 'failing test' can be the BDD for the expected behaviour. Then, once that works properly, additional BDD scenarios can be added as new failing tests to be implemented.

Definitions of ready and done

'Quality cannot be inspected into a product or service. It must be built into it', W. Edwards Deming.[197]

---

197   Deming, W. E. (2000) *Out of the Crisis*. MIT Press, Cambridge, MA.

The definition of ready (DoR) and definition of done (DoD) are mechanisms designed to reinforce transparency and assure built-in quality (see Table 10.13). They provide an agreed set of rules that smooths the transition of the work item into the development team and onto the user, and ensures that expectations of the work item to be planned, developed and completed are set and clear for the whole team.

Table 10.13 Definitions of ready and done

Definition of ready	Provides a set of value-focused criteria that needs to be in place before work can commence on a work item, capability or product release.
Definition of done	Provides a set of criteria to verify that quality driven activities are in place and completed for a work item, capability or product release.

The DoR ensures that once the team starts working on the item there should be nothing external that stops them completing it. They have all the information, data, permissions, access to customers and so on. that they need, including from wider stakeholders (users, auditors, marketing, security, etc.).

The DoD ensures that once the team thinks they are complete there is nothing to prevent the product being used by the real customer to meet their real goals. It will be tested, safe and legal to use, secure, in the right environment, documented enough, using the right branding, marketed, accessible and so on.

The definitions are owned by the whole team (including the customer or Product Owner), which makes everyone more likely to adhere to them. They evolve as the development proceeds and should push increased quality standards over time. This can make them an indicator of the maturity of the Agile team.

The DoR and DoD can be seen to represent the agreement of the boundary between the development team and customer. The DoR represents what the customer will do in order to prepare the work item ready for the team to start work on it straight away. The DoD represents what the team will to ensure that the work item can be used by the customer straight away.

They can also be seen as setting entry (DoR) and exit (DoD) criteria for work items, although they must not be confused with stage gates. Their purpose is to aid flow of work, not impede it. Examples of DoR and DoD for a work item such as a user story are shown in Table 10.14.

Both DoR and DoD can and should be applied at all levels of abstraction that the team use, for example a work item, feature and release levels. Some aspects may only be relevant at higher levels, but, more importantly, we need to test and accept higher-level elements independently. We can't assume that a story is done just because its low-level work items are done. Similarly, headline features or capabilities in a product should be tested explicitly, not just assumed to work because the underlying stories are finished.

Table 10.14 Example of DoR and DoD for a user story

Definition of ready	In user story format 'As a ..., I want ..., so that ...'.
	Meets the INVEST[198] criteria (independent, negotiable, valuable, estimable, small, testable).
	Written in collaboration with user/customer/Product Owner/development team.
	Is small enough to be delivered within an iteration.
	Has acceptance criteria that can be tested.
	Is documented in the appropriate tool/environment.
	User available to test story with test data and permission to access it.
Definition of done	Is tested using BDD scenarios.
	Is tested for software/hardware.
	Demonstrated to user/customer/Product Owner.
	Documented.
	No must-fix defects outstanding.
	Accepted by the Product Owner.
	Included in a version that the customer can use.

MANAGING THE BACKLOG

A critically important Agile practice is the creation and maintenance of one or more backlogs. The Product Backlog is the main one and it contains the things that we think will be necessary to deliver the value to the customer.

In some methods, there is also a backlog for the current iteration. This backlog contains a lower level of detail that helps the team to ensure that they know what they need to do to meet the iteration goals. There may also be higher-level, strategic backlogs with portfolio or programme level items. Generally speaking, the fewer backlogs the better.

Sometimes, there may not be an obvious backlog at all. The minimum necessary, assuming the team isn't working on the final story, is that the team knows what the next highest priority work is and that it is elaborated enough for them to complete in their next iteration. Whether you have one or multiple backlogs, and whether they are called a backlog or not, the product's queue of future requirements needs to be managed and maintained. In simple terms, the backlog is a prioritised list of work items that contains the most important work items at the top and less important work items at the bottom (see Figure 10.21).

---

[198] The INVEST mnemonic was coined by Bill Wake in 2003. https://xp123.com/articles/invest-in-good-stories-and-smart-tasks/. It is sometimes adapted, for instance by replacing 'small' with 'small enough'.

Figure 10.21 Product Backlog

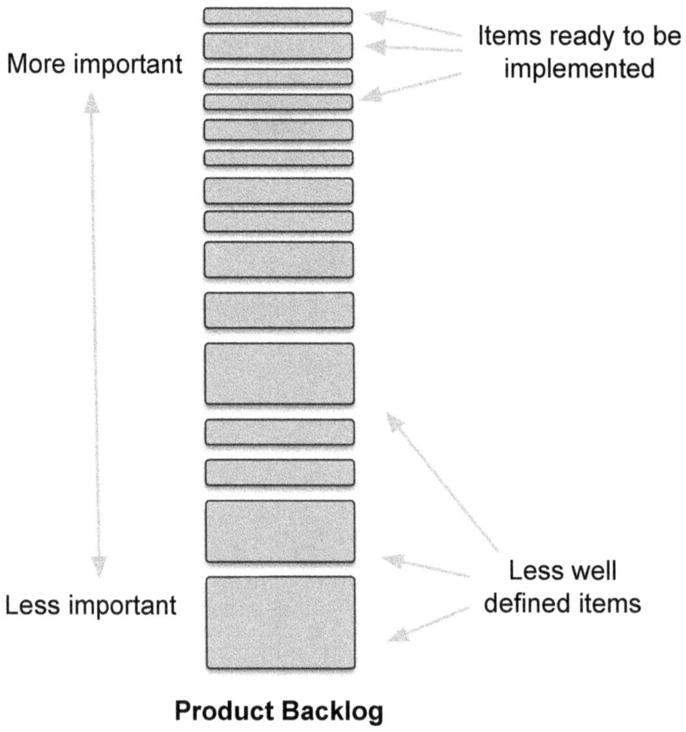

Product Backlog

In Mike Cohn's book, *User Stories Applied*,[199] he refers to the backlog as an iceberg because the work items at the bottom are less developed than the work items at the top (see Figure 10.22). Only the work items at the top, above the water line, will be developed to the point at which they can be accepted into an iteration. Similarly, the items below the water line are more likely to be big stories (i.e. epics) and will need further work and analysis to break them down.

Prioritising the backlog

The iceberg metaphor is also a helpful prioritisation technique, since it provides a simple, two-state priority system: above water or below water. Items above water are prioritised for delivery and should be prepared so that the team can pull them into their next iteration. If an item is below water, we should not elaborate it further until it rises above the water. As the above-water items deplete, a 'backlog refinement' session will assess the items below and select which ones should be prioritised higher.

You will note that Figure 10.22 also shows small stories below the water line. This is not unusual; sometimes, even low priority stories are small. However, this also occurs when

---

199   Cohn, M. (2004) *User Stories Applied: For Agile Software Development*. Addison-Wesley, Boston, MA.

an epic is split into three or four smaller stories, but only one or two of those stories are deemed important enough to be above the water line. The remaining stories then take their rightful place in the prioritisation order, which may be anywhere depending on importance.

Figure 10.22 Backlog iceberg (Adapted from Cohn, 2004)

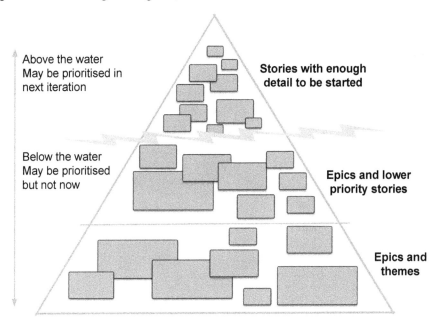

Above the water
May be prioritised in
next iteration

Stories with enough
detail to be started

Below the water
May be prioritised
but not now

Epics and lower
priority stories

Epics and
themes

This approach is also useful for backlogs with more detailed prioritisation systems. Many backlogs employ a unique priority system, as shown in Figure 10.23. The position of the item determines its priority. During backlog refinement we apply a similar approach to splitting epics as before. An epic may occupy a unique priority, but once split each story that emerges is independently prioritised.

The original epic could have been near the top of the backlog, but needed splitting since it was too big for the next iteration. Despite this, some of the stories could end up quite low priority, for example we may have an epic that allows customers to pay through their app. We wish to prioritise this to test its popularity. We split the epic into smaller stories and prioritise the easiest one that allows payment. The others will only be prioritised if the experiment is a success, until then they are low priority.

Chapter 8 describes several prioritisation techniques that we can apply to help us prioritise and split stories or epics on the backlog. Whichever technique(s) you use, remember that the most important part of a backlog is the top. At the top is the most valuable work the team can do next, of a size and level of detail that they can start immediately. Any work elaborating work items beyond that is potentially wasteful.

Figure 10.23 Splitting an epic and reprioritising the stories

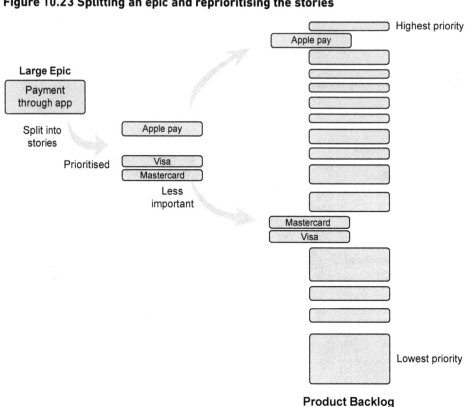

Product Backlog

Judging how much work needs to be in this state means knowing something about how much work the team can do in each iteration. This is dependent on several factors, including team capacity, complexity of the work and size of the work. If the complexity of the work items is very variable, then including some estimate of complexity alongside size and value can be helpful when prioritising the work. However, remember the simplicity principle: only do this if you need to, and even then do 'just enough'.

Backlog refinement

The order of the backlog is likely to change over time and so needs careful and constant management. We refer to this as 'backlog refinement' and it is an activity that should be carried out by the whole team as and when necessary, as follows:

- when a change happens that affects the work to be done next;
- when the number of 'ready' backlog items starts to run out;
- when a refinement event is scheduled;
- when the backlog gets too big.

Managing changes to the backlog in this way ensures constant review of the backlog so that it is always up to date but minimises unnecessary work. The fact an item is below the water line should be an indicator that there is little value in doing any work on it at the moment.

Managing a large backlog is an anti-pattern as it indicates that more customer needs and work items have been elicited and documented than are necessary. This results in effort having been spent organising and managing work items that may never find their way into a working solution.

To avoid this, and to keep the backlog lean, it is good practice to regularly remove items from the backlog. Some criteria you may want to apply when considering whether items should be removed from the backlog are:

- The work item has been in the backlog for more than six months and never been deemed important. (If you are wrong, it will soon get noticed and it will return.)
- The work item does not meet feasibility criteria.
- The work item is not aligned with the product/service vision.

SUMMARY

The backlog is where a customer need begins its journey to fulfilment and careful management, refinement and prioritisation will help you to ensure that the most valuable customer needs are always ready to be implemented next.

The backlog is also an important vector to good stakeholder engagement. Using innovative or creative ways to capture a backlog, such as user story mapping, can help to bring the product to life for stakeholders. However, we must also be careful to avoid setting unrealistic expectations or allowing stakeholders to view backlog items as commitments. Avoiding dates, maintaining short backlogs and regular refinement can help with this.

There are a great many techniques available to help with managing the backlog, not least because techniques from product innovation, prototyping and traditional requirements engineering can be used alongside Agile techniques.

Understanding and applying a number of these practices, including knowing when not to apply them, will help you to understand and document the product scope, customer needs and customer interactions with the product. They can allow you to create a backlog of small, value-centric goals that contribute towards the overall product through increments that customers find valuable. Achieving this is the domain of successful product and backlog management.

This chapter has just scratched the surface of the plethora of techniques available in this topic. We don't expect all team members to be adept or experienced in these techniques as many of them can take years to hone. There may be specialists such as business analysts, product managers, user researchers or customer experience designers who may be available to help or coach.

11 BEYOND THE BASICS

Now you have mastered Agile from first principles, what next?

So far, we have covered Agile in a fair amount of detail; covering it from first principles has led us to explore a lot of ground. We have introduced you to a wide range of ideas, models, practices and approaches, and have reiterated that Agile is a simple concept to comprehend but fiendishly difficult to apply well. And yet we have really only covered the basics. We haven't discussed things in a great deal of depth, and we have consciously steered clear of the hot topic of scaling Agile.

This is because we feel it is really important to properly understand what underpins a good Agile mindset before trying to complicate things further. When many teams struggle even with simple, single-team Agile, they will only find things more difficult if they try to scale.

This chapter starts the discussion on a few areas where you can start building on your Agile foundations and still remain true to an Agile mindset. We will discuss ways teams can avoid the need to scale, but also introduce you to some scaled approaches. We will help you to tailor approaches in ways that make them more suitable for your environment but without compromising them, and we will describe when self-organising teams may need some specialist skills and people.

Having a good handle on how the culture and psychology that we have already explained underpins the Agile mindset will be important.

HOW NOT TO SCALE AGILE

There isn't a typo in the section heading. Before even contemplating scaling Agile, we must first exhaust all the ways that we can avoid needing to scale in the first place. However, that isn't where most organisations start. Most organisations begin assuming they need to scale, pick a scaling approach, book the training and sit back to wait for the results.

However, if you have followed the trends in this book, you will realise that this isn't likely to be a successful path. With single-team Agile so hard to do well, we should expect scaled Agile to be even more difficult. Additionally, if simple Agile hasn't been mastered then it is likely that bad practices will also be scaled and will be much harder to address and fix too.

This isn't just our opinion. Every good scaled Agile class will start with the same message: **If you don't have to scale, don't scale.** However, because this message is delivered in the first 30 minutes of a two- or four-day class, it doesn't tend to be the message that participants leave with. Instead, they leave with some knowledge about all the additional things that teams can do on top of simpler Agile. These extra things also usually come with the caveat that, before scaling Agile, teams must already be highly skilled at single-team Agile. However, both these core messages are often overlooked in favour of careering into a scaled Agile method with freshly trained, enthusiastic people, perhaps supported by some consultants.

We want to help you to avoid this by considering some of the factors that drive teams and organisations towards scaling and what you can to do to solve those problems in other ways.

Why do we want to scale in the first place?

Agile works well with relatively small, co-located teams of less than 10 people who are working collaboratively with their customers to deliver a product or solution. The most common reason for scaling is that multiple teams are working on the same product – perhaps to deliver it faster, perhaps because it is highly complex or perhaps because of the range of skills required. Scaled approaches are also commonly adopted because the teams are in the same cost centre, governed by the same higher-level programme or managed by the same people.

Reduce the drivers of scaling

Before committing to a scaled Agile approach, we should be absolutely sure that it is necessary. To do this, we need to understand the drivers for scaling and what we can do to reduce or remove them. Only then can we reassess whether we still need to scale and select the most appropriate approach to adopt.

Some common justifications for needing a scaled approach include:

- The product is too big.
- Our team has grown and is becoming hard to manage.
- We have lots of teams able to work on this product.
- There are too many features required for one team to deliver in time.
- Our teams are specialists, each focused on a single component – they need to be coordinated.
- All this work is governed by the same budget and must be managed the same way.
- We depend on other teams or departments.
- These products are used by the same customers.

These factors can be reduced by applying some or all of the following practices. Ideally, we can use a combination of these to result in work that can be delivered by multiple single teams without requiring them to follow a formal scaled method.

Reduce complexity

Fundamentally, any factor that increases complexity can also be manipulated to reduce complexity. To help understand this, it is helpful to consider all the aspects of a delivery as an interconnected and interdependent system – the people, their processes, the environment, the solution, tools, the stakeholders, other departments, other products, everything. Changing any aspect of the system will affect other parts of the system, sometimes in counter-intuitive or unexpected ways. Considering and solving problems in this way is called systems thinking or systems theory.

As we bring in more people to a delivery endeavour or try to solve bigger problems, the system gains more parts and more lines of communication and dependencies. Luckily, just because we have complexity in one part of the system doesn't mean that the system as a whole needs to be complex. However, left unchecked, as teams and product scope grow, their complexity will also often increase.

By applying systems thinking, we can help to avoid this. For instance, using feature teams rather than component teams reduces inter-team dependencies because each feature team operates independently from the others. Using open-source architectures and practices reduces inter-team dependencies since any team can change or add to a system component, not just the team or developer who created it. Setting principles and standards rather than writing rules and processes enables teams to interpret and apply them taking account of their own circumstances, reducing lines of communication and bureaucratic control.

In Chapter 6 we introduced the Lean wastes of transportation, inventory, motion, waiting, overproduction, over-processing, defects and unused talent. Identifying and reducing any of these wastes is likely to help reduce complexity in your overall system.

Decouple everything

Complexity is often the result of highly coupled architectures, requirements, teams or governance processes. Decoupling these will significantly reduce the complexity and usually results in solution elements that are able to be developed independently.

Architectures can be decoupled by using interfaces, standards-based data formats, object-oriented design, domain-driven development, component architectures, services and micro-services, serverless functions and so on. These approaches help to separate solution elements from one another. This makes each element simpler and easier to develop, and that development can be done in isolation of the development of other elements. It also promotes reuse and helps with scalability.

Requirements can be decoupled by making them small and simpler – perhaps by using the story splitting techniques from Chapter 10. Ensuring that they are independent from one another (including their acceptance criteria or DoD) will decouple them from other requirements, help to make their prioritisation easier and allow them to be developed in parallel by independent teams.

The obvious way to decouple teams is to form teams that are fully empowered to deliver value to the customers. This means that they include all the skills and authority to carry out all the tasks necessary to deploy the solution, which could include legal, marketing, sales or security skills. Where this isn't possible (or isn't palatable), then we should identify each of these external dependencies and get agreement on how they will be accessed in advance of starting the work. This helps to avoid delays and bottlenecks later.

Governance processes can be decoupled by abstracting them to the highest level possible and empowering teams within those higher-level structures. Only mandate what is essential. Allow teams to set their own ways of working that can adapt to their unique environment. Guide them with principles and standards. Where possible, pull existing data from teams for higher-level reporting and aggregation rather than creating additional data for reporting upwards; this is not only wasteful but risks diverging from the truth and being out of date quickly. Pulling existing data also makes it easy to decouple business rhythms from team delivery cadence. This lets each team optimise their cadence for their situation, including higher-level governance teams.

Manage products
Most scaling approaches assume that multiple teams are working on a single product with a single Product Backlog. They then help manage this complexity by finding ways for the teams to split out the work in a sensible fashion and communicate with one another to ensure they can integrate their work together into a new increment each iteration. However, if teams are working on separate products, the need to collaborate and integrate disappears. Each separate product has its own backlog and Product Owner.

If the products are related or funded in the same way, a higher-level product management function is often helpful to guide relative priority between products and perhaps adjust investment. This is done in the same way as a single team would prioritise and adjust effort against backlog items, just at a higher level of abstraction.

Managing the set of products in this way allows each product team to remain independent and autonomous, but also allows the organisation to adapt and change priorities. It is important to ensure that each product is still delivering tangible value to its users. This means splitting the higher-level problem by user value, not by component.

Decompose goals
As we discussed in Chapter 10, decomposing goals into small goals, or splitting epics into stories, is an effective way to ensure that teams are delivering valuable work to their customers. This approach can also be taken to larger endeavours. Ensuring the smaller goals are independent from one another will create discrete goals that can be delivered in parallel by multiple teams without needing high levels of overhead. It is helpful for teams to understand the high-level goal their team is contributing to, and to know what is being progressed by other teams, but they should still be able to deliver their goal on their own.

Amazon famously uses the 'two-pizza team rule'[200] to size their development teams – they try to create teams that are no larger than can be fed by two pizzas. In doing this they tried to split large goals into goals that could each be given to a 'two-pizza' team to implement.

---

200 https://docs.aws.amazon.com/whitepapers/latest/introduction-devops-aws/two-pizza-teams.html.

Refactor architectures

Where teams are working on the same large product, the feasibility of being able to work independently may depend on the architecture of their product. Particularly with software systems, how a product is architected and designed can have a profound impact on how it must be developed. Monolithic systems with lots of components and tight integration can be hard to work on with multiple teams. Conversely, systems with loosely coupled services, open interfaces and standards-based data are easier for multiple teams to work on.

Most organisations and architects don't set out to create products that are hard to develop and maintain, but we often see products where this has been the result. The DevOps practices advocated by Dr Nicole Forsgren, Jez Humble and Gene Kim in their book *Accelerate*[201] are good ways to create better architectures.

Create feature teams

A feature team is a team that can develop a new feature on a product themselves. Multiple feature teams can each develop features concurrently (see Figure 11.1). This means that they are each able to make changes to all elements and components of the product that need to change.

Sometimes this will mean that multiple teams are making changes to the same part of the system, for example our loyalty card system may have two feature teams working on two new features:

- Feature Team 1 – Forecast demand for chilled convenience foods.
- Feature Team 2 – Report marketing promotion results for in-app discount codes.

These two features are independent from one another, but they will both require changes to the part of the system that extracts data from customer purchases and makes them available to the data analytics component.

This is surprisingly difficult to achieve for many organisations but the preceding practices in this section make it much easier.

We often see component teams in organisations. A component team is solely responsible for one or more parts of the product (see Figure 11.2), for example data extraction, data storage or UI. While this can seem sensible because it concentrates the knowledge and experience in one team, it leads to other, more serious problems.

Component teams don't deliver end-to-end value to the customer. Value is only realised from the work of several teams. The more teams that are involved, the higher the risk that one or more will have problems and the value is not realised. Component teams can become silos of knowledge and single points of failure. This is because they know how their component works and they aren't often inclined to make it easy for others to learn.

---

201 Forsgren, N., Humble, J. and Kim, G. (2018) *Accelerate: The Science of Lean Software and DevOps: Building and Scaling High Performing Technology Organizations.* Trade Select, Portland, OR.

Figure 11.1 Feature teams

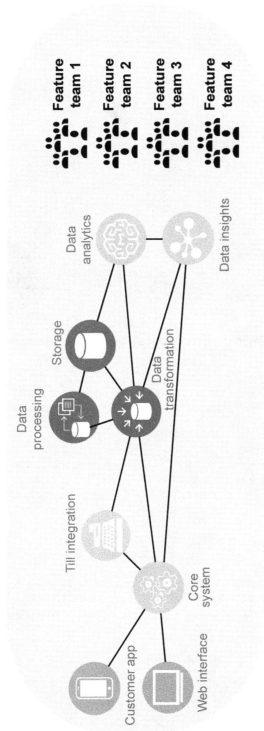

Figure 11.2 Component teams

| Front-end team | Business logic team | Database team | Analysis team |

Converting a component team organisation to feature teams can be a challenge, but the rewards are worth it. Particularly since doing so usually requires other changes such as those described earlier in this section.

Shorten cycle time

Longer increments contain more work and more risk than shorter increments. More work means more detail and more interdependencies. This leads to more risk, but so too does trying to plan and predict further into the future. Our guesses will be less accurate, and we will fail to foresee more things than can affect our ability to deliver value.

As we said in Chapters 8 and 10, there is still a need for longer-term planning, but we can balance long-term release planning with short, value-centric iterative delivery.

It is easy to assume that larger, more complex endeavours need longer iterations because there is so much to do. Even though most scaled methods permit or advocate releasing value frequently, in practice in many scaled implementations we wait until the end of the planned iteration to release.

BUT I REALLY WANT TO SCALE

While we always recommend attempting to negate the need to scale with the suggestions from the previous section, there will still be occasions when a scaled approach is necessary. Sadly, it is more common to see organisations, teams or managers decide they need a scaled approach without trying any ways to avoid the need.

In either case, there are a few options. As we outline later, there are several scaled Agile frameworks and models. Despite the marketing, they generally have more in common with one another than they would admit, and if adopted with the Agile mindset we advocate in this book, any of them ought to give good results. Some may suit your management, governance or enterprise architecture better than others, but you may find that the decision on which one to use has already been made for you. As with any other Agile method or framework, they each promote continuous improvement and undergo regular updates, so any advice we could include here to help you select one would quickly be out of date.

Apply an Agile approach

The risk of applying an off-the-shelf scaled approach is that one size doesn't fit all. The method authors and training providers cannot possibly know your particular situation, so the scaled practices they advocate may work well for you, but they may not. An alternative is to apply the principles of Agile described in this book to the problem of how to scale your endeavour.

- Start by identifying why you need to scale. Which practices or elements of your approach need to change and which are still okay?
- Identify additional practices that will address the challenges you have identified.
- Try them out to see if they work. If not, try something else.
- Continue to inspect and adapt your processes.

This seemingly simple approach will be more successful when conducted by experienced Agile practitioners. Having knowledge and experience of a wide range of Agile practices and frameworks will provide the richest set of options to choose between and help to identify both practices that need support and those that do not.

Sometimes all that is necessary is some simple team of teams coordination events and a common backlog to guide the work of several teams.[202] Try not to over-complicate things. It's always easier to add practices than to take them away.

The golden rule

No matter how you choose to scale, the most important thing to remember is that scaled Agile approaches are still Agile approaches. All the advice and guidance in this book still applies, including the pitfalls and anti-patterns.

There is a general rule for scaling anything: be really good first before attempting to scale. This is certainly true with Agile. It is hard enough itself without the added complexity of trying to scale. Starting from a weak position will make your scaling endeavour much more likely to fail.

---

202 For example, a regular stand-up meeting with some members from each team, common backlog refinement or teams attending each other's end of iteration reviews.

TAILORING YOUR APPROACH

This book has focused on helping you to understand the fundamentals of Agile without attempting to teach a particular method or approach. You can take this knowledge and apply it directly to your work. However, there are many methods and frameworks available that will help you to apply Agile by providing pre-packaged guidance, techniques and practices. Some of the most common are discussed later in this chapter.

They provide varying amounts of content and rigour, but none of them claim to tell you everything you need to do in every situation. They all permit and expect some amount of tailoring to match your specific situation. While this is sensible, pragmatic and empowering, it can also be a dangerous path. As we have reinforced repeatedly in this book, Agile is difficult to get right and easy to do badly. The same is true for the tailoring of any practice. It must be executed with care, considering the wider system and the second or third order impacts that changes can create.

Shu Ha Ri

The Japanese phrase *Shu Ha Ri* (see Figure 11.3) is a useful way of thinking about how you learn and evolve your learning of a technique. With roots from 14th-century Japanese Noh theatre and popularity in martial arts, as Agile Manifesto author Alistair Cockburn explains in *Agile Software Development*,[203] it is a powerful model to explain Agile learning.

Figure 11.3 *Shu Ha Ri*

Shu — Follow   Ha — Master   Ri — Transcend

Shu roughly translates as 'follow'. In this stage, the student follows the master or recipe and doesn't diverge. The rule is followed repeatedly without divergence.

Ha means 'detach'. In this stage the student learns as much as they can about the technique. They gain a deeper understanding and may begin to teach others. In their quest to advance, the student begins to break free of the rigid instruction, questions more and develops new ways to apply the technique while remaining true to its principles.

Finally, in *Ri*, which roughly means 'leave', the student knows the technique so well that they respond differently in each situation, inventing and blending new techniques. They still apply the rigid methods, but they create new elements. They progress more through self-discovery than instruction.

---

203 Cockburn, A. (2001) *Agile Software Development*. Addison-Wesley, Boston, MA.

Shu Ha Ri can also be described as 'follow-master-transcend' or '*Shu*: follow the rule; *Ha*: break the rule; *Ri*: be the rule'. You cannot move from one stage until you have completed the previous stage; and you may well move back to *Shu* several times.

When it comes to adapting or tailoring a process, this model is particularly important. We see many people try to tailor an Agile framework from a position of low experience and little understanding – often as part of their first attempt to use it. They aren't even accomplished in the *Shu* state, let alone *Ha* or *Ri*.

You should be at least at the *Ha* and preferably *Ri* stage before considering tailoring or adapting an Agile method. Only once you truly understand the process as designed will be you able to safely tailor it without risking damage.

Essence

In Chapter 8 we discussed Essence,[204] the OMG standard for describing methods and practices. Essence provides a way of comparing practices from various methods and allowing teams to pick those that work for them. For instance, one team may prefer to manage their requirements with use cases while another prefers user stories. One team may like estimating with Story Points where another uses WSJF.

Mapping our practices with Essence allows us to see how we can advance each of the important elements of our endeavour. It provides clarity on areas we may have overlooked and allows us to see other ways to advance those elements that may suit our situation better. In this way we can easily compose our own method, but do so by building on established practices from a wide range of experts and methodologists whose practices have been essentialised.

Kaizen

Kaizen in Japanese means 'change for the better' or 'continuous improvement' and is central to the Lean approach and the Kanban Method. Importantly, *kaizen* is about small changes rather than big changes (the word *kaikaku* means 'radical change'), which means they should be easier to apply, quicker to show results and easier to reverse or alter if they don't behave as expected.

When tailoring a process, make small changes, test that works and don't be afraid to change back. Making lots of changes at once makes it hard to tell which ones are working and which are not.

We often see people being very keen to adapt or tailor their process as soon as things start to get difficult, especially when they are using a complicated method. It's easy to remember the advice on tailoring from the training courses and assume that you need to diverge from the usual approach. This is rarely the case; most often, the practice you propose changing isn't actually being applied properly in the first place. Before you consider tailoring, make sure you are doing things properly to start with. Then, once you are certain that it isn't working for you, apply *kaizen* and make small changes.

---

204   https://essence.ivarjacobson.com/publications/essence-pocket-guide.

THE CASE FOR SPECIALISTS

In Chapter 7 and elsewhere we describe how Agile teams consist of cross-functional team members that are T-shaped or generalising specialists. We explain that having teams of multi-skilled people makes them more flexible and increases the chances that we can always work on the most valuable thing for our customer, whether that requires technology X, skill Y or authority to do Z.

This is true, but like most rules it has exceptions.

Specialist roles

Specialists bring experience and knowledge, and ought to be able to tackle problems within their specialism of far greater scale or complexity. They often bring a wider and more diverse network and the ability to reach out to their peers within their current organisation and more widely. They should be keeping track of innovations and developments in their field and be able to advise when to adopt new approaches. They can provide mentoring, support and development advice to other staff, both aspiring specialists and more cross-functional team members. They can provide some degree of quality control for all activities in their specialism, whoever is carrying them out.

Of these unique attributes, the most significant one is their ability to tackle more complex work. Sometimes the problem being solved requires the talent of a specialist with years of dedicated experience to solve it. While a cross-functional team of T-shaped professionals could perhaps have a go, they bring higher risk and more chance that they will inadvertently make poor decisions or omit important tasks. In this situation, you should consider bringing a specialist onto the team.

Generalising specialists

The T-shaped professional metaphor described in Chapter 7 is helpful to describe teams where the members each have a range of skills and can each carry out a range of different types of work. In many cases, people in the team have some skill in which they have higher competence and can carry out more complex tasks.

Scott Ambler takes this a step further and introduces the term 'generalizing specialist'[205] to describe people who don't just have an area where they are more competent, but one in which they can actually be regarded as a 'specialist'. In addition to this specialism, they also have other skills. This means that:

- Like a T-shaped professional, they can step in and do the highest priority work for the team, even if that isn't their specialist area.

- Like a specialist, they can lead, mentor, coach and train others in their specialism and provide oversight and assurance of that kind of work.

---

205 http://agilemodeling.com/essays/generalizingSpecialists.htm.

Hiring or developing people into generalising specialists for the types of work likely to be more complex can be a good strategy. It balances the need for specialist skill with the ability to retain focus on the most valuable work at each point of time.

Specialist teams

Feature teams can take any feature or story from the backlog and deliver it. This ensures that we are always able to prioritise the work that will deliver the most value for the customer.

However, there are some occasions when specialist teams are required either temporarily or on a sustained basis. Some examples of when we recommend a specialist team include:

- The work is so bespoke or specialist that teams cannot be expected to succeed without developing deep knowledge and experience. For example,
  - complex cryptographic or mathematically intensive systems;
  - systems with complicated integrations, for instance with legacy systems;
  - components or systems implemented with legacy, bespoke or particularly complex languages or technologies.
- Legacy components that are highly coupled, bespoke, fragile or otherwise hard for multiple teams to work on, particularly where those components are critical to most value streams (e.g. payment systems, data aggregation or data collection and processing systems). Often this is a temporary situation, and the specialist team is also responsible for re-architecting the component.
- Business critical components or systems, particularly those that are also in the value stream for other (non-Agile) systems.

Specialist teams, like individuals, can be purely specialist – in other words, they focus 100 per cent on the system or component – or can also behave more like a generalising specialist: when work on their component needs to be done, they are responsible for it, but if other work is more important, they can work on that instead.

COMMON AGILE METHODS AND FRAMEWORKS

This book has focused on the fundamentals of Agile and we have tried to describe things in a generic and method-agnostic way. Some Agile approaches have been mentioned in passing, but there are others that you may come across that are also worth mentioning.

It shouldn't come as a surprise that Agile approaches usually demonstrate the principle of iterative development and continuous improvement themselves. This means that any detailed description will quickly become out of date. For this reason, we will describe them very briefly and expect you to refer to them directly for an up-to-date description.

Scrum is by far the most popular method, with 66 per cent of teams in the 15th State of Agile Report (2021)[206] stating that it was the approach they followed most closely. Of the scaled approaches, SAFe is the most popular, with 37 per cent of teams saying they use it, with Scrum@Scale or Scrum of Scrums second at 9 per cent. Here, we present them in alphabetical order.

Agile portfolio management

This is not so much a documented method as a phrase that organisations and consultancies are increasingly using to describe an evolution of classic, linear portfolio management towards more Agile practices.

Targeted at organisations with a heritage from project and programme management, it tends to advocate a focus on value over cost, shorter-term decision making and applying Agile and Lean techniques to existing portfolio and programme management approaches.

Disciplined Agile

Disciplined Agile[207] is a framework of tools, practices and strategies that can be composed together to match your specific circumstances. In contrast to more prescriptive frameworks such as SAFe or Scrum, Disciplined Agile allows you to combine elements with other practices. Created by Scott Ambler and now owned by the Project Management Institute, the Disciplined Agile toolkit is arranged as a series of 'blades' that provide a range of options for how to proceed.

Examples of blades include People Management, Transformation and Governance, in addition to more technical blades such as Security, Data Management and Research and Development. The blades are underpinned by foundation practices such as principles, promises, Agile, Lean and teams.

Enterprise Scrum

Mike Beedle, one of the Agile Manifesto authors, used his experience on numerous Agile adoptions to develop the Enterprise Scrum Framework for Business Agility[208] to take Scrum and generalise it for any domain, any sized initiative and any organisation. It has a strong focus on value, visualisation and iteration.

Since his death in 2018, Enterprise Scrum has lost momentum and training is hard to find, but some organisations are still using it.

---

206 https://stateofagile.com/#ufh-i-661275008-15th-state-of-agile-report/7027494.

207 https://www.pmi.org/disciplined-agile.

208 https://www.michaelherman.com/publications/agile/EnterpriseScrumIntro_v4.0.pdf; Beedle, M. (2020) *Enterprise Scrum: Agile Management for the 21st Century*. Addison-Wesley, Boston, MA.

FAST

FAST[207] stands for Fluid Scaling Technology and is a process that dynamically creates teams each iteration that are each optimised for that specific iteration's work.

Everybody is in a single Tribe that visually represents its business goals on a wall. The Tribe self-organises into dynamic teams to break down and do the work. At the end of the cycle, the Tribe comes back together to share their progress and repeats the cycle. It is a flow system (like Kanban) and the cadences for doing the work are short – they recommend starting with a two-day cadence.

The Kanban Method

The Kanban Method is described in more detail in Chapter 8, in the book *Essential Kanban Condensed*[210] and on the Kanban University website.[211] It is a pull-based flow system for optimising the flow of work through a system. Work is represented on a visual board with each column representing the stage of development it is in (for example, Analysis or Testing).

It applies Lean and queuing theory to optimise flow through the system by limiting the WiP and advocating small batches of work. It is frequently combined with Scrum (and sometimes called ScrumBan), although teams often omit some of its elements.

LeSS

Large-Scale Scrum (LeSS)[212] was founded by Craig Larman and Bas Vodde in 2005 and is based on some of their experiences consulting at Nokia on how to scale their Agile development.

LeSS scales Scrum by keeping as much Scrum as possible within the teams and adding a few additional events where all the teams come together at a whole product level. It is designed for single products that are being developed by multiple feature teams and requires a product architecture that supports this model. It places value on experiments and using their results to provide guidance and evolve the method.

The philosophy of LeSS is to scale up rather than tailor down. That is, rather than define lots of potential activities that organisations can pick and choose from, it focuses on augmenting the Scrum elements that struggle when scaled and creating concrete additional elements to support them.

---

209   https://www.fastagile.io/home.

210   Anderson, D. and Carmichael, A. (2016) *Essential Kanban Condensed*. Blue Hole Press Sequim, WA.

211   https://resources.kanban.university/kanban-guide/.

212   Larman, C. and Vodde, B. (2016) *Large-Scale Scrum: More with LeSS*. Addison-Wesley, Boston, MA. https://less.works.

Nexus

Nexus[213] is a framework for delivering a single product with a 'nexus' of three to nine Scrum teams. It was developed by scrum.org and Ken Schwaber, one of the founders of Scrum. Nexus builds on the empirical foundation of Scrum and focuses on reducing the complexity of the Scrum teams by helping them collaborate to deliver an integrated, valuable and useful product increment each Sprint. It does this by creating an additional team – the Nexus integration team – and some Nexus level events similar to the team Scrum events. The Nexus Sprint is the same cadence as the team Sprints.

SAFe

SAFe[214] is the most popular framework chosen by organisations wanting to scale and has certified more than 1 million people in one of its many certifications. SAFe was developed by Dean Leffingwell in 2011 based on his experiences with the RUP and with scaling development teams at Nokia.

SAFe is described in 'big pictures' at several levels of scale, including 'essential', 'large solution', 'portfolio' and 'full'. There are also views for government projects.

SAFe uses a train metaphor with an 'Agile release train' that is loaded with the work of the teams in each 'planning increment' (PI). PIs are generally longer than most Agile iterations at 8–12 weeks, as they are intended to deliver larger amounts of value.

SAFe draws on four main sources for its guidance and content: Agile development, Lean product development, systems thinking and DevOps. In theory, this means that it should be able to operate in a very Lean and Agile way. In practice, achieving high levels of agility with SAFe can be a challenge that requires large amounts of business change, training and shifts of mindset.

Despite this, SAFe is popular with large organisations, particularly where they have established programme and project management functions. Unlike most of the other scaling approaches, it is easy to identify roles and responsibilities in SAFe that appear to be a good fit for programme and project managers. It has well marketed, comprehensive training and certification that is globally available.

Scrum

Scrum[215] is described in more detail in Chapter 8 and is by far the most popular Agile framework being used today. It is a simple framework that uses a rugby metaphor to describe an iterative and incremental approach to delivering value in short sprints of less than four weeks.

---

213 https://www.scrum.org/resources/online-nexus-guide.

214 https://www.scaledagileframework.com.

215 https://scrumguides.org.

It is built on empiricism, and mandates events that allow teams to inspect and adapt their process regularly, even daily. Scrum has introduced some vocabulary that is commonly used throughout Agile development such as retrospective, Sprint and backlog.

Most scaled Agile approaches encourage or allow Scrum to be applied at the team level, although some, such as SAFe, have customised their version of it. Scrum is often combined with other approaches such as XP or Kanban.

Scrum@Scale

Scrum@Scale[216] is a framework for scaling Scrum developed by Jeff Sutherland, one of the founders of Scrum. It is based on the fundamental principles of Scrum, complex adaptive systems, game theory and object-oriented technology. It allows Scrum to be scaled up to whole organisation level, and beyond software or technology problems.

Unlike some other scaled approaches, it applies beyond large single product endeavours. Rather than focus on managing the work through higher-level backlogs, it focuses on coordinating multiple Scrum teams, who may or may not be working on the same product, on high-level prioritised goals and adds the minimum viable bureaucracy (MVB) to do so.

MVB means having the least number of governing bodies possible, reducing the latency of decision making and increasing business agility. The two leadership groups added are Executive MetaScrum to focus on the value being created and Executive Action Team to help remove higher-level blockers and help teams to deliver faster.

'Spotify model'

There isn't really a Spotify model, although many teams still report using it. What people think of as 'the Spotify model' is the set of practices, ideas and experiments conducted by Spotify engineers around 2013 and popularised through blogs, presentations and articles by some of the coaches who worked there at the time, such as Henrik Kniberg[217] and Joakim Sundén.[218]

The best descriptions are probably the videos and rich pictures created by Henrik Kniberg in January 2014 explaining the engineering culture at Spotify.[219] Part 1 describes some of the practices and principles;[220] part 2 focuses more on the experimental nature and their fail-friendly environment.[221]

---

216   https://www.scrumatscale.com/scrum-at-scale-guide/.

217   https://blog.crisp.se/2015/06/07/henrikkniberg/no-i-didnt-invent-the-spotify-model.

218   http://joakimsunden.com/spotify-staying-lean-from-small-start-up-through-rapid-growth/.

219   Note that these are descriptions of some of the things happening at Spotify in 2014, not necessarily what they did later or do now.

220   https://youtu.be/Yvfz4HGtoPc.

221   https://youtu.be/vOt4BbWLWQw.

They describe a wide range of practices followed with a focus on people, motivation, community and trust rather than structure and control. Spotify deploy quickly and frequently. They enable this with small teams, a decoupled architecture and an internal open-source model. They call their teams Squads, which are grouped into Tribes. 'Chapters' represent competence areas such as Agile coaching, quality or web development and decouple line management from the Squads. 'Guilds' are lightweight communities focusing on a particular area of interest that help to share knowledge and experience across the Tribes.

Despite Henrik saying that culture is more important than structure, many organisations trying to implement a 'Spotify model' focus on just the structure; they use the language of Squads, Tribes and Guilds, but don't focus so much on the architecture practices, the autonomy or the experiments.

XP

The first XP project was started in March 1996 when Don Wells and Kent Beck radically changed how software development was being done on the Chrysler Comprehensive Compensation (C3) project.[222] Kent Beck subsequently documented their approach in the book *Extreme Programming Explained*.[223]

Unsurprisingly, given that it was XP leaders who initiated the meeting where the Agile Manifesto was born (see Chapter 2), XP includes many of the core principles and practices of Agile, including short iterations, team empowerment, iterative planning, planning by feature, user stories, stand-up meetings and a focus on delivering working software. It also includes many technical practices and guidance, including code refactoring, pair programming, modelling and continuous testing.

Although XP can be a method in its own right, it is commonly used alongside other frameworks such as Scrum, Kanban or SAFe and regarded as a toolkit of practices rather than a complete approach.

Hybrid and bespoke methods

The methods and frameworks we have just explained are some of the more common approaches that you may come across based on responses to the State of Agile survey.[224] There are others we could also have included.

However, in practice we often observe teams using a combination of approaches or something bespoke. As mentioned earlier, Scrum is often combined with other approaches such as Kanban or XP. Most scaled approaches also use Scrum, Kanban or XP at a team level and add extra layers above or around them.

---

222 http://www.extremeprogramming.org.

223 Beck, K. and Andres, C. (2004) *Extreme Programming Explained: Embrace Change* (2nd edn). Addison-Wesley, Boston, MA.

224 https://stateofagile.com/#ufh-i-661275008-15th-state-of-agile-report/7027494.

Bespoke methods are very common, and we usually see them as the result of one of three circumstances:

- An existing process (often an in-house one) is evolved and adapted to make it 'Agile', often by adding Agile methods or frameworks into it.

- An Agile approach is modified by adding additional processes into, above or around it to cater for specific local needs, for example additional security or compliance elements, or specific governance or reporting processes.

- An Agile framework or method is implemented, tailored or customised in such a way that it is no longer recognisable.

Of these three approaches, the last is the most worrying, particularly when the modifications have been made by people who are not deep experts in Agile or in the method.

The Scrum Guide states that Scrum, as it describes it, is immutable – in other words, if you aren't doing everything in the guide, then you aren't doing Scrum. So, when we see teams who don't bother with Daily Scrums or conduct Sprint Retrospectives, we know they aren't doing Scrum, but we also wonder about what else they are omitting or doing poorly.

Similarly, with large-scaled frameworks such as SAFe it is very clear what is required to adopt and apply it. It states the principles that each practice is based on and how it should be applied, yet we frequently see even core SAFe practices misapplied and misunderstood.

While tailoring a process and adapting it to local conditions is important, it is more important to conduct this tailoring from a position of experience and knowledge, and with the wider consequences understood, from the *Ha* or preferably *Ri* position in the *Shu Ha Ri* model explained earlier. When this is done, the first and second bespoke patterns above can be applied very successfully.

SUMMARY

This book has given you a broad understanding of Agile, which should allow you to adopt or improve your Agile mindset and skills. However, as our numerous references suggest, there is a lot more to mastering Agile than we can include in this one book.

The topic of scaling Agile is popular at the moment and there are plenty of organisations keen to sell training and certifications to help you scale. Before you sign up, however, there are several things you can do that might remove the need to scale in the first place. Applying the Agile Manifesto values and principles is a good start, but we sometimes require more wholesale changes, such as refactoring architecture, changing product management models, and restructuring teams. However, given how hard single-team

Agile is, scaling it also scales the complexity and difficulty, so avoiding the need to scale can really pay dividends in team productivity and time to market.

As good as rules and guidance are, sometimes they need to be broken. Including introducing specialists and changing or tailoring processes are two such examples where sometimes we need to break some rules. When we are considering this, however, the Japanese martial arts model for personal development, *Shu Ha Ri*, can be a helpful metaphor. Before we seek to diverge or break the rules, we must first build mastery and expertise through applying the rules properly many times. Only then can we trust ourselves (or be trusted) to make changes that build on the process we are changing rather than break it.

There are many methods and frameworks that you can choose to help you deliver value in an Agile way. As you would expect, they apply iterative development and the inspect and adapt model to themselves, so frequently change and evolve. We have therefore chosen not to explain the methods and frameworks in any depth as they will become out of date too quickly. However, we have listed some of the more common approaches and provided references to their latest guidance.

INDEX